John Ruskin, Henry James and the Shropshire Lads

John Ruskin, Henry James and the Shropshire Lads

Cynthia Gamble

Published in the United Kingdom in 2008 by

New European Publications Limited
14-16 Carroun Road
London SW8 1JT, England

in association with European Atlantic Publications Ltd.

British Library Cataloguing in Publication Data

ISBN 978-1-872410-68-5

Cover and page design: orbitgraphic.co.uk

Printed and bound in Great Britain by Imprint Academic, Exeter.

Contents

List of Illustrations

Author's preface and acknowledgements

The inception of this book was due to a "pin-prick", a casual remark by a staunch Salopian who, after attending a talk given by Principal Librarian Gordon Dickins, asked me one day: "By the way, did you know that Henry James came to Much Wenlock?" I began by writing what I thought was a book solely about Henry James. But a dripstone and decorative arch at Wenlock Priory (known locally as Wenlock Abbey) led me also to John Ruskin and his Shropshire circle of friends. Among them, I was particularly interested in Osborne Gordon who had been a pupil at Bridgnorth School that I myself attended. This led to Mr and Mrs Pritchard: while Edward Cheney's close connection with Ruskin and Effie in Venice took me to Badger Hall, his country residence.

In the course of unravelling the intricate network of Ruskinian connections, and constructing the web with Ruskin at the centre, I examined original documents and engaged in dialogue with local people whose knowledge has been invaluable. My quest took me to Oxford (in particular Christ Church) and to Easthampstead in my pursuit of primary sources. In Shropshire, I explored Broseley Parish Church where I discovered memorial tablets to the Gordons and the Pritchards whose lives and destinies became so inextricably interwoven. In St Leonard's Church, Bridgnorth, I found more memorials to the

Pritchards and to Thomas Rowley, Osborne Gordon's Headmaster. I derived much pleasure from following and untangling Henry James's hidden itinerary of his essay "Abbeys and Castles" in places richly laden with medieval history: Much Wenlock, Buildwas, Stokesay and Ludlow.

The background for much of my Ruskin work has been the Ruskin Centre at Lancaster University, with the stimulating weekly Thursday seminars, the engagement with colleagues and friends, and the resources of the unique Ruskin Library, a treasure store of manuscripts, paintings, books, journals and other items relating to Ruskin.

I am most grateful to many friends, old and new, colleagues and acquaintances for their wholehearted support. My particular thanks go to Jeffrey Richards, Professor of Cultural History, Lancaster University, for his inspired choice of title during an engaging dinner at the Royal Over-seas Club, London, and for his helpful comments and support during the writing of this book. Dr John F. A. Mason, former pupil of Bridgnorth Grammar School, Emeritus Student, former History tutor and Librarian at Christ Church, Oxford, has been a constant source of inspiration and of much practical help. He kindly introduced me to George C. Baugh, formerly county editor of the *Victoria County History, Shropshire*, who generously shared his meticulous research with me. The Rev. Guy Cole, rector of the church of St Michael and St Mary Magdalene, Easthampstead, Berkshire, inheritor of Osborne Gordon's mantle, willingly and enthusiastically supported this book and responded generously to my many queries, particularly those of a theological nature. The Rev. Béatrice Pearson kindly welcomed me on my first visit.

In Broseley, Mel Mars, owner of The Lawns, Church Street, allowed me to explore the house in which George Pritchard lived and died, while Mike Starkey showed me the home of John Pritchard (now Broseley Social Club) and Pritchard's unusual Victorian flush toilet. I was warmly received by the Rev. Michael Kinna and by the Rev. David Shinton at the rectory in Broseley where, in the drawing-room, we experienced the buzz of the discovery of the burial records of John and Jane Pritchard as we searched through the ancient parish registers.

Other Salopians provided invaluable local insights: Margaret Bennett of Harley, Pat and Granville Goobert of Badger, and last but not least the person who drew my attention to the lavabo. Suzanne Boulos helped immensely and went out of her way to find answers to obscure queries. I am also indebted to Tom Foxall and John Smith for their photographic help. I have enjoyed stimulating conversations and tea at the Hotel Russell, London, with Dr Elinor Shaffer, Director of The Reception of British and Irish Authors in Europe (RBAE). Sir Richard Body and John Coleman provided steady, gentle support and thoughtful guidance throughout.

I would like to thank the Ruskin Foundation for permission to use material in their care in the Ruskin Library, Lancaster University. Stephen Wildman, Director and Curator of the Ruskin Library, Rebecca Patterson, Deputy Curator, Diane Tyler, Assistant Curator and Jen Shepherd, Secretary, have always welcomed me with unfailing courtesy and responded generously to requests for documents and information, as well as for jugs of water. I have also been greatly assisted by archivists and staff at Shropshire Newspapers; Shropshire Archives, in Shrewsbury; Bridgnorth Library; Broseley Library; Much Wenlock Library; Much Wenlock Museum; Berkshire County Archives; City of Westminster Archives Centre, London; the British Library, London; the National Art Collection Library (NAL) housed in the Victoria and Albert Museum, London; the Warburg Institute, London; the Institute of Historical Research (IHR),University of London. These institutions are a priceless source of information, which would otherwise be lost, and should be preserved for the enrichment of our society. Their loss would be a national disaster. Philip Dunne MP, whose constituency of Ludlow and South Shropshire covers almost all the places mentioned in this book, kindly agreed to write the foreword.

Who's Who of the main characters

Henry Wentworth Acland (1815-1900), one of Ruskin's closest friends, from Christ Church. He had a medical practice in Oxford and eventually became Regius Professor of Medicine.

Henry Brooks Adams (1838-1918), American historian, grandson of John Quincy Adams 6th President of the United States. He was a lifelong friend of the Gaskell family and of Henry James.

Joan Agnew – see Severn

Rawdon Lubbock Brown (1803-1883), Venetian resident from 1833 until his death. Eccentric bachelor, antiquarian and archivist: friend of Edward Cheney. He delighted in the flirtatious company of Effie Ruskin.

Edward Cheney (1803-1884), collector of art and *objets d'art*, painter, lover of Venice, inherited Badger Hall in 1866. He had a love-hate relationship with Ruskin.

Harriet Cheney (1771-1848), talented painter and mother of Robert Henry, Ralph, Edward, Harriet Margaret and Frederica.

Robert Henry Cheney (1799-1866), eldest of Cheney brothers, painter.

William Gershom Collingwood (1854-1932), Oxford graduate, artist, Ruskin's indispensable secretary, devoted friend, confidant and first biographer.

Richard Whiteman Fall (1820-1878), Ruskin's first boyhood friend who was a boarder at Shrewsbury School and who initiated him into the delights of the Shropshire landscape.

George Forester (c. 1738-1811), Shropshire landowner whose country estate was Willey Hall. His agent was John Pritchard Senior.

Charles George Milnes Gaskell (1842-1919), barrister, son of James Milnes Gaskell. Close friend of Henry James.

James Milnes Gaskell (1810-1873), MP for the Borough of Wenlock between 1832-1868.

Lady Catherine Milnes Gaskell (1857-1935) *née* Wallop, daughter of the Earl of Portsmouth. After her marriage to Charles George Milnes Gaskell, she lived at Wenlock Priory from 1876 until her death. Lady Catherine was Henry James's much-admired hostess in both Shropshire and Yorkshire.

George Osborne Gordon (c.1779-1822), wine merchant, father of Osborne Gordon.

Osborne Gordon (1813-1883), whose studies at Bridgnorth School and Christ Church were central to his life. Rector of the church of St Michael and St Mary Magdalene, Easthampstead, from 1860 until his death. He was a lifelong and greatly valued friend of Ruskin.

Jane Gordon, see Jane Pritchard.

Constance (Connie) Hilliard (1852-1915), daughter of the Rev. Hilliard of Cowley Rectory and Mrs Hilliard (sister of Lady Trevelyan). Ruskin first met Connie as an eleven-year-old girl.

Henry James (1843-1916), American novelist whose stay at Wenlock Priory ("Abbey") inspired much of his writing.

Rose La Touche (1848 -1875), Irish girl with whom Ruskin fell hopelessly in love.

Henry George Liddell (1811-1898), Fellow (1836) and Censor (1845) of Christ Church, Headmaster of Westminster School (1846-1855), Dean of Christ Church 1855-1891 and Vice-Chancellor of Oxford University (1870-1874). Author of a scholarly *Greek-English Lexicon* (1843).

John Everett Millais (1829-1896), talented and successful painter. Fell in love with Ruskin's wife, Effie, whom he married in 1855.

Richard Monckton Milnes, Lord Houghton from 1863 (1809-1885), MP for Pontefract 1837-1863. A flamboyant character, a collector of erotica and people among whom were Laurence Oliphant, Tennyson, Swinburne, Henry Adams and Henry James. He died of angina pectoris at a hotel in Vichy and is buried at St Andrew's Church, Ferry Fryston.

Charles Thomas Newton (1816-1894), born in Clungunford, Shropshire, son of a clergyman. Writer, archaeologist, Keeper of Greek and Roman Antiquities at the British Museum, Professor of Archaeology at the University of London (1880-1888).

Charles Eliot Norton (1827-1908), American writer and art historian. Influential friend of Ruskin and many other Victorian writers (the Brownings, Thackeray, Mrs Gaskell). He launched Henry James on the London literary scene in 1869.

Jane Pritchard (1816-1892), *née* Gordon, sister of Osborne Gordon. Wife of John Pritchard MP.

John Pritchard Senior (c.1759-1837), attorney and banker, agent for George Forester and his Willey Estate: father of John Pritchard MP.

John Pritchard (1796-1891), barrister, banker, MP for the Borough of Bridgnorth (1853-1868), married Jane Gordon in 1845. Executor for John James Ruskin's will and trusted friend of the Ruskin family.

Effie Ruskin, *née* **Gray** (1828-1897) married 1) John Ruskin, marriage annulled in 1854 on grounds of non-consummation 2) John Everett Millais in 1855. She gave birth to eight children.

John Ruskin (1819-1900), a great political, social and environmental thinker who played an important part in the early development of the Labour Party.

John James Ruskin (1785-1864), wine merchant and shrewd businessman, father of John Ruskin.

Margaret Ruskin, *née* Cock (1781-1871), evangelical matriarch who ruled her son John with a rod of iron.

Joseph Arthur Palliser Severn (1842-1931), painter whose talents deserve wider recognition. He was the son of Joseph Severn (1793-1879), friend of Keats and British Consul in Rome 1860-1872.

Joan Severn, *née* **Agnew** (1846-1924), companion to Margaret Ruskin and to John Ruskin until their deaths. She married Arthur Severn in 1871. Both Arthur and Joan Severn benefited greatly from Ruskin's generosity and inherited his Lakeland home at Brantwood.

Frequently used abbreviations

– Burd, *The Ruskin Family Letters*. Van Akin Burd (ed.), *The Ruskin Family Letters. The Correspondence of John James Ruskin, His Wife, and Their Son, John, 1801-1843*, in two volumes, Cornell University Press, Ithaca and London, 1973.

– CW. E.T.Cook and Alexander Wedderburn (eds.), *The Works of John Ruskin*, George Allen, London, in thirty-nine volumes, 1903-1912.

– *Diaries*. Joan Evans and John Howard Whitehouse (eds.), *The Diaries of John Ruskin*, Clarendon Press, Oxford, three volumes, 1956-1959.

– Lancaster RF. The Ruskin Foundation (Ruskin Library, Lancaster University).

– S.A. Shropshire Archives, Castle Gates, Shrewsbury (formerly Shropshire Record Office).

– VCH *Shropshire. The Victoria History of the Counties of England*, edited by C.R.J.Currie, published for the University of London Institute of Historical Research by Oxford University Press relating to Shropshire. *VCH Shropshire*, volumes iii (1979), iv (1989), x (1998) and xi (1985) are edited by George C. Baugh.

Foreword

On Wenlock Edge the wood's in trouble
His forest fleece the Wrekin heaves;
The gale, it plies the saplings double,
And thick on Severn snow the leaves.

A. E. Housman

The beauty of the Shropshire landscape has been the inspiration for generations of writers and artists. Over the years, Shropshire has provided a backdrop to English literature rightly gaining an important place in our literary heritage.

Shropshire's own literary pedigree is rich and varied. It includes many of the well-known names in English literature who have either stayed in Shropshire or who have just passed through.

Cynthia Gamble's book is a scholarly contribution to help ensure that the literary connections of Shropshire are recognised today and will continue to thrive for generations to come.

Philip Dunne MP

PART ONE

Chapter 1

John Ruskin's formative Shropshire experiences

Ruskin possessed one of the most prolific brains of this century.
Few lives have been more literally spent in the service of duty.

The Times obituary 22 January 1900

When the great Victorian critic, writer, teacher, polemicist, environmental campaigner, painter, draughtsman, philanthropist died from influenza at his beautiful but badly heated, draughty home at Brantwood, overlooking Coniston Lake and his beloved Lakeland hills and fells, at the age of eighty, on 20 January 1900, *The Times* paid him due homage over several pages of that prestigious newspaper. There was a sense of national and international loss and grief at the death of this towering, bearded figure whose life spanned that of Queen Victoria. In accordance with his wishes, a simple burial took place in the little churchyard attached to St Andrew's Church, Coniston.

John Ruskin, the only child of a Scot, John James Ruskin (1785-1864) and his cousin Margaret, *née* Cock (later changed to the less sexually charged name of Cox), was born on 8 February 1819 at 54 Hunter Street, near Russell Square in central London. The house was demolished in the 1960s to make way for property development. Ruskin had the good fortune to have a father who was a shrewd and wealthy wine merchant and active partner in the wine and sherry firm Ruskin, Telford & Domecq that he had established in 1815. Although the offices were in Billiter Lane, in the heart of the City of London, John James needed to be in frequent face-to-face contact with stockists, outlets and customers throughout Britain and abroad. This involved a great deal of travelling and hard work acquiring orders, conducting business and tasting the vintages.

In 1831, the Ruskin family – father, mother, twelve-year-old son John and Mary Richardson his sixteen-year-old Scottish cousin – journeyed slowly in their horse-drawn private carriage, on a circular route from the south of England, through Wales, returning via Oswestry in north Shropshire on their way back to their home in Herne Hill, in south London.[1] The journey took several months. Their itinerary included Dover, Margate, Southampton, Portsmouth, Stonehenge, Hereford, Devil's Bridge, Hafod, the mountain of Plynlimmon that marks the source of the river Severn,[2] Aberystwyth, Dolgelly, Cader Idris "a king of mountains" climbed with the help of ponies,[3] Pont-y-Monach and the Rheidol Falls, Barmouth, Harlech, Tan-y-Bwlch, Caernarvon, Snowdon the highest peak in Wales, Bangor, Conway, Llangollen, back into Shropshire at Oswestry (only three miles from the Welsh border), Monmouth, Chepstow, Clifton, Bath and Newbury. Scant information is available about that trip, but that first taste of Shropshire and the wild border country, the "blue mountains" of Wales,[4] as Ruskin described them, did not leave the budding geologist indifferent. Ruskin always travelled for a purpose, to learn through seeing and sketching: landscape, geology and botany fascinated him. He incorporated some of his scientific observations about Snowdon and its lakes in his first article "Enquiries on the Causes of the Colour of the Water of the Rhine" published in 1834 in the *Magazine of Natural History.*[5] In a letter to his father the following year, he used the metaphor of the force of the conjunction of the gushing rivers Myach and Rheidol linked by the bridge of Pont-y-Monach over the deep gorge (an impressive and picturesque sight popularly known as the Rheidol Falls) to exemplify the power and passion of being reunited with his father on the latter's return home after a long absence.[6] Many decades later in his autobiographical work *Praeterita*, he remembered fondly "the drive from Hereford to Rhaiadyr, and under Plynlimmon to Pont-y-Monach" and "the joy of a walk [...] towards Hafod", "gathering pebbles on the beach at Aberystwyth", "Harlech and its sands, Festiniog, the pass of Aberglaslyn, and marvel of Menai Straits and Bridge".[7]

* * *

The year after that trip to a country and borderland that was even more remote than the *Wild Wales* of George Borrow,[8] John James was in Shrewsbury, on his own, on business, in late February.[9] We have no more information about the visit.

When away from home, John James wrote frequently – usually daily – to his wife Margaret and son: thus we know that he visited Shrewsbury again, in 1840. He set out from Chester at 3 o'clock in "a Unicorn Coach – that is 3 horses", he explained to Margaret, from Hereford, on 22 March 1840: there was no railway in Shrewsbury until 1848. Stagecoach journeys were often dangerous, slow and unpredictable and it is not surprising to learn that an accident happened *en route*. South of Chester, about seven miles into a forty-three-mile journey, an encounter with a dozen or so piebald ponies belonging to a circus company so terrified the three horses pulling John James's Unicorn Coach that the latter turned around "like a coach coming in the opposite way" and broke the pole on the coach. The repairs were long and tedious and delayed considerably his arrival at (most likely) the famous old coaching-inn, The Lion, standing on a steep thoroughfare called Wyle Cop, in central Shrewsbury.

His main purpose was to conduct business with the wine and spirit merchants John Jones and Son, and Peter Beck & Co., in Claremont Street.[10] But he also found time to attend a service at the Abbey Church (Holy Cross), at Abbey Foregate a suburb to the east of the town, close to the English Bridge (the subject of one of Turner's picturesque paintings), one of several bridges over the loop of the Severn. This was the site of a former Benedictine monastery founded by Roger de Montgomery in c. 1080. Only a few years before John James's visit, many of the monastic buildings were destroyed to enable the main Shrewsbury-Holyhead (A5) road to be built close by.

John James described to his wife his delight in both the architecture of the Abbey Church and the religious service. The building was "a remarkable beauty in old Saxon columns & such twisting & nice rusting notching & nicking in a Stone Skreen". The preacher, who impressed him greatly, was "a capital young Clergyman – Bickerstaff [sic]". Comparing the experience to a service in the University Church of St Mary the Virgin in Oxford, at the Abbey Church the "Voices & Music [were] sweeter [...] – perfectly heavenly. Never did I hear in home Church or foreign Cathedral anything so sweet. After Rome please to take Shrewsbury – you will wonder at what you have missed".[11] One can but speculate on how these high church leanings would have been received by his Puritanical wife, then in lodgings in the High Street, Oxford, where she was chaperoning her son, an undergraduate at Christ Church.

The "capital young clergyman" was the Rev. Edward Bickersteth (1814-1892). Bickersteth had graduated from Sidney Sussex College, Cambridge in 1836: after studies at Durham University, he was ordained deacon in 1837. John James had correctly spotted a high churchman and a high-flyer, for Bickersteth rose quickly in the ranks of the Church of England. From being a humble curate at the village church of St Giles, Chetton, near Bridgnorth, Shropshire, in 1838, he moved the following year to be curate at the Abbey Church in Shrewsbury. Subsequently he was appointed vicar in Aylesbury and archdeacon of Buckinghamshire, finally becoming Dean of Lichfield Cathedral in 1875 where he remained until his death. His appointment as honorary canon of Christ Church, Oxford, in 1866, enabled him to have contact with Ruskin's circle of friends and acquaintances. One of these was George Richmond RA (1809-1896) who painted a portrait of *The Venerable Archdeacon Bickersteth* in 1869 depicting a handsome, youthful, kindly, clean-shaven fifty-five-year-old. Bickersteth maintained strong links with Shropshire on account of his two marriages with local girls: firstly to Martha Mary Anne (or Marianne?) Vickers of Cranmere, (married in 1840, she died in 1881) and secondly to Mary Anne, daughter of Thomas Whitmore Wylde-Browne of The Woodlands, Bridgnorth. He was a prolific writer on religious subjects.[12]

John James added the following slightly enigmatic postscript to this letter: "They said at Shrewsbury they had no Oxford paper but they have told lies in this Town since Falstaff's days." John James's allusion to their being "no Oxford paper" in Shrewsbury may be an attempt to reassure his evangelical wife that, in spite of the High Church service at the Abbey, the town has not really come under the influence of the Oxford Movement or Tractarians (hence John James's reference to an "Oxford paper" or Tract) seeking to restore ceremonial and some Catholic teachings within the Church of England. The mention of St Mary's, Oxford is poignant for that was the church at which John Henry Newman, who later converted to Catholicism, was preaching and promoting his Tractarianism. St Mary's was also situated only a few yards from Margaret Ruskin's lodgings. John James concludes by almost teasingly suggesting that their being "no Oxford paper" might not be true!

The reference to lies and Falstaff embeds Shrewsbury in a historical context, for it was the site of the famous Battle of Shrewsbury on 21 July 1403 between Henry Percy (Hotspur) and King Henry IV of England. In Shakespeare's play *Henry IV, part I*, Sir John Falstaff is depicted as a fat, jolly, debauched knight, greedy and cowardly despite his joviality, a larger than life character. On the battlefield at Shrewsbury, he feigns death when attacked, then rises up, picks up the body of Hotspur who had been slain by Prince Harry (Hal) and makes the false boast to have killed him. He also untruthfully asserted that he and Hotspur had "fought a long hour by Shrewsbury clock".[13] Here is the relevant Shakespearean dialogue:

Prince Harry: Why, Percy I killed myself, and saw thee dead.

Falstaff: Didst thou? Lord, Lord, how this world is given to lying! I grant you I was down and out of breath, and so was he; but we rose both at an instant, and fought a long hour by Shrewsbury clock. If I may be believed, so; if not, let them that should reward valour bear the sin upon their own heads. I'll take't on my death I gave him this wound in the thigh. If the man were alive and would deny it, zounds, I would make him eat a piece of my sword.[14]

The following year 1841, John James Ruskin, in London, wrote to his son who was visiting the Rev. Walter L. Brown at Wendlebury, and commenced: "Enclosed a full hour by Shrewsbury Clock & one Dr Acland opened by Mama." The Shakespearean allusion to Falstaff's claim to have "fought a long hour by Shrewsbury clock" is clear, but what does John James really mean in this context? He may be implying that the letter took one hour to write. Van Akin Burd has suggested that he appears to be enclosing a long letter to his son from someone (unidentified) in Shrewsbury.[15] The other letter enclosed would seem to have been sent to Ruskin by his college friend Dr Henry Wentworth Acland (1815-1900). It was a common practice for Ruskin's parents to open their son's mail.

* * *

Richard Whiteman Fall (1820-1878) was a close, boyhood friend of Ruskin: the two families lived near each other at Herne Hill. The friendship started in 1832 when both sets of parents agreed that their sons of more or less the same age could spend time together during holidays.[16] During term time, Richard was away at Shrewsbury School (his father's old school).[17] Ruskin recalls that Richard was already at Shrewsbury School when they first met: however, records confirm that he was there between 1834 and 1837.[18] This ancient school, founded by King Edward VI in 1552 as the Free Grammar School for boys, was situated off a steep slope at Castle Gates, close to Shrewsbury castle. It possessed stately and lavish premises, only surpassed by those at Eton and Winchester.[19] In 1882 it transferred to its present site and the solid old school building (in front of which is a late nineteenth-century seated statue of Charles Darwin a former student of the school) was used as a library.

Ruskin, at the time, was educated mainly at home, by his mother and father and by many private tutors among whom were John Rowbotham (1798?-1846) for mathematics,[20] Charles Runciman (1798-1864) for drawing lessons, and the evangelical preacher the Rev. Edward Andrews, for Hebrew and fencing lessons.[21] For a short period, from September 1833 until spring 1835, he attended classes, mornings only, at a little school in Grove Lane, Camberwell, run by the Rev. Dr Thomas Dale. From February until December 1836, Ruskin was enrolled as an occasional student at King's College, London, for a course in English literature,[22] and had further intensive tuition from Thomas Dale in order to prepare for Oxford.

Richard Fall was, Ruskin wrote, "extremely gentle and good-natured […] entirely good-humoured, sensible and practical; but had no particular tastes; a distaste, if anything, for *my* styles both of art and poetry. […] He was never unkind or sarcastic".[23] The two boys seemed to get on well and complemented each other: they studied Greek and Latin together at Ruskin's home in the morning and often enjoyed walking in the afternoon. In an undated letter to Henry Acland, Ruskin described Richard as his "first playfellow and unfailing friend".[24]

When apart, they corresponded. In 1835 Ruskin, touring

through France and Switzerland with his parents, sent a regular diary in the form of rhyming letters to Richard in Shrewsbury.[25] Even at the top of Mount Rigi near Lucerne, he was thinking of Richard, playing cricket or in his schoolroom. The verse begins:

> I hope all this is entertaining!
> I think, if lesson-time's gone by
> And play-time come, and it is raining,
> It may be so, at Shrewsbury.[26]

From the Refuge or Hospice on the Grimsel Pass, in the Bernese Alps, at a height of 6000′, on "a terrible day" 25 August 1835, Ruskin's thoughts were of the Shropshire countryside, of the river Severn (of which Richard was reputed to know every mile)[27] and Shrewsbury:

> I wonder much what sort of day
> This 25th of August may be
> In dear old England far away!
> Perhaps the sun is shining gaily,
> And you may see, by Severn's stream,
> The city basking in the beam,
> And sloping fields with harvest white,
> And distant mountains, bluely bright.[28]

He then contrasted the Shropshire scene with the Swiss views before him from which he composed a lyrical recollection of different moments and moods at sunrise and sunset; moonlight, storm, darkness, thunderclouds and terror. Elements of this poem to Richard and recollections of the Rigi were later incorporated into *Modern Painters*, in a descriptive passage beginning: "Stand upon the peak of some isolated mountain at daybreak, when the night mists first rise from off the plains […]."[29] Shortly after matriculating at Oxford in the autumn of 1836, Ruskin composed another rhyming letter to "My dearest Richard".[30]

Ruskin's early attempts at poetry were openly mocked by

Richard Fall. Ruskin recalled in *Praeterita* that he "laughed me inexorably out of writing bad English for rhyme's sake, or demonstrable nonsense either in prose or rhyme".[31] However, poet *manqué* perhaps, Ruskin won the Newdigate Prize with his poem "Salsette and Elephanta" that he read at Commemoration on 12 June 1839 in Oxford.[32]

In August 1841, Richard and Ruskin went on holiday in Wales, as far as Pont-y-Monach, the little bridge at the Rheidol Falls, at which point Ruskin, in poor health, had to return to the spa town of Leamington to be treated by the physician Dr Jephson.[33] One can imagine the many conversations between the young men about life in Shrewsbury and the county so steeped in history and legend. They shared both a practical and theoretical interest in the new and often controversial science of Geology and on several occasions attended lectures at the Geological Society in London.[34] Their friendship remained steady and constant, at least until 1849.

In the summer of 1849, Richard Fall joined Ruskin for a walking holiday in the Alps. Ruskin was by now the celebrated author of *Modern Painters* and *The Seven Lamps of Architecture*: he was also in the second year of his ill-fated marriage to Effie Gray who on this occasion remained for several months in Scotland. Richard and Ruskin travelled to Vevey on the Lake of Geneva, and to the village of Chamonix at the foot of Mont Blanc. With Ruskin's faithful guide Joseph Couttet and servant George Hobbs they went in deep snow up the Montanvert, but did not venture on the potentially very dangerous glacier of the *Mer de Glace* "in its robe of winter ermine".[35] In the steps of Turner, they descended to the source of the river Arveyron.[36] These were places that Ruskin already knew well from both practical experience (his first Swiss visit was in 1833) and from his study of geological works, in particular Horace-Bénédict de Saussure's *Voyages dans les Alpes*, his fifteenth-birthday present.

Although Ruskin declared in *Praeterita* that this "was the last of [their] winter walks together",[37] it was not the end of their

friendship, even though their paths and lifestyles were beginning to diverge significantly. Ruskin summarises succintly and
not a little uncritically Richard's adult life:

> [Fall] married a wife, very nice and pretty; then grew rich; held a
> rich man's faiths in political economy; and bought bad prints of
> clipper packets in green sea; and so we gradually gave each other
> up – with all good wishes on both sides. But Richard, having no
> more winter walks, became too fat and well liking when he was
> past fifty – and *did* die, then; to his sister's great surprise and
> mine.[38]

Richard became a businessman and a partner in the mercan-
tile house of Palmer, Mackillop, Dent & Co.[39] at 11 King's Arms
Yard,[40] a small street behind the Bank of England in the City, and
not far from John James Ruskin's office in Billiter Street. Ruskin
maintained a close friendship with Eliza Fall, Richard's only
sister: they often dined or lunched together or with friends.

Richard Fall was one of the first of Ruskin's contemporaries to
initiate him into some of the mysteries of Shropshire.

Chapter 2

Osborne Gordon: from Broseley to Bridgnorth and Christ Church

Osborne Gordon was the third of six children (five boys and a girl)[1] all born and baptised in the parish church in the little town of Broseley, in Shropshire. The name Broseley is thought to mean "woodland clearing" as much of the area was wooded in the Middle Ages.[2] He was born on 21 April 1813. His father, George Osborne Gordon, was a wine merchant. His only sister, Jane, born on 27 July 1816, outlived all the siblings: she died on 25 February 1892, aged 75. It is Jane and her husband John Pritchard who will play a role in the life of John Ruskin.

Controversy surrounded the legality of Jane's baptism on 24 August at St Leonard's Church, Broseley. The curate who officiated, the "Rev. W. C. [H. S?] Gregory",[3] was revealed to be a bogus cleric and impostor whose real name was Lawrence Hynes ('Henry') Halloran (1764-1831). He was curate to the rector, the Rev. Townsend Forester. "Gregory" may have continued for a considerable time as "curate" at Broseley if a particular misdemeanour had not been discovered. In 1818, he was charged, at the Old Bailey no less, with forging a frank on a letter that he sent to his rector and of defrauding the revenue of 10d. He argued in his defence that he had acted in such a manner because he had had a quarrel with his rector. He lost his case and was sentenced to seven years' transportation to New South

Wales where he remained until his death in Sydney on 8 March 1831. Little hard information is available about Halloran. He was of Irish origin, persuasive, with a talent for preaching, although he was not ordained: he claimed to be a Doctor of Divinity. His background prior to coming to Broseley was colourful: he was often in debt, he published sermons and, probably to escape attention, lived in several places, not only in England but in South Africa. In Sydney, he seems to have made a name for himself as a pioneer schoolmaster! How he arrived in Broseley is unclear. However, like Gordon (and Ruskin), he was immortalised in the *Dictionary of National Biography*[4] and in its successor the *Oxford Dictionary of National Biography*, published in 2004.[5]

During Gordon's lifetime, there were two parish churches in Broseley – the centuries-old parish church of St Leonard and the "new" church, renamed All Saints, rebuilt on the same site between 1843-1845. It was designed by Harvey Eginton – he also designed Holy Trinity Church at nearby Dawley – and re-built by William Exley & Sons at a cost of approximately £9,500, a sum raised mainly by subscriptions. The estimated cost of £3000 in 1841 had more than tripled.[6] It was a relatively large church for a dwindling population.

Gordon was but nine years old when his father died on 1 April 1822,[7] at the early age of forty-three. Elizabeth, his mother, was left to bring up three sons and a daughter aged ten, nine, seven and five respectively, as well as a baby (William Pierson).

Elizabeth sought help and solace from her widowed mother, Jane Onions, and from her (Elizabeth's) sisters Mary and Martha.[8] It was fortunate that Elizabeth had been born into a comfortable middle class family. The large, powerful Onions family – there were many branches and members often had the same names, hence the likelihood of confusion – were ironmasters and pioneers of the industrial revolution. They owned and developed huge ironworks with blazing coal furnaces in and around Broseley, Ironbridge and the Black Country. In 1801,

John Onions's new Broseley foundry was the envy of the rival industrialist John Wilkinson who reputedly described Onions's products as the neatest he had seen anywhere.[9] Their accumulated wealth enabled some members of the Onions family to live in the spacious, square-shaped Queen Anne house called White Hall, near the parish church in residential Church Street.[10] This solid residence was still standing at the beginning of the 21st century.

Only two years before his untimely death, George Osborne Gordon had taken on much extra work and responsibility – the management of his father-in-law's ironworks at Brierley, near Dudley, in Staffordshire. He placed the following public announcement in the Classified Advertising columns of *The Times* of Tuesday 13 June 1820, page 3:

> Brierley Iron-Works for Castings, Engine Work, Bar Iron, and Tire. – GEORGE OSBORNE GORDON, Son-in-law and successor to the late Mr. John Onions, respectfully informs Brewers, Distillers, Sugar-bakers, Soap-boilers, and the Public in general, that he has undertaken the BUSINESS of his late father-in-law, at Brierley, and solicits the continuance of the favours conferred on Mr. Onions, which he assures them they may depend upon being executed with the greatest attention, punctuality, and despatch, and upon the lowest terms. All letters and orders are requested to be addressed to him, at Brierley, near Dudley.

In the early nineteenth century, Broseley was a small, but fairly self-sufficient town of approximately 4500 inhabitants. In 1811, it consisted mainly of one long street, at the top of an eminence, with narrow lanes and paths (known as "jitties") branching off and going down the slopes to collieries, furnaces, brick works, tile works, pipe works and small holdings. There were rows and rows of tiny, brick houses, often one-up-one-down – or one-and-a-half-up-and-down – and a group of large houses and Broseley Hall in Church Street. There was no street lighting until 1847. The town declined rapidly throughout the nineteenth and twentieth centuries: in 1870, Murray's *Handbook for Shropshire, Cheshire and Lancashire* described Broseley as "an unattractive town, principally dependent on its potteries and brick-yards". The entry remained unchanged in the 1879 and 1897 editions. The absence of a railway and the closure of furnaces contributed to this decline. The author recalls a visit on the Wednesday afternoon of 1 March 2006, on a bitterly cold day, when all the shops and cafés were closed, and no public transport was available (not even taxis responded to calls): through ice and snow we trod back on foot for four miles through narrow lanes to Much Wenlock. Only a wild hare darted across a snow-covered field, trying to find shelter on the wind-swept heights. But in 1828, sixteen butchers were listed, as well as numerous taverns and public houses and a variety of shops and occupations (hatter, draper, grocer and tea dealer, cabinet maker, boot and shoemaker, basket maker, attorney, baker and flour dealer, blacksmith, brick and tile manufacturers, coalmaster, corn miller, draper, cooper, maltster, sadler, tallow chandler). There was a fine Town Hall, a brick building with pillars and arches and rooms on the first floor that had originally opened in 1779 as a market hall in the High Street. But the lack of fresh water was a constant problem and drinking water was so scarce that it was considered acceptable to give a butt of fresh water as a present.

The town's great prosperity in the 18th and early 19th centuries was due to abundant iron and coal in the vicinity. It was but three miles down steep winding roads to the wooded narrow gorge of the river Severn traversed by means of the western world's first single-span cast iron bridge (hence the name of the village of Ironbridge) designed by Abraham Darby (1750-1791) and inaugurated in 1779. Adjoining Ironbridge were the Coalbrookdale (an evocative name written as Coalbrook dale/Dale in early documents) coalfield and blast furnaces, romantic subject matter for many artists. The Strasbourg-born painter Philippe Jacques de Loutherbourg (1740-1812) made a series of watercolours of industrial subjects in Shropshire: in his dramatic oil painting *Coalbrookdale by Night* (1801),[11] he captured the terrific heat of those furnaces that operated non-stop, day and night, as the orange-red blaze rises up into the sky against a profile of the factory, the workers' dwellings on the hillside as well as the workers themselves. While cataloguing the thousands of paintings and drawings by Turner that he had bequeathed to the Nation (the Turner Bequest), Ruskin identified and catalogued the following four Shropshire sketches: nos. 13, 15,16 and 17 are entitled respectively *Large Fire-Engin (sic) in Coalbrook Dale; Fire-Engin, Coalbrook Dale; Iron Foundry, Maidly Wood, at the Top of the Hill* (this is Madeley Wood, a village adjoining Coalbrookdale); *Largest Fire-Engine of Coalbrook Dale*.[12] These were part of a series of "manufactory subjects" depicting what Ruskin called the "manufacturing picturesque"[13] of that mining community with its plentiful supplies of coal and clay, and its iron smelting works, furnaces and foundries. Turner may have executed these when he was in Shropshire in 1794 or when crossing the county on his way to or from Wales at a later date. Turner's interest in scientific and industrial developments drew him to the birthplace of heavy industry and the cradle of the Industrial Revolution in the gorge of the river Severn at Ironbridge, Coalbrookdale and Madeley, places within a few miles of rural Much Wenlock. Particularly striking is his rendering of the dramatic moment of the opening of a furnace at night in his *Limekiln at Coalbrookdale* (c. 1797),[14] a masterpiece that is couched, according to James Hamilton, "deliberately and fashionably, in the visual language of Rembrandt".[15]

The bridge at Ironbridge, weighing 378 tons, described by Viscount Torrington as "one of the wonders of the world",[16] quickly became a tourist attraction – this was the beginning of industrial tourism – in the little eponymous town advertised as the "Brighton of the Midlands".[17] This feat of engineering was painted by William Williams (active 1758-1797) in his oil on canvas *The Cast Iron Bridge near Coalbrookdale* (1780).[18] The bridge linked the south and north banks of the river and gorge and provided an indispensable means of communication. Some of the finest ironwork of the Coalbrookdale Company was exhibited at the Great Exhibition in Hyde Park, London, in 1851.

The name of the wealthy industrialist John Wilkinson (1728-1808), "the Father of the Iron Trade", is synonymous with Broseley. He lived at The Lawns, a fine Georgian house in Church Road, opposite the parish church. The house, originally called New House, was built in 1727 for Thomas Stephens, a local mine owner, and remodelled by John Wilkinson in the 1760s. The quality of the building was very high and included features by the Shrewsbury architect Thomas Farnolls Pritchard.[19] He owned several furnaces in the vicinity producing weapons – grenades, shells and cannon – as well as castings for domestic and industrial use. Not only was he an astute and to some extent ruthless businessman, he was also the inventor of an accurate cannon-boring machine that was used to bore cylinders for steam engines. He built and launched at Willey Wharf (on the Severn) the first iron barge, a precursor of the iron vessels on the Thames and Tyne. The threat of an invasion by France in 1803 sent Wilkinson's furnaces into a frenzy of production: men worked day and night to push the manufacture of ammunition for the British forces. Wilkinson's profits soared and he was even suspected of selling artillery to Britain's enemy or "bogey" Napoleon Bonaparte. A later notable resident of The Lawns was John Rose (died 1841), who owned factories at nearby Caughley and Coalport producing fine porcelain, often of distinctive blue and white hues, with the famous designs of the "Willow Pattern" and "Broseley Blue Dragon" that acquired a worldwide reputation.

After a sharp decline in the area's fortunes with the closure of the coalfields and rail branch lines, Ironbridge – but not Broseley – enjoyed a revival in the late 20th century when it was designated a World Heritage Site and became a flourishing tourist centre. The old mills and furnaces were converted into museums and the former industries gained historical and cultural importance. The heritage industry had replaced heavy industry.

*   *   *

When Gordon was a boy, there was no recognised academic school in Broseley, apart from a few privately run establishments: a National [i.e. Anglican] School was not built until 1854/5. So from 1825 until 1831 young Osborne Gordon, between the ages of twelve and eighteen, attended the ancient (16th century) fee-paying and notable Bridgnorth School or Free Grammar School ("free" meaning "free from ecclesiastical oversight") in the pretty and prosperous market town some ten miles away.

Bridgnorth, with a population of approximately 6000 inhabitants,[20] was an attractive place in which to spend those six formative years. It had (and still has) immense character – a Low Town on the banks of the river Severn in a valley bounded by precipitous rocks covered with wood, and a High Town with an eleventh-century fortress castle, a seventeenth-century Town Hall astride the High Street, innumerable black and white houses and ancient taverns. Murray's *Handbook for Shropshire, Cheshire and Lancashire* extolled its situation: "Few towns are more picturesquely placed."[21] From the terraced walk around the castle remains, from the top of the cliff, there is a sheer drop of almost 200 feet. When King Charles 1st of England visited the town he was awestruck and famously declared: "The finest view in all my Kingdom!" Turner was attracted to its unique features and as part of his first Midland tour in 1794, he worked from the Low Town and sketched in pencil and watercolour a *View of Bridgnorth on the River Severn, Shropshire*[22] with the church of St Mary Magdalene in the distance.

Bridgnorth School was located in a quiet part of the High Town, in an ecclesiastical close adjoining St Leonard's Church. Gordon was most likely a boarder, one of just over a hundred at the time. Each day started early: boarders rose at six o'clock, followed by prayers at six-thirty, then the first lesson at seven o'clock. In addition to the academic programme, there were organised sports – swimming in the river Severn in Low Town, cricket, twenty-mile walks – and a weekly visit to the theatre. Older pupils were encouraged to read for pleasure and self-improvement Ancient and Modern History, Poetry and Shakespeare.[23] Gordon's Headmaster during his entire school years was the Rev. Thomas Rowley (1797-1877), regarded as a staunch Tory. Rowley had good academic credentials: he had studied first at Shrewsbury School under the headship of Samuel Butler and then at Christ Church, Oxford. Gordon was immensely talented and had a reputation at Bridgnorth School for being a "genius who could dispense with work, and who occupied an unapproachable position of his own", according to the recollections of his younger fellow school student (later Sir) Ralph Robert Wheeler Lingen (1819-1905).[24]

In his final year, Gordon became Head Boy. Lingen recalls the eighteen-year-old's traits:

> the long, thick, soft, and dark hair, the refined features, and the large expressive eyes, the look rather absent and dreamy when at rest, but always with a lurking mockery about it, instantly called by occasion into characteristic and witty comments, – the rather sauntering gait, the head somewhat on one side, and the hand somewhat raised.[25]

A photograph of Gordon in the spring of 1857,[26] taken by fellow Christ Church scholar and lecturer in mathematics (from 1855) Charles Lutwidge Dodgson, better known later by his pseudonym Lewis Carroll and as author of *Alice's Adventures in Wonderland* (1865), reflects some of those characteristics. It depicts a pensive, studious, relaxed forty-four-year-old: slim, well dressed, with dark hair and sideburns (no beard), and seated reading a book propped against a table covered with a decorative cloth. He is a handsome man. However, one must treat photographs with caution: well before the era of digital enhancement, they were sometimes retouched to ameliorate the qualities, health and youth of the sitter. Nadar, working in France, was a master of this technique. Another undated photograph shows a slightly older Gordon, still beardless, holding a walking stick in his left hand, seated in an upright armchair and facing the camera with a strong, direct gaze.[27]

Bridgnorth School had a special relationship with Christ Church through the Careswell Exhibition – so named after the benefactor Edward Careswell – an endowment financing the University studies of a small number of very talented boys. Preparation for the scholarship was based on a classical curriculum and there was no better teacher of classics than Rowley. Osborne Gordon won the scholarship. He matriculated on 25 October 1832, a ceremony that required him to present himself at Oxford before his college Dean and Vice-Chancellor.[28] Perhaps there is a missing letter by Gordon describing the ceremony? However, one of the most vibrant accounts of matriculation at Oxford is provided by A.[lfred] E.[dward] Housman, writing to his stepmother from St John's College on Sunday 21 October 1877:

At a quarter to five on the Saturday afternoon all the freshmen of this college, twenty-two in number, were collected in Mr Ewing's [tutor of St John's College] rooms, and were there instructed how to write our names in Latin in the Vice-Chancellor's book. Alfred, he said, became Alfredus, Edward, Edvardus, and so on; the surnames of course remaining unchanged. Then he marched us off to New College, where we found the Vice-Chancellor [James Edwards Sewell] seated in dim religious light at the top of the hall. Another college was just concluding the ceremony, and when they had finished, we one by one inscribed our names in a large book, in this wise. 'Alfredus Edvardus Housman, e Coll. Di.

Joh. Bapt. Gen. Fil. natu max.' which is, being interpreted, 'A. E. Housman, of the College of St John the Baptist, eldest son of a gentleman'. Sons of clergymen write 'Cler. Fil.' and sons of officers write 'arm. Fil.' Then I wrote my name in English in a smaller and less dignified book, and then paid £2 10s. 0d. to a man at the table, and then we sat down one by one in a row till all had written their names and paid their fee. Then an attendant brought in twenty-two copies of the Statutes of the University, bound in violet, and piled them on the table, hiding the Vice-Chancellor from the eye. Presently his head appeared over the top, and we got up and stood in a sort of semicircle in front of him. Then he called up each of us by name and presented each with a copy of the Statutes, and with a paper on which was written in Latin, or what passes for Latin at Oxford:-

'At Oxford, in the Michaelmas term A.D. 1877, on the 13th day of the month of October: on which day Alfred Edward Housman of the College of St John the Baptist, gentleman's son, appeared in my presence, and was admonished to keep the laws of this University, and was enrolled in the register (matricula) of the University.

J. E. Sewell
Vice-Chancellor'

Then he settled his gown over his shoulders and said, 'Gentlemen of St John's College, attend to me.' We attended. He said, in Latin, 'Allow me to inform you that you have this day been enrolled in the register of the University, and that you are bound to keep all the statutes contained in this book' (with the violet cover) 'as far as they may concern you.' Then we went. As to keeping the statutes contained in the violet cover, you may judge what a farce that is when I tell you that you are forbidden to wear any coat save a black one, or to use fire-arms, or to trundle a hoop, among other things.[29]

Normally a student matriculating in the autumn would commence at Oxford in the following January – as did Ruskin[30] – but Gordon is listed in Foster's *Alumni Oxonienses* as being a "senior student" from 1834 (until 1861). Could he have enrolled as a "student" in 1833?

On the first leg of the journey, Gordon would have travelled by coach and horses to Birmingham, then changed to the Oxford coach. The Emerald provided a regular service between Shrewsbury and Birmingham, calling at the White Hart Inn, in nearby Ironbridge, every morning at ten o'clock. It was a huge step from life with his widowed mother in the small town of Broseley to the great Oxford college, founded in 1525 as Cardinal College by Cardinal Wolsey and re-founded as Christ Church in 1546 by King Henry VIII with a chapel designated as a cathedral. That College was to play a central role throughout Gordon's life.

Osborne Gordon had had such a thorough academic grounding at Bridgnorth School that he easily outshone the Christ Church undergraduates, many of whom had been admitted on the grounds of their noble birth. Gordon was registered at Oxford as being from a family, like Ruskin's, entitled to bear heraldic arms. But it was not necessarily an easy environment for a true scholar with aspirations, and the lack of order and cleanliness must have been a shock. Tim Hilton describes the undergraduates in the 1830s as "idle and riotous" with "wines, gambling and hunting" being the chief amusements, and concludes, with reference to Ruskin, that "it was not an inspiring environment for such an eager young man".[31]

Gordon excelled in Greek, a passion nurtured and inspired by Thomas Rowley, and by 1835, he gained the Ireland university scholarship, "chiefly through the merits of eight exquisite lines of Doric Greek on the subject of Sir F. Chantrey's monument to two children in Lichfield Cathedral".[32] This was Francis Chantrey's sculpture of the children of the Rev. W. Robinson that Ruskin praised so highly many years later in his lecture on the Sienese sculptor Jacopo della Quercia (1374/5-1438) at Oxford on 24 November 1874: it was, he proclaimed, an example of a "portrait-statue still retaining the recumbent position, [...] very touching and lovely".[33] Winning the Ireland scholarship was a considerable feat that caused some astonishment, admiration and no doubt some jealousy among his peers but quickly set Gordon apart as an intellectual force to be reckoned with. It also caused a flurry of excitement and much pride among the staff and students at Bridgnorth School.[34]

In 1836, Gordon obtained a BA, taking a double first in Classics and Mathematics. According to his contemporaries and local tradition mixed with a degree of malice and envy, this double first was obtained "after being idle for the greater part of his undergraduate's career, and then working a fabulous number of hours daily in the last year, especially towards the end of it, when the less critical spirits spoke of sixteen hours out of the twenty-four".[35] He remained at Christ Church as a tutor.

Chapter 3

Gordon, Ruskin's wise tutor and friend

It was a family affair when John Ruskin went up to Christ Church in January 1837 and remained so throughout the three years of his undergraduate studies. Margaret Ruskin, his ever vigilant and overprotective mother, and his cousin Mary Richardson took lodgings in the High Street, Oxford, where they were joined by John James Ruskin at weekends.

It was at Christ Church that Ruskin first met Osborne Gordon (or Gordon as he always called him): indeed, the whole family made his acquaintance. This was the beginning of a mutually enriching, lifelong friendship. The Ruskin family liked Gordon very much and judged that he was a most suitable person to invite to their home at Herne Hill, a few miles south of London. John James, himself a wine merchant, felt a particular affinity with the Broseley wine merchant's son. He may have traded with Gordon's father or with the prominent Broseley wine and spirit merchant Slaney & Son, established in 1780. He and Margaret reached out to this scholar who had been deprived of a father at the age of nine.

Gordon, "a pearl among tutors",[1] was Ruskin's tutor at Christ Church. The young undergraduate was highly independent, a characteristic he maintained throughout his life. In a letter of 1837, Henry George Liddell (1811-1898), then a tutor at Christ Church, described Ruskin as "a very strange fellow, always dressing in a great-coat with a brown velvet collar, and a large neckcloth tied over his mouth, and living quite in his own way".[2] The fact that Ruskin was chaperoned by his mother during all his Oxford studies would surely have been sufficient for him to be ragged, or at least teased by fellow students. But Ruskin did not seem to care. Gordon sensed Ruskin's potential vulnerability: he told William Holman Hunt (1827-1910), during the latter's Commemoration visit in 1852, that Ruskin "had been made the subject of a great deal of horse-play on account of his avoidance of sports".[3] Ruskin in later life described Gordon at that time as "a man of curious intellectual power and simple virtue",[4] and on another occasion as an "entirely right-minded and accomplished scholar".[5] He emerged as a kindly, caring, almost paternal figure, giving Ruskin reassurance about his examinations and helping the nervous undergraduate to overcome his apprehension.[6] Ruskin passed and Gordon was singled out for praise in Margaret Ruskin's letter of 4 March 1838: "Mr Gordon was early with him [John Ruskin] in the morning and accompanied him to the door of School and afterwards run to secure his testamur [certificate for having passed an examination] as soon as possible showing himself all through much interested and very kind."[7]

By late autumn, Gordon was giving Ruskin extra private tuition. "Mr Gordon now very frequently reads from nine till ten with John after he leaves us", Margaret informed her husband. This was a source of great enjoyment for she added: "John assures me he has never felt the slightest degree of head ake fatigue or weariness of Brain from what he does at present."[8]

At the beginning of the Hilary term, Ruskin attended lectures given by Robert Hussey, then Censor of Christ Church, the Rev. Edward Hill and Gordon. Gordon was by now on more intimate terms with Ruskin and confided to him that he had had to return to Shropshire as he had been worried about the health of his widowed mother, Elizabeth. He "came up yesterday" Margaret Ruskin wrote to her husband, "in great spirits, his mother quite well again".[9] Occasionally, during vacations, Gordon also returned to his old school at Bridgnorth.[10]

Later that term, we learn that Ruskin has "gone to his rooms to study with Mr Gordon".[11] The details of his performance at the end of term were relayed by Gordon, as Margaret wrote on 5 June 1839 to her husband: "Mr Brown told Gordon John had done very well indeed – he answered every divinity question – and the greater part of all in Mathematiks &c."[12]

At some point in their conversations, it was agreed that Gordon would give Ruskin some extra tuition and coaching during vacations. We do not know whose initiative this was or on what terms the lessons took place. Was there a financial incentive or did John James repay the tutor with cases of sherry and fine wines, gifts of Turner paintings and travel abroad? Perhaps Gordon's altruism and a desire to satisfy his pedagogical needs played a part. He recognised in the young student qualities and talents that could be developed and stretched even beyond what Oxford offered.

Twenty-six-year-old Gordon stayed at the Ruskin family home at Herne Hill in the Long Vacation or early autumn of 1839 – we do not know exactly when or for how long. He came, Ruskin recalled in *Praeterita*, "to be my private tutor, and read with me in our little nursery".[13] Gordon was preparing Ruskin for "the last push",[14] the twenty-year-old's Oxford finals due in 1840. Ruskin had been overworking and was under considerable pressure, not only from his parents but also from the effects of his unrequited and clumsy, unrealistic love affair with young Adèle-Clothilde Domecq, one of the daughters of his father's Spanish, Roman Catholic business partner. Gordon's first and urgent task was to make him relax and unwind. The rustic metaphor of ravelled ends of flax that need to be twisted and reshaped is Ruskin's own: "Taking up the ravelled ends of yet workable and spinnable flax in me, [Gordon] began to twist them, at first through much wholesome pain, into such tenor as they were really capable of."[15] These could also have been symptoms of one of many breakdowns that plagued Ruskin with increasing intensity throughout his life. Gordon was an excellent teacher and his first advice to his pupil and *protégé* in order to relieve the pressure was: "When you have got too much to do, don't do it."[16] We know that Ruskin rarely followed this advice, but he certainly remembered it. It became almost a catch phrase, as Collingwood recalled many years later and gave an instance of Ruskin actually heeding Gordon's advice. When confronted by great difficulty in landing his boat on Coniston Lake, Ruskin refused to struggle:

> Now Ruskin was a very practical man in some things. 'When you have too much to do, don't do it,' he used to say. So after a wild water-gallop, he simply landed and walked home. When the wind changed he could bring back his boat. There was no use in making a pain of a pleasure.[17]

Only six years in age separated Ruskin and Gordon, a divide that narrowed and eventually became unimportant as time passed. The relationship of tutor-student evolved and changed to that of two good friends who mutually respected each other. At Herne Hill, they walked and talked ... about religion, about art, about Turner, about his *Richmond Bridge, Surrey* that Ruskin had received as a present from his father. A second Turner painting, *Gosport*, was acquired during Gordon's 1839 stay.[18] It is difficult to find fault with Gordon: he was, wrote Ruskin, "a practical Englishman, of the shrewdest, yet gentlest type; keenly perceptive of folly, but disposed to pardon most human failings as little more".[19] The former University College Oxford student William Gershom Collingwood (1854-1932), who became Ruskin's secretary, friend and biographer, described Gordon as "famous for his scholarship but still more for his tact [and] was always regarded with affectionate respect".[20]

Gordon was a rigorous tutor whose questioning style of instruction and belief in grammatical analysis provided Ruskin with the realisation not only of its importance in literature and language but also its relevance to the technique or grammar of drawing. In a letter to Henry Acland (c. 1840), Ruskin recalled Gordon's method: "One day I was declaiming to Gordon on the poetical merits of a noble passage in one of the Dramatists, but could not construe the first line accurately, when requested so to do. In Drawing only, I learned by *grammar* thoroughly [...].”[21] Ruskin's *Elements of Drawing* of 1857 would demonstrate these principles: likewise, the grammar of architecture is a subject that permeates his writings.

Ruskin himself provided a perceptive and praiseworthy snapshot of his tutor in *Praeterita*:

> In his proper work with me, no tutor could have been more diligent or patient. His own scholarly power was of the highest order; his memory (the necessary instrument of great scholarship) errorless and effortless; his judgment and feeling in literature sound; his interpretation of political events always rational, and founded on wide detail of well-balanced knowledge; and all this without in the least priding himself on his classic power, or wishing to check any of my impulses in other directions. He had taken his double first with the half of his strength, and would have taken a triple one without priding himself on it: he was amused by my facility in rhyming, recognized my instinct in painting, and sympathised with me in love of country life and picturesque towns, but always in a quieting and reposeful manner.[22]

Ruskin returned to Oxford in the following January and extra tutorials and "very steady work"[23] continued under Gordon's "wholesome moderatorship". In a letter John James wrote, from London, to his wife in Oxford, he refers to having been with Gordon, but the circumstances are not clear: "I came in with Gordon & felt sorry at parting & the entire break up, but we never know our pleasures till they are gone."[24]

While the entire country was preoccupied with the forthcoming controversial royal wedding between Queen Victoria and her German cousin Prince Albert of Saxe-Coburg-Gotha, John James and Margaret Ruskin were planning a party to celebrate their son's coming of age. It was held in Oxford on Saturday 8 February and guests included two much loved college tutors who became lifelong friends, Walter Lucas Brown (c. 1805-1862) Reader in Rhetoric, and Osborne Gordon.[25] His father purchased a new set of clothes, ordered quantities of wine, gave his son Turner's drawing of *Winchelsea*, the ancient seaside town in Sussex about two miles south west of Rye, (Ruskin was disappointed in the choice) and shares valued at £7500 producing an annual interest of £315.[26] Although this grand occasion marked a legal threshold in Ruskin's life, it did not give him the much-needed psychological independence from his parents. Ruskin remained a boy in their eyes. Similarly, John James regarded Victoria and Albert as children – they were both aged twenty – and disapproved of their marriage. Of Queen Victoria he wrote that she "is but a silly child & seems to have no Character": and of Albert he expressed the wish that "the Boy may grow into something better".[27]

A recreational interest that Ruskin and Gordon shared was fencing: they may even have fenced together. Ruskin's father paid for his son to have both fencing and archery lessons.[28] Gordon was a skilled fencer and on one occasion in 1840 his opponent was Shropshire-born (from Clungunford)[29] Charles Thomas Newton (1816-1894), a senior at Christ Church when Ruskin was a freshman: Newton later became an archaeologist, Keeper at the British Museum and a lifelong friend of Ruskin. John James comments on Gordon's prowess and agility: "I do not see that Mr Newton was *foiled* by Gordon who attacks in a fashion that no man however cunning in fence has learned to cope with. It is like having a man at one side to run you through Sideways."[30]

At the very beginning of March 1840, a glimpse of some acrimony, or at the very least a degree of tension between Gordon and the Ruskins became apparent, revealed in John James Ruskin's letter of 4 March. It is in connection with Ruskin's studies and the parents' desire to travel during clement weather. The situation regarding Ruskin's studies at this time is unclear. In a letter of 3 March 1840, John James Ruskin informed W. H. Harrison that Ruskin was "not going up for Degree until later which is a great relief to us as he was Killing himself with reading".[31] It appears that in view of Ruskin's high intelligence, knowledge and capacity to work hard, it was decided, in consultation with his tutor Walter Brown, that Ruskin's time at Oxford could be reduced. He could aim for a high class degree by the end of the next term, but that naturally meant that he would be subject to intense pressure. Ruskin became the subject of conflicting pressures and victim of an impending nervous breakdown.

One can surmise that Gordon had formulated a plan to keep Ruskin in England, perhaps at Oxford, during the autumn of 1840, no doubt hoping that he could perhaps extend the period of his studies at a more leisurely pace. Perhaps take his degree later, in the autumn? Mr and Mrs Ruskin had other plans for their precious child – to leave for the Continent while the weather was sufficiently clement for travelling. If Ruskin continued his Oxford studies at a more leisurely pace, as Gordon suggested, it "derange[d]" the travel habits of the Ruskin family. This was a most selfish reason and emphasised the rigidity of the habits of this close family unit. John James Ruskin asked his wife, still at Oxford, to clear up any misunderstanding:

> Will you say distinctly to Mr Gordon that although it deranges our plan of going abroad by making us travel in depth of winter in place of in mild autumn – I mind nothing so much as Johns continuing a member of Ch Church & terminating Studies there with Credit. I wish this conveyed because I think G[ordon] expected me to be greatly annoyed & now tries to please us by saying it might have been worse. I am sorry for anything being done even by ignorance or omission against College rules. I am greatly obliged by so rigid an Enforcer of rules as the Dean treating my Son with lenity & consideration.[32]

The pressure of work was intense, "until twelve at night [and] from six in the morning, with little exercise, no cheerfulness, and no sense of any use in what I read", Ruskin recalled in *Praeterita*.[33] When Ruskin heard that his first young love, Adèle Domecq, had married another suitor, Baron Duquesne, he became severely agitated and appeared to be on the verge of a serious illness. Barely had the term started when, late one evening during the weekend of 18-19 April,[34] after Gordon had left at about ten o'clock, he experienced "a short tickling cough [...] preceded by a curious sensation in the throat, and followed by a curious taste in the mouth".[35] It was blood.

Ruskin had headaches, eye problems and was suffering from nervous exhaustion: the nature of his illness remains obscure. Medical opinion concurred that he needed rest and a complete change of environment. The court physician Sir James Clark (1788-1870) advised wintering abroad, in Italy, and being "as much in open carriages as possible".[36] This was advice that would have suited Mr and Mrs Ruskin. One wonders to what extent his parents and others overreacted and put pressure on the young undergraduate.

So Ruskin left Oxford, only returning some eighteen months later to complete his period of residence and receive a degree. That is a fairly bland statement that conceals much argument, discussion and soul-searching. It was not crowning Ruskin in glory to leave his Oxford studies before completion and he remained bitter about having to leave in such circumstances. His father was disappointed.

The Ruskins left England on 15 September 1840 for a continental journey that lasted for nine months: an entire gap year. They went to Rouen, Chartres, the Loire Valley, the Auvergne, Nice, into Italy, to Rome, as far south as Naples "1651 miles from London" noted John James in his diary, returning via Venice, Turin, Chambéry, Geneva, Nancy, Châlons-sur-Marne, Rheims and Laon. They did not return to England until late June 1841.[37]

* * *

Ruskin had still not recovered from his bout of illness and doctors advised a "cure" at the fashionable spa town of Leamington, in Warwickshire. Ruskin stayed there, first at the Bedford Hotel, then later in lodgings at 53 Russell Terrace – a blue plaque was erected to mark the event in 2006 – for much of the summer and early autumn, apart from a short walking holiday with Richard Fall. He was under the care of physician Dr Henry Jephson who recommended a special diet, warm baths and spa water.[38] The regime did not have the desired effect and by early October Ruskin's health was a cause of great concern to his father: "Your letter today causes me some anxiety. You do not say you are well."[39] The isolation Ruskin felt was also detrimental to his recovery.

His solitary state was broken by a welcome visit from Gordon, now the Rev. Osborne Gordon, on Wednesday 6 October 1841.[40] Far from being harmful as John James Ruskin suggested, this contributed to his intellectual well-being. They spent at least the evening together – it was a happy and stimulating occasion – as Ruskin records in his diary:

> Gordon with me last night; very glad to see him again and looking well. I was sorry to find that in talking with him on philosophical subjects I seemed to be far less clear in my thoughts and language than I used to be. It may be want of practice.[41]

Ruskin was fascinated by spiritualism and by dreams and their interpretation. So it is perhaps significant that what interested him in particular was Gordon's account, in 1841 during his visit to Leamington, of an identical dream experienced by Earl Grey[42] and his daughter:

> Curious story he told me about Earl Grey and his daughter: That they saw the same head appear at the foot of their beds without a body; the daughter merely thought of it as a vivid and disagreeable dream, mentioned it to her sister in the morning as she

was dressing. At breakfast Earl Grey mentioned his having seen it also, and his daughter fainted instantly. This Gordon had from a lady who heard it from his daughter's own lips. It is reported that Earl G. has since been haunted constantly by this head – Whitbread's, Gordon thought.[43]

Ruskin does not comment on the dream with its foreboding overtones. Unconsciously did he make a homonymic connection with Effie Gray, his wife-to-be? The teenager was at that time very much on his mind, for he was composing a fairy story, *The King of the Golden River*, to amuse her. Did the dream so terrify him that he conveyed his anxiety to his father? John James Ruskin expressed further concern in his letter, and went so far as to blame Gordon for his growing influence, saying: "I am afraid you have exposed yourself too much with Gordon." There were many unanswered questions in John James's mind, particularly about his son's health and studies: "Why not have said if Gordon Said anything of your appearance – [...] Has Gordon changed your Intention as to time of going to Oxford?"[44]

On the same day, 7 October, Margaret Ruskin was writing independently to her son expressing her confidence in Gordon and inviting the tutor to stay (again) with them at Herne Hill: "I am delighted to find your regard for Gordon unabated and that he has done something toward Removal of your difficulties – we would try and find means of accommodating him [...] if he would pay us a visit – you will see him when you go to Oxford."[45]

In a reply to his father on 8 October, Ruskin had mentioned Gordon's high praise of him at Oxford. But in a somewhat cursory and cutting response that must have angered his son, John James commented dismissively: "Gordon remembered you at your best at Oxford – if he remembered at all. People say something at times considered at other times unconsidered trifles."[46] These extracts are typical of the undercurrent of tension apparent between father and son, mother and son in much of the correspondence.

A month later, Ruskin was back at Herne Hill "with his wise tutor",[47] Osborne Gordon. It was an almost futile effort to catch up on eighteen months of missed tuition of an academic kind, particularly in Greek, Latin and Mathematics. Ruskin had already begun his education at the University of Life, sketching, writing, observing, criticising, studying geology, botany, history and geography during that nine-month tour of France and Italy in 1840-1841. *Modern Painters* was germinating in his mind, a seminal work that would hit the headlines in May 1843. Gordon guided Ruskin judiciously along the right path at this critical time. He was extremely sensitive to Ruskin's needs and knew how to get the best out of his student. He sensed that if he had forced him to study Greek at the level required for the Oxford honours examination, his *protégé* would most probably have had a complete nervous breakdown. Whereas other Oxford dons regarded Greek constructions as essential for life, Gordon simply replied, "with Delphic *double-entendre*", to Ruskin: "I think it would hardly be worth your while."[48] Pressure was relieved by Gordon's steadying presence and also by the pleasure in being taught drawing by James Duffield Harding.

In April 1842 Ruskin was awarded an honorary degree, a Double Fourth. He could now legitimately call himself "A Graduate of Oxford". Soon after, the family departed on 24 May for another continental tour, returning on 19 August 1842. He was leaving behind an atmosphere of theological debate with the Oxford Movement at its height. The question of Sundays, the subject of heated discussion between Ruskin and Gordon, left Gordon in a sorrowful state, dramatically described by John James as "troubled in Spirit for he looks like Niobe weeping for her Children".[49] This is an allusion to the Greek myth of Niobe whose seven sons and seven daughters were killed by Apollo and Artemis, as a punishment for her arrogance. Niobe in her grief was turned to stone, which continued to shed tears. John James's hyperbolic portrayal of Gordon suggests both the Shakespearean overtones of Hamlet's mother's grief at the death of her husband "Like Niobe, all tears"[50] and the painting in Dulwich Picture Gallery, near the Ruskin family home, of *The Destruction of Niobe and her Children*.

Planning for the tour abroad had started in the spring. Ruskin asked his father for permission for Gordon to join the family in Chamonix, most likely as their guest (but we do not know the terms of the arrangement). John James Ruskin happily agreed and wrote to his son: "I shall be very glad to see Gordon at Chamouni." He added, with perhaps a reference to Gordon's dry humour: "Some of his dry things will be very agreeable in that wet & snowy Region."[51] So he was invited to join the party during some of his Long Vacation, partly as a recompense for his help and sound advice at a critical moment in Ruskin's life, but also as a congenial companion for the young Ruskin in particular.

Gordon stayed on to honour his academic commitments at Christ Church and joined the Ruskin family in Chamonix in late June 1842. We do not know which route he took or whether he travelled alone. Chamonix at the time was under Sardinian rule and Savoia (Savoy), in which it is situated, was not annexed to France until 1860. Savoy belonged to Piedmont from 1815 until 1860, with the administrative capital at Turin. Ruskin's long engagement with Savoy led him to believe that its annexation to France would "be an immense benefit to Savoy".[52] For it was a particularly poor region, one that Ruskin described in terms of "miasma" when writing to his friend Dr John Brown, the Edinburgh doctor and writer, on 6 August 1860: "A few million of francs judiciously spent will gain to Savoy as many millions of acres of fruitfullest land and healthy air instead of miasma."[53]

When Ruskin had first discovered Chamonix – he usually preferred the old spelling of Chamouni – in 1833 it was a remote, isolated hamlet nestling in the great Alpine Valley. It remained one of his favourite places. He returned time and time again, until his last visit in 1888, and found there enjoyment, stimulation and solace. It satisfied so many of his needs. But over fifty years he witnessed dramatic and irreversible changes in landscape (the disappearance of the *Glacier des Bois*) and in society (the development of organised tourism and the construction of hotels and the railway).

Ruskin and Gordon were both vigorous, athletic young men. They went climbing in the Alps, scaling the Bréven – within 300 feet of the top – some 8284 feet above sea level, north-west of the village of Chamonix. The Bréven provided some of the finest views of Mont Blanc and its Massif. A registered, competent local guide, a member of the *Compagnie des guides* their regulatory and professional body, was always advisable and Ruskin engaged Jean-Michel Dévouassoud (1787-1864). He was one of the most renowned guides who had participated in several ascents of Mont Blanc. In 1825, he had escorted Victor and Adèle Hugo up the peaks. Dévouassoud was now fifty-five years old and according to the regulations for guides would have to retire at sixty. Ruskin's recollections of Dévouassoud in *Praeterita* in which he refers to him as a guide of "average standard […] who knew his way to the show places, and little more" are, to say the least, ungenerous.[54]

He noted in his diary on Wednesday 29 June 1842: "Up to within three hundred feet of top of Bréven, with Gordon, on a perfect day, cloudless and windless, and mistless till 12."[55] It was beautiful but dangerous for Ruskin had spotted a threatening avalanche and had not, it seemed, drawn Gordon's attention to it. Writing his diary entry a few weeks later from Schaffhausen, in Switzerland, and now with a certain detachment, he reflected on its majesty:

> I consider myself, looking back, as more fortunate in the single avalanche I saw from the Bréven with Gordon than even in all the fine weather I had at Chamouni. Its dense, symmetrical, globular, multitudinous masses of foamy smoke; their majestic yet lightning advance along the level field of the Glacier des Pèlerins; the sharp edges with which each volume was defined, and depth of shadow between them and the snow beneath, were

all characteristics which I never saw approached – even in kind, much less in degree – by any of the numberless falls I saw in the rest of the month. That I saw on the morning of the 26th was remarkable for the height and extent of its rising vapour, but had no defined masses.[56]

Ruskin's watercolour entitled *Chamouni* sketched during his 1842 stay captures some of the "foamy smoke" and threatening avalanches.[57]

Against this backcloth Ruskin was seething with concealed anger that was to goad him into action as an art critic and spring to the defence of Turner. The reason was the way in which critics had reviewed Turner's paintings in the Royal Academy exhibition of 1842. Ruskin only read some of these reports when he arrived in Geneva on his tour. Many treated Turner's works in a mocking, ribald and derisory way, seeming not to have any understanding of the great artist's intentions. Nor did they make any attempt to understand. A reviewer in *The Literary Gazette* of 14 May 1842 wrote: "No 52, 'The Dogano' (*sic*), and 73, 'Campo Santo', have a gorgeous *ensemble*, and produced by wonderful art, but they mean nothing. They are produced as if by throwing handfuls of white, and blue, and red, at the canvas, letting what chanced to stick, stick." That same reviewer's hostility increased: *Burial at Sea* excited "ridicule" and *War: the Exile and the Rock-Limpet* (the subject was Napoleon) was "truly ludicrous".[58]

Ruskin did not, at this stage, share these thoughts about the role of art and the artist with Gordon. It was not until March 1844 that he revealed to Gordon how incensed he had been in 1842 about the ignorance of the so-called art critics and how the idea for *Modern Painters* had germinated. His original idea was to respond in a pamphlet but the deeper he reflected, the bigger the project became and grew like the heads on the mythological Hydra. It seemed almost out of control and Ruskin must have found it a daunting task, fearing that he would never complete it. He tried to delay writing but by so doing, the size of the task increased. He explained his dilemma to Gordon:

> I put off my pamphlet till I got home. I meditated all the way
> down the Rhine, found that *demonstration* in matters of art was
> no such easy matter, and the pamphlet turned into a volume.
> Before the volume was half way dealt with it hydraized into three
> heads, and each head became a volume. Finding that nothing
> could be done except on such enormous scale, I determined to
> take the hydra by the horns, and produce a complete treatise on
> landscape art.[59]

That led on to questions: "what is the real end of landscape
art?" and reflections as to whether art "might become an instru-
ment of gigantic moral power".

Chapter 4

The maturing friendship

In October 1842, the upwardly mobile Ruskin family acquired the remaining thirty-six years' lease, on payment of £4800, on a more spacious house and garden at 163 Denmark Hill, only a mile or so from their previous house at Herne Hill. This was a much more comfortable property in which the Ruskins could entertain more freely and provide good hospitality. The cool wine cellar alone was one of the most comprehensive and of the highest quality, as befitted a good wine merchant. John James Ruskin's stock included thirty dozen Cockburn Port bottled in 1840, twenty-three dozen Harris Port bottled in 1830, twelve dozen Muscatel, sixteen dozen pints and over thirteen gallons of Paxarete (a sweet wine used for blending sherry), and one hundred and nine dozen bottles and fifty-four gallons of sherry.[1] In addition there were large stocks of fine wines. Over nearly three decades, until 1871, many famous writers, artists, politicians, friends and acquaintances would be welcomed at this house. Among these were Turner, Samuel Prout, Charles Eliot Norton, Henry James, Richard Fall and Robert Browning. Gordon was one of the first guests and stayed for almost a week in January 1843. His arrival was recorded in Ruskin's diary entry of 21 January:

Gordon came today – and always full of mind. He says when

anything like the planned assassination of Sir R. Peel in papers to-night – takes place, nobody does anything naturally – nobody asks, but every body inquires.[2]

One of their conversations centred on religion. Ruskin's report reveals Gordon's High-Church leanings, recounting his dislike of Martin Luther and his repudiation of the doctrine of justification by Faith to which Luther adhered:

> I am quite sleepy and tired to-night, though I have had some interesting conversation with Gordon – who doesn't like Luther at all – [...] in one of his last letters to a friend [...] he [i.e. Luther, ed.] says – pecca fortiter – [3][...] Great point of dispute. G[ordon] says, is [...] not worship of images, nor of Virgin – but doctrine of justification[4] in which the Romanists are right.[5]

Both men attended a service at Camden Chapel in Walworth Road, Camberwell, where the Rev. Henry Melvill was the incumbent. Melvill's lengthy, evangelical sermons – although perhaps not quite rivalling the four-hour orations of the seventeenth-century French churchman Louis Bourdaloue whose name was given to a ladies' chamber pot – were structured according to a regular pattern familiar to his parishioners, with pauses enabling them to cough and clear their throats.[6] This was one of his last appearances at Camden Chapel. His fame as a Ciceronian orator spread far and wide – Gladstone was among his admirers[7] – and he was soon promoted to the Principalship of the East India College, Haileybury, a post he held until the college closed in 1858.[8] He was also Chaplain to Queen Victoria. Gordon did not share Melvill's Puritanism, preferring Pusey's Oxford Tractarianism:

> Sermon from Melville [sic] showing the duty of rejoicing. Gordon didn't like it – said it was not so positive a command as M[elvill] wanted to make out – preferred one of Pusey's, which affirmed that the Christian posture was one of constant humiliation.

Melville said finely of the phrase – rejoice <u>in the Lord</u> – That the want of joy was caused only by looking for the cause of it to our-selves – for the real cause was, not that our faith was too strong to let Christ go – but that Christ was too faithful to let <u>us</u> go.[9]

Out among the "nasty blue mist at Norwood" and "cold wind", Ruskin enjoyed a "pleasant walk with Gordon", perhaps peppered with theological questions.[10] In *Praeterita* Ruskin recalled how, only a few years before during their walks over the Norwood hills, he had tried to engage Gordon, unsuccessfully, in his [i.e. Ruskin's] "favourite topic of conversation, namely, the torpor of the Protestant churches, and their duty [...] before any thought of missionary work [...] or comfortable settling to pastoral work at home, to trample finally out the smouldering 'diabolic fire' of the Papacy, in all Papal-Catholic lands". Gordon, although about to be ordained, surprised Ruskin by avoiding the topic "with the sense of its being useless bother".[11] He knew that any such discussion at the time would have been futile and would have led to much friction for Ruskin was totally under the influence of his evangelical and anti-Catholic mother. Ruskin was always trying to change the world, whereas Gordon's approach was more realistic. Gordon's attitude had been formed, Ruskin wrote in *Praeterita*, very early when "a keen, though entirely benevolent, sense of the absurdity of the world took away his heart in working for it" or, Ruskin added, "perhaps I should rather have said, the density and unmalleability of the world, than absurdity. He thought there was nothing to be done with it, and that after all it would get on by itself".[12]

Ruskin was an avid theatregoer and he took Gordon to Drury Lane to see *Macbeth* with the great Shakespearean actor William Charles Macready in the central tragic role. Ruskin and Gordon reacted quite differently to the play: Ruskin with detached but hyperbolic dislike as demonstrated by the underlining in his diary, Gordon with strong emotional attachment and sensitivi-ty. Late on the evening of 24 January, while politely waiting for his guest to return from a christening, Ruskin wrote in his diary:

> I am getting quite dissipated – out at Drury Lane last night.
> <u>Macready in Macbeth – wretched beyond all I had conceived</u>
> <u>possible.</u> – quite tired and bored – but Gordon liked it – and as
> it was for him I went, I was well pleased. I was surprised to see
> him completely affected and upset by the scene where Macduff
> hears of the death of his children. [...] I am sitting up now only
> for Gordon, who has been out to a christening and mayn't be
> back till midnight, I dare say.[13]

Gordon's reaction to the stage deaths may have been due to
the revival of thoughts of how his own grandmother had
responded to the death of her only surviving son, George
Osborne Gordon (Gordon's father) in 1822 and his funeral at
Broseley Parish Church on 8 April. Perhaps in the course of their
many conversations Gordon shed light on his reaction?

The weather had turned unusually mild for mid-January: it
was 65 degrees Fahrenheit (the equivalent of 17.5 degrees
Celsius) in the hall of 163 Denmark Hill "but with a small fire".
Gordon and Ruskin enjoyed both the warm weather and "a
pleasant saunter" to the zoological gardens with "many new
animals".[14]

On the last "pleasant evening"[15] of Gordon's stay, two other
friends were present: Gordon's only sister, Jane then aged
twenty-six and Richard Fall. We do not know whether Jane was
also staying at Denmark Hill or whether she had been invited
solely for the evening. Richard Fall lived nearby at 44 Herne Hill.
One of Ruskin's favourite places in the vicinity was Dulwich
Gallery and on Gordon's last day, they "sauntered" there. On
this, the diary is laconic. How interesting it would have been to
know Gordon's opinions on *The Destruction of Niobe and her
Children*, or Salvator Rosa's *Mountainous Landscape with a
River*, the subject of discussion in Ruskin's chapter "On Inferior
Mountains" in *Modern Painters*?[16]

27 January 1843 marked Gordon's departure and left Ruskin

feeling alone and bereft of his company. He wrote: "Gordon left us today, […] I miss him very much, kind fellow, and clever as kind."[17] Ruskin accompanied Gordon into central London, probably by coach and horses, from where he would have travelled back to Oxford. Perhaps to counteract his feelings of loneliness and sadness, Ruskin immediately called on Turner. Fortunately, he "found him in – & in excellent humour".[18] But the visit was not entirely for palliative reasons. Turner was very much on Ruskin's mind, for he was in the throes of completing his first major work *Modern Painters*, a defence of the great English landscape painter. It was more than "<u>beginning to assume form</u>" as Ruskin suggested, but nevertheless emphasised, in his diary on 26 January 1843,[19] for it was published in the first week of May 1843.

For part of the summer term, Ruskin returned to Oxford, without "Mama", to satisfy residential requirements relating to the award of his MA. This was an opportunity, at last, to be alone in Oxford with Gordon. They discussed religion and it would have been more sensible if Ruskin had shown more discretion and had not conveyed Gordon's religious beliefs to his mother. There was a strong difference of opinion between Margaret Ruskin's dogmatic, self-righteous, evangelical views and those of Gordon. She admonished her twenty-four-year-old son, and Gordon, in a letter (to her son) of 12 June 1843:

What strange whims even men of first rate talents get into their heads. Does Mr. Gordon forget that we have an Almighty Intercessor? … I am sorry, very sorry, that such differences should take place anywhere, but more especially that they should have arisen in Oxford. What are the real doctrines of what is termed Puseyism? Why do they not state them fairly and in such plain terms as may enable people of ordinary understandings to know what they think the truth? Any time I have heard Mr Newman preach, he seemed to me like Oliver Cromwell to talk that he might not be understood … Surely our Saviour's consecration must have effected a change in the elements if an

ordinary minister can; [...] and I beseech you to take nothing for
granted that you hear from these people, but think and search for
yourself. As I have said, I have little fear of you, but I shall be glad
when you get from among them.[20]

Her hypocritical order to "think and search for yourself" was
really "think as I do".

*   *   *

Any differences of opinion were set aside, and Gordon was
invited again to stay at Denmark Hill the following year, 15-19
January. Details are sketchy. The two friends enjoyed their
shared interests in art and geology and, as before, Ruskin was
deeply sorry when Gordon left. They went to the Geological
Society of which Ruskin had been made a Fellow in 1839.
Ruskin did "a little oil painting and drawing, and some brushing
up of head with G[ordon]".[21]

In spite of suffering from a "horrid cold" which got worse and
worse, Ruskin was not deterred from making the journey to
Tottenham Green, then a pleasant village to the north of
London. He wanted to introduce Gordon to Benjamin Godfrey
Windus (1790-1867) and to his large collection of Turner paintings. Windus was a retired coachmaker who was an avid and
astute collector of Turner's works and those of other artists. He
had acquired a substantial collection, housed in the library of
his villa at Tottenham Green, that he allowed people to visit,
usually once a week. It was almost a private Turner gallery but
Ruskin had "the run of his rooms at any time",[22] enabling him to
have access to source material for *Modern Painters*. Ruskin considered that apart from himself, Windus was the only other
person who "*cared*, in the true sense of the word, for Turner".[23]
It was Ruskin's second visit that week to Windus's: his obsession
with Turner was unabated. Among the many drawings, water-
colours and oils, Gordon may have seen *Glaucus and Scylla*,
Tynemouth, and *The Lake of Zug*.[24] Ruskin's diary entry records

that they had a "pleasant day".[25]

The scarcity of diary entries during Gordon's stay may to some extent be due to Ruskin being incapacitated by the severity of his cold. "I haven't had so bad a cold for years: thoroughly incapacitated for everything to-day", he wrote on 19 January.

But something was troubling Gordon during that short, winter stay. Ruskin was aware of it, but so tactful and sensitive was he to his friend's emotional state that he refrained from violating Gordon's need for privacy. It was not until several weeks later that Gordon confided to Ruskin what must have been his doubts about the latter's pursuit of art as a career and a lifetime occupation:[26] that was what had been on his mind during the Denmark Hill stay in January. It is through Ruskin's lengthy response (of 10 March 1844)[27] that we not only surmise Gordon's problem but we enter deeply into Ruskin's mind. He reveals for the first time the tensions he felt about commencing what became *Modern Painters* and his dilemma about his future career. He asks Gordon for advice and lists, in a penetrating study of self-analysis, seven reasons why he is not suited to be a clergyman, as his mother wished. Broadly the main characteristics of his mind are, he writes, "to mystery in what it contemplates and analysis in what it studies". He continues like a performer on stage in an entertaining, yet self-mocking manner. One can almost hear the laughter at the end of each cadence:

It [Ruskin's mind] is externally occupied in watching vapours and splitting straws (Query, an unfavourable tendency in a sermon).

Secondly, it has a rooted horror of neat windows and clean walls (Query, a dangerous disposition in a village).

Thirdly, it is slightly heretical as to the possibility of anybody's being damned (Q. an immoral state of feeling in a clergyman).

Fourthly, it has an inveterate hatred of people who turn up the white of their eyes (Q. an uncharitable state of feeling towards a pious congregation).

Fifthly, it likes not the company of clowns – except in a pantomime (Q. an improper state of feeling towards country squires).

Sixthly and seventhly, it likes solitude better than company, and stones better than sermons.[28]

Gordon already knew these aspects of Ruskin's personality and would not have been in the least surprised. Ruskin's letter ends with a mention of an unknown lady: "We are all glad to hear Miss G. is better." Miss Jane Gordon, perhaps?

During the Easter Vacation, two days before Good Friday on 3 April 1844, Gordon and an unnamed male friend, "a pleasant fellow", were invited to lunch at Denmark Hill. Gordon stayed on for dinner where he met some of Ruskin's distant Scottish relatives, the Tweddales. "I enjoyed myself much", Ruskin wrote in his diary, "though the Tweddales were rather stupid company for him [Gordon] at dinner".[29] "It was", Ruskin continued, "a glorious day – for weather – cloudless sky, intense blue, but wind a little cold – though from the west". At the end of this happy day, in which Ruskin had also sketched "a bit of fine trunk", he walked with his guests as far as the Elephant and Castle – a distance of about three miles in the direction of central London – "and sauntered back in great luxury".[30]

Saturday 28 April 1844 marked an important step, demonstrating Ruskin's celebrity status as a sought-after young writer, author of two editions of *Modern Painters*, I, published within a year of each other.[31] He was invited, without his parents, to the home of Sir Robert Harry Inglis (1786-1855) in fashionable, aristocratic Bedford Square in central London, a stone's throw from the British Museum. Sir Robert Inglis was at the time MP for Oxford University (a seat he held between 1829-1854). The invitation was most likely to a breakfast party, for Ruskin was back at Denmark Hill the same day by two o'clock. Sir Robert had gathered together around his table a glittering array of interesting and influential people of varying ages: twenty-five-year-old Ruskin was the youngest member of the party. Among these were

Lord Northampton – Spencer Alwynne Compton, second Marquis of Northampton (1790-1851) who was President of the Royal Society between 1838-1849[32] –, Lord Arundel and the historian and politician Lord Mahon, afterwards 5th Earl Stanhope (1805-1875). There was the eighty-one-year-old poet Samuel Rogers (1763-1855) whose book of poems *Italy* with illustrations by Turner had first aroused Ruskin's interest in that country. Another guest was the arctic explorer Sir John Franklin (1786-1847), "the North Sea man"[33] as Ruskin reminded his father. Franklin, after a distinguished naval career in the Napoleonic wars, was best known as a national figure who had brought fame to his country through his exploration of vast, unknown wastes in northern Canada. He had recently returned from a nine-year spell (1834-1843) as governor of the penal colony of Tasmania (known as Van Diemen's Land until 1855). Franklin never returned from an expedition attempting unsuccessfully to break through the North-West Passage: he died heroically frozen in the packed ice in 1847 where his body remained until it was discovered in 1859. Sitting immediately next to Ruskin was the MP for Pontefract, Yorkshire, Richard Monckton Milnes, later Lord Houghton (1809-1885). The presence of this charismatic, often larger-than-life figure filled the dining room: he liked young Ruskin and "talked away most pleasantly"[34] to him, asking him to go and see him. They exchanged visiting cards, but when did they next meet?

Ruskin was showered with other invitations, from Rogers,[35] from Lord Northampton to breakfasts and *soirées*. He was launched. However, writing required solitariness and single-mindedness and Ruskin sensed the perils ahead if he accepted all the invitations. This party served as an early warning to him. For in the following year, his need to be alone in order to concentrate on a second volume of *Modern Painters* was uppermost in his mind.

* * *

The annual Ruskin family continental tour in 1844 lasted over three months. After setting sail from Dover on 14 May, the family did not see the white cliffs again until 23 August. Geology was Ruskin's main interest for most of this tour, so much of the time was spent in Savoy and Switzerland. Chamonix was the ideal base for four weeks in June and early July from which to explore mountains and their anatomy. Once again, Gordon joined the party but this time at intervals. In Chamonix Ruskin made a drawing, *Chamouni in Afternoon Sunshine*, as a gift for Gordon. During the execution of the picture, Ruskin had expressed to Gordon the "constant vexation [he] suffered because [he] could not draw better", whereupon Gordon replied, simply: "And I should be very content if I could draw at all."[36] Gordon later gave this painting to his sister Jane who likewise enjoyed mountain scenery and walking.[37] On his Alpine rambles, Ruskin was also collecting samples of plants and flowers that he saved in a green leather bound book, with a clasp, his *Flora of Chamouni*. His album contains dried samples of meadow plants, alpine plants, mosses, varieties of orchids, gentians and saxifrage accompanied by records and descriptions. Of the *Saxifraga Cuneifolia* he wrote: "This saxifrage, common everywhere, was growing in great luxuriance (June 9th) in the lower woods of the Pèlerins, whence I gathered these in my evening walk. But all the form of the flower is now lost."[38]

On 7 July 1844, Ruskin and Gordon spent the day in Geneva, but Gordon, much to Ruskin's chagrin and irritation, could not stay longer and had to return to Chamonix "with a stick of a pupil". Ruskin wrote in his diary (on 8 July) from St Gingoulph, a small town nestling in the southeast corner of the Lake of Geneva:

> Yesterday at Geneva a dull day, though spent with Gordon; Everything going wrong – Tug[39] ill: no letter from Griffith – bad weather – Mont B[lanc] invisible – Gordon unable to go with us: forced to go to Chamonix with a stick of a pupil. I was very sulky all the way here – […].[40]

This suggests that Gordon was accompanied by one of his less robust students, "a stick of a pupil"!

Gordon travelled from Chamonix and met Ruskin and his parents on 19 July 1844 at Zermatt, then a tiny Swiss town at the foot of the Matterhorn. Chamonix is to Mont Blanc what Zermatt is to the Matterhorn. As the crow flies, over the peaks, the distance between the two resorts is approximately 69 km/44 miles. But the only route possible for a human being would be via Martigny (meeting the Rhône), Sion, Sierre, Visp to Zermatt, a total of approximately 140 km.[41] The journey, on foot, would have taken several days: it would not have been easy. Gordon would have had to negotiate several cols and rugged, rocky terrain, through glacier passes: he may occasionally have used mules. Chamonix to Martigny was an eight-hour journey on mule-back.[42] If Gordon broke the journey halfway, very basic accommodation was available at the inn at Trient.[43] From Martigny to Sion he may have posted.[44] We know that Gordon spent one night *en route* at Visp (Viège in French) in the very Catholic Canton of the Valais in south-west Switzerland. From Visp to Zermatt it was at least an eight-hour walk such as that undertaken by the Scottish physicist and writer on the Alps, James Forbes, in 1841.[45] There was no railway from Visp to Zermatt until 1891: that reduced the journey time to two and a half hours. Gordon arrived first at Zermatt, not surprisingly tired and hungry and his first thoughts on greeting the Ruskins were connected with food rather than the beauty of the Matterhorn "in full ruby, with a wreath of crimson cloud drifting from its top"[46] that so enchanted Ruskin. Gordon, Ruskin recalled, "met us with his most settledly practical and constitutional face" and the following dialogue ensued:

'Yes, the Matterhorn is all very fine; but do you know there's nothing to eat?' said Gordon
'Nonsense; we can eat anything here.' Ruskin
'Well, the black bread's two months old, and there's nothing else but potatoes.' Gordon

'There must be milk, anyhow.' Ruskin
Yes, there was milk, he supposed.
'You can sop your bread in it then; what could be nicer?'
Gordon.[47]

Gordon was thoroughly disappointed with the meagre menu
– the hotel too was so very uncomfortable that the party only
stayed one night – and Ruskin had to admit, although somewhat
reluctantly, his agreement:

> But Gordon's downcast mien did not change; and I had to admit
> myself, when supper-time came, that one might almost as hope-
> lessly have sopped the Matterhorn as the loaf.[48]

This unrefined but nutritional and healthy rye bread or rye loaf
– the six-month-old *pain de seigle* that Henri de Saussure had
described in his report on the region in 1796[49] – formed a staple
part of the diet of these mountain people.

What an impressive sight the sunset was against the
Matterhorn when the clouds eventually lifted and revealed
"playing crimson lights over the sky, and the Matterhorn
appeared in full ruby, with a wreath of fiery cloud drifting from
its top". For Gordon this sunset had religious (high church) significance and overtones: it was "like incense from a large altar".[50]

* * *

1845 was the year in which Gordon was appointed University
Reader in Rhetoric. It was also the year in which the twenty-six-
year-old Ruskin set off on his first continental journey (for
seven months between 2 April and 4 November 1845) without
his parents. But he never travelled alone. His valet George
Hobbs accompanied him: Joseph Couttet, his faithful guide and
fatherly factotum joined his entourage in Geneva. It was a
stately, measured journey for the most part in Ruskin's private
black and gilt *calèche* and horses: all the evidence pointed to a

wealthy, well-educated, perhaps rather spoilt, pampered young English gentleman travelling in a grand style. Young Ruskin was totally in charge and his well-paid staff (Couttet received four francs a day clear for himself and in addition had free board and lodging) attended to his every whim. Couttet held an umbrella over him while he sketched, and made sure his master always took "a squeeze of lemon in his water".[51] As Ruskin journeyed across France, the Alps and Italy,[52] as was his wont he arranged to travel with or meet up with different congenial friends and companions at various places *en route*. He needed the intellectual stimulation: he met his drawing teacher and artist James Duffield Harding in Baveno and went with him for several weeks across North Italy to Como, Bergamo, Desenzano, Verona and Venice.[53] Ruskin was, as always, very busy and totally absorbed in his work for this tour was the foundation of the second volume of *Modern Painters*, published in April 1846.

Gordon had recommended that Ruskin read, with care and attention, *The Laws of Ecclesiastical Polity* by the sixteenth-century theologian Richard Hooker (1554-1600), "for its arguments and its English".[54] This Ruskin did, recalling in *Praeterita* that he left "no passage till [he] had put as much thought into it as it could be made to carry, and chosen the words with the utmost precision and tune [he] could give them".[55] Gordon's wise counsel was, Ruskin claimed, the basis of the style of *Modern Painters*, II: "the style of the book was formed on a new model, given me by Osborne Gordon."[56] Ruskin attempted partly to imitate Hooker, whose style he admired, and also Samuel Johnson.[57] However, there is a hint that Ruskin may have regretted his overdependence on Hooker, when, as John Batchelor points out in his biography, Ruskin wrote in 1883 of the shame and indignation felt on re-reading the somewhat pedantic *Modern Painters*, II, "at finding the most solemn of all objects of human thought [God, presumably?] handled at once with the presumption of a youth, and the affectations of an anonymous writer".[58]

Five weeks of the tour were spent in Florence, between 29 May and 6 July. This was Ruskin's third visit and his appreciation of its art and architecture was in stark contrast to his first impressions in November 1840 when he was grievously disappointed in many things – "the Uffizi collection in general, an unbecoming medley, got together by people who knew nothing, and cared less than nothing, about the arts":[59] the church of Santa Maria Novella seemed to him ugly and he could not understand Michelangelo's admiration for it. "Glad to get out of stupid Florence", was his pointed diary entry on 25 November 1840. But now, five years later, Ruskin was seeing Florence with different eyes. On revisiting the church of Santa Maria Novella, he was "very much taken aback".[60] There were Cimabue's *Madonna*, Orcagna's *Last Judgment* in the chapel, Domenico Ghirlandaio's frescoes and "three *perfectly* preserved works of Fra Angelico".[61] He studied Rubens in the Pitti Palace.[62] He was desperately short of time, in spite of often working from five o'clock in the morning until late at night. The long daylight hours of early and mid-summer could not be wasted. Florence was a particularly rich storehouse for the subject of his next book and Ruskin worked relentlessly as the oppressive heat increased. The mosquitoes were a problem and Ruskin attempted to fend them off with some essence of lavender purchased from the monks' *Spezieria* at Santa Maria Novella.[63] He revisited Masaccio's frescoes in the Brancaci Chapel in the church of Santa Maria del Carmine: on a previous occasion he had sketched the background landscape of *The Tribute Money* and discussed it in *Modern Painters*, I.[64] The realisation that Masaccio had achieved such greatness in art at such an early age and had died in his mid-twenties (more or less Ruskin's age) goaded him to do more work. Gordon was never far from Ruskin's fertile, cross-referential mind and in this chapel he endowed his friend with a kind of eternity by connecting him with Florentine art. As he looked intently at a fresco of a self-portrait of Masaccio, he saw in it "a kind of mixture of Osborne Gordon and Lorenzo

dei Medici (the Magnifico)".[65] Giorgio Vasari (1511-1574) identified the self-portrait as being that of St Thomas, the last figure
on the right of the central group in *The Tribute Money*. Which
painting of Lorenzo dei Medici did Ruskin have in mind?

Developing themes on concepts of beauty and imagination in
art for *Modern Painters*, II, was a vast comparative undertaking
that required extensive and intensive knowledge of paintings. As
always, Ruskin combined the hand and the eye in order to
remember and see. So he recorded detailed descriptions of his
discoveries – Giotto's frescoes of the story of *Job* in the Cappella
dei Medici in the church of Santa Croce,[66] works by Orcagna,
Giotto's *Crucifix* in the church of San Marco,[67] Benozzo
Gozzoli's frescoes in the Riccardi Palace,[68] tombs sculpted by
Mino da Fiesole in the Badia.[69] The aim of *Modern Painters*, II,
was twofold, as Ruskin explained later in *Praeterita*:

> I had two distinct instincts to be satisfied, rather than ends in
> view, as I wrote day by day with higher-kindled feeling the
> second volume of *Modern Painters*. The first, to explain to
> myself, and then demonstrate to others, the nature of that quality
> of beauty which I now saw to exist through all the happy condi-
> tions of living organism; and down to the minutest detail and
> finished material structure naturally produced. The second, to
> explain and illustrate the power of two schools of art unknown
> to the British public, that of Angelico in Florence, and Tintoret
> in Venice.[70]

*   *   *

It was about two o'clock on Wednesday 18 June 1845. Ruskin
was in the Uffizi,[71] studying the paintings, when he met, coinci-
dentally or by design, a "Mr and Mrs Pritchard". This was forty-
nine-year-old barrister John Pritchard on honeymoon with his
young bride, the former Miss Jane Gordon – aged twenty-nine –
sister of Osborne Gordon. Ruskin had known Jane since at least
January 1843 when he had entertained her at the Herne Hill

family home.[72] But for reasons unknown, he had never been introduced to her husband whom she married in 1845. It was a brief encounter – the Pritchards were leaving for Switzerland the following day – but a favourable one as Ruskin commented to his father: "She is looking very well; he seems a nice person."[73]

Who was "Mr Pritchard", the middle-aged barrister who was enjoying art on that hot summer's day in Florence?

Chapter 5

Pritchard, Effie, Gordon and the Ruskins

His amours were notorious, and some of his mistresses were rare specimens of rustic beauty.

John Randall

Thus the Broseley-born historian and artist John Randall (1810-1910) described local landowner George Forester in his book of country life, *Old Sports and Sportsmen*, published in 1873. George Forester (c. 1738-1811), known as the great hunting "Willey Squire" or "the Squire", was of a prestigious lineage that could be traced back to the 13th century when the family were originally "foresters" in Shropshire, a much coveted office that gave the holder control over large tracts of land. He had inherited estates, known as "the Willey estates" stretching for many miles around the village of Willey. A stream of members of the Forester family had represented the Borough of Wenlock in Parliament almost continuously from the reign of Charles II.[1] The family also frequently held office as bailiffs or mayors of Wenlock and sheriffs of Shropshire.

The family seat was Willey Hall, known later as the Old Hall to distinguish it from the New Hall built in 1813-1815. This was George Forester's country seat, set in a large park – a portion of the ancient forest of Shirlot/Shirlett – situated close to Willey Church (St John's). It was a solid stone and brick 'Queen Anne' mansion with a distinctive octagonal tower at one end.

The "Squire", who never married, had the reputation of being a womaniser. Jealousy arose inevitably among his paramours and on one occasion was of such vehemence that one "Phœbe Higgs" threatened to shoot him unless he gave her "maintenance equal to that of Miss Cal–t".[2] On another occasion when Phœbe Higgs attempted to kill him, his life was only spared when, at dead of night, as she was on her way to do the deed, she became unnerved by her favourite monkey who jumped on her shoulder just as she was opening a gate. However, he provided for his many illegitimate children and treated them with care and consideration. But his dissolute life style, ribald language and behaviour were tempered by his concern for the poor and hungry whom he supplied with corn, butter and coal during shortages. His favourite sport was fox-hunting, dressed in his red coat, riding with his own packs of hounds and with his famous whipper-in Tom Moody.

This is a snapshot of the man who employed Pritchard's father (John Pritchard Senior as I shall refer to him) as his agent from 1794. When he accepted this extra responsibility, Pritchard Senior was already established as an attorney in Broseley, in partnership with John Harper and Thomas Mytton.[3] Country attorneys needed to be linked with and represented by London solicitors in order to have a presence in the capital. By 1805, Pritchard Senior and his partner James Griffiths had acquired two London agents, Presland and John Tarrant. Like John James Ruskin, John Pritchard Senior had achieved his wealth and public esteem by sheer hard work and determination: by 1799, in addition to his legal practice, he was also a partner in the bank Vickers, Son and Pritchard with branches in Broseley and Bridgnorth. The professional worlds of attorneys and bankers were closely interwoven in a lucrative partnership: they had a monopoly in Broseley. There were no other solicitors or bankers in the town.

Not only was Pritchard Senior Forester's trusted agent, but

was also his legal advisor. When there was a disagreement with the vicar of nearby Barrow Church – "Parson Jones" – about the chancel and pews, Forester wrote a letter to Pritchard Senior asking him for a legal opinion about certain encroachments upon what he conceived to be his rights as patron.[4]

Forester's trust in Pritchard Senior was absolute, even after his death as his will demonstrates. "I do hereby request", he wrote, "my Cousin Cecil Forester and the said John Pritchard [Senior], as soon as conveniently may be after my decease, to look over and inspect the letters, papers, and writings belonging to me at the time of my decease, and such of them as they shall deem to be useless I desire them to destroy". There is an interesting parallel here, for it was to be John James Ruskin who, many years later, had such trust in Pritchard Senior's son that he instructed him to be one of the executors of his will.

* * *

As a boy, John experienced many family deaths. His younger brother William died aged ten months in 1801 and his mother, Ann, died in 1809, at the age of forty-four. Six young children were left without a mother: George, the eldest, then aged sixteen; John, thirteen; Thomas, eleven; Emma, six; Eliza, five and Mary Anne. John and Thomas were sent, the following year (1810), as boarders to Shrewsbury School where their elder brother George was already a pupil. John enrolled at the same time as Thomas Rowley who rose to become Headmaster of Bridgnorth School (Osborne Gordon's influential Headmaster). More sorrow hit the family when John's sister Eliza died at the age of seven.[5] John's widowed father found a new wife and remarried on 20 September,[6] two years after Anne's death. Pritchard Senior's second wife was Fanny Wilkinson (1760-1839), daughter of Mr Wilkinson of Buildwas. It appears that no more children were born: Fanny was fifty-one years old at the time of her marriage and probably past childbearing age.

After Shrewsbury School, John Pritchard joined the family firm of attorneys and worked alongside his elder brother George (1793 -1861) and his father. He is first listed in Clarke's Law List of 1824 in which the entry reads: "Broseley – John Pritchard, George Pritchard and John Pritchard, junior". Their London agents were Bigg, and Mayhew & Co. That situation remained stable for twelve years. Two more family deaths ensued: his brother Thomas, also a solicitor and banker, in 1829 at the age of thirty-one, and sister Emma in 1832 at the age of twenty-nine. They may have been victims of a terrible cholera epidemic in Broseley and the surrounding area that was at its peak in 1832 and 1833 and of such severity that a special burial ground was created.

In 1837, Pritchard Senior died at the age of seventy-eight at his residence, the Bank House, Broseley, on 14 June: his death was recorded in *The Gentleman's Magazine*. His death was followed two years later by that of his second wife, Fanny. In her will, she showed that same generosity of spirit found in the Pritchard family: she left £100 to be invested in government securities, the interest of which to be used for the purchase of warm clothing for ten poor women, to be given on St Thomas's Day (21 December).[7] George Pritchard took over the practice as sole attorney in Broseley for several years.[8] Left without any surviving parents, John and George Pritchard took responsibility for the only remaining sibling, Mary Anne. Mary Anne never married: she was a robust woman who lived to a considerable age and died on 5 March 1882, four days before her eighty-seventh birthday. A portrait of Pritchard Senior, painted by Devis, was engraved by Cousins.[9]

After his "apprenticeship" in the family firm and increasing responsibility, John's position was more formally recognised when, on 10 June 1841, he was called to the bar at Lincoln's Inn.[10] His marriage to Jane Gordon in 1845 opened many doors. Jane's brother George (1815-1865) was also a banker/attorney and became a partner in the firm of Pritchard, Nicholas, Gordon and Co. Through Jane and her brother Osborne Gordon, Pritchard entered not only the Ruskin family circle where he was warmly welcomed by all, but the enriching network of a non-banking, non-legal community. Ruskin's many political, artistic, literary and academic contacts would have been stimulating and useful in furthering Pritchard's ambition to be a MP. Ruskin enabled John Pritchard to become a national figure, whereas his solicitor/attorney brother George remained essentially embedded in Shropshire life, his work focussed on the town and county of his birth (Under-Sheriff of Shropshire, Deputy-Lieutenant of Shropshire, Mayor of Much Wenlock, local phi-lanthropist). He remained a loyal, trusted lifelong friend of Ruskin and his parents.

*   *   *

Back to the summer of 1845 and the *chassé-croisé* between Gordon and Ruskin ...

Gordon was also planning to spend much of the summer vacation of 1845 abroad, on a lengthened tour in the Alps, Switzerland and Italy. His main companion was George Marshall (1817-1897),[11] also of Christ Church. Marshall, five years younger than Gordon, matriculated in 1836 at the age of 18, obtained his BA in 1840 and MA in 1842, and held various posts in the college – Reader in Greek in 1846, Censor 1849-1857 – until he left to become vicar of Pyrton, Oxon in 1857. Marshall remained a lifelong friend of Gordon's and wrote the first and only biography of him. Gordon and Ruskin were due to meet: the problem was where and when. Ruskin was not entirely free to choose his own itinerary: his father controlled the purse strings and so regarded it as his right and parental duty to influence the shape and timing of the tour. Each day Ruskin was under the irksome obligation to write to his parents and report fully on his activities. If he missed, there would be recriminations and questions. However, this obligation ensured a plentiful supply of letters and information enabling us to reconstruct events.

In a strange way, responsibility for arranging the meeting with Gordon became dependent on the whim of John James Ruskin. When Ruskin was in Florence at the beginning of June, Gordon was staying with his mother Elizabeth Gordon at her home at Linley Hall, about three miles from Broseley on the road to Bridgnorth, where she had lived since at least 1841.[12] Instead of contacting Gordon directly and discussing the matter with him, Ruskin wrote to his father via his mother:

> Would you tell my father that if he thinks it best for me to go to the Alps at once, to write to *Gordon* at Linly [sic] Hall, near Broseley, Shropshire, and apologize to him for the letter I sent which I ordered to be paid, but which couldn't be paid, I found afterwards, & to tell him that after the 15th July, I am to be found at Val Anzasca, or near it, for a month & that I will leave a letter for him at the post office Domo d'Ossola, saying where to find me, and that if he can take the mountains first, we will go to Venice together in September.[13]

In an age without the telephone or telegraph, making such uncertain arrangements seemed doomed to failure – and that is exactly what happened. One can but imagine Gordon's reaction and how stretched his tolerance must have been towards his good friend. Gordon had already sketched out his route with Marshall, taking into account an agreed meeting with Ruskin. Now things had changed.

On Friday morning 13 June, Ruskin informed his father: "I write to Gordon immediately, telling him to write me here, with his probable address (on the 1st July)."[14] Because Gordon had changed his itinerary, at the last minute, to try and accommodate Ruskin's, he had not had time to inform his sister and her new husband. Hence the comment in Ruskin's letter, of 17 and 18 June, from Florence, to his father: "They didn't know of Gordon's change of route."[15]

Meanwhile, Gordon had reached Geneva! Ruskin recognised

the confusion his letters were causing and commented to his father, from Florence on 3 July: "I've a letter from Gordon, at Geneva – nearly as unintelligible as mine."[16]

From Florence, Ruskin went in a northerly direction to Milan, then towards Como and the northern Italian lakes. They reached Macugnaga, in Val Anzasca, on 23 July (he had told Gordon that he would be there "after the 15th July [...] for a month"). Ruskin was now among the Pennine Alps "up in the clouds again", in view of his favourite peak Monte Rosa that "showed off tonight, brilliantly, like a good creature as she is". He was happy and looking forward to Gordon's arrival: "Gordon wrote me from Geneva he should drop down on me here some day soon – perhaps he is pastured up by the weather at Saas."[17] The Swiss village of Saas was almost directly north of Macugnaga but separated by fairly inhospitable terrain. It was at least a full day's walk from Saas to Macugnaga, via the desolate Mattmark See and a climb over the pass of Monte Moro. Gordon did not arrive.

By 19 August, in Baveno, Ruskin's anxiety was mounting. He was jittery, upset at having missed Gordon and fearful that the same thing might happen with his water colourist friend J. D. Harding. He was also desperate – the word is not too strong – to have company and expressed his uncertainty and helplessness – "I don't know what to do" was his heartfelt *cri de cœur* – in a letter to his father:

> I am fidgetty about Harding, for I have missed Gordon, who is now on his way home – and Acland is at the Shetland islands – and I want to see somebody. I have been a little too much alone.[18]

It was not until 23 August that light was shed on the Gordon mystery and the unfortunate way in which they had missed each other. In his letter to his father, Ruskin blamed Gordon, unfairly I think:

> I have a letter from Gordon – he is going home from Lucerne. We missed each other in a most clumsy way, but it was more his fault

than mine, for he never told me in his letter from Geneva where to write to him, so that I couldn't tell him where I should be – the consequence was that he arrived at Milan on the Sunday [i.e. 20 July], I having left on the Saturday [i.e. 19 July] – he followed me to Como on Tuesday [i.e. 22 July], by accident, saw my name in the book as off for Val Anzasca, & went off the other way, for Venice – and he would have been at Milan on the Saturday but that he got out of the steamer at Arona by mistake for Sesto Calende.[19]

Gordon had taken a boat on Lago Maggiore aiming to disembark at the most southerly point on the Lake (Sesto Calende) from where there was a direct route to Milan. Arona is a small port further up on the western shore of the lake. This seems to have been Gordon's first visit to Italy and his mistake can easily be understood in the circumstances. He certainly tried very hard to find Ruskin. What Ruskin did not seem to understand was that Gordon's vacation was of a limited duration and that he needed to return to Oxford. Ruskin's journey was of an almost indefinite length and with almost unlimited resources.

Ruskin continued to correspond with Gordon during this continental tour and sometimes shared these letters with his parents. There is an echo of this in Ruskin's letter from Venice in which he told his father: "I enclose a letter to Gordon which perhaps may interest you a little."[20]

Gordon was drawn to Chamonix in particular (he had been there with Ruskin in 1842 and 1844) and returned there with Marshall in 1845. But by now, the Oxford tutor was behaving like a student of Ruskin! As such, with his "keen perception and critical judgment", he was already Marshall's guide in matters of Art and Nature. He knew Chamonix well and memories of observing Ruskin closely the previous year as he sketched the mountain scenery, in particular *The Valley of Chamouni* (Ruskin's gift to Gordon), were fresh in his mind. He had shared Ruskin's thoughts, had learned how to see through Ruskin's eyes: Gordon knew Ruskin's mind and personality more intimately than anyone. Marshall confirms Ruskin's influence on Gordon:

Though Mr Gordon was not of a robust frame, he had an exquisite enjoyment of mountain scenery; and without attempting any dangerous ascents he had, perhaps, a truer appreciation of the peculiar beauties of rocks and glaciers than many who had penetrated further into their secrets. He took great interest in Mr Ruskin's studies of nature, which he greatly valued, and was constantly bringing his old pupil's theories to the test of experience.[21]

Gordon gave the impression that he was not physically strong – as photographs imply – but his slight frame belied great strength and powers of endurance. He needed stamina for all those mountain walks and climbs with Ruskin. At Chamonix (during this 1845 tour) Gordon was joined by several other Oxford friends: he took them on a Ruskinian pilgrimage to spend the day on the famous *Mer de Glace*. But Gordon did not engage a skilled and accredited guide – Couttet, one of the best, was away in Ruskin's service at the time – or indeed any guide other than himself. It was foolhardy and, not surprisingly, a near disaster happened. On the return journey, the party lost their way and found themselves off the main tracks and had "carelessly come to a fork in the river, one branch of which lay between them and the Inn at Chamounix, only a short distance off in a straight line".[22] There was at that point a difference of opinion between the young men: realising the danger, all except Gordon wanted to "make a considerable detour, and cross by a bridge further up the stream".[23] Gordon, impetuously, acted otherwise and, "divesting himself of part of his clothing, tried to wade, but, as the rest of the party feared, was swept away by the torrent, icy cold, and running with great rapidity".[24] His companions acted instantly and with great presence of mind ran as fast as they could down stream to a point where "the river narrowed considerably, and where they hoped to rescue him".[25] They waited in vain, fearing the worst. Eventually, they returned to the inn where they were staying and, to their great relief, found Gordon alive and well. His great physical strength had enabled him to reach the opposite bank of the dangerous stretch of water. Marshall adds a poignant touch of local colour to the episode:

> A Savoyard peasant-woman, who had witnessed the adventure, took him under her special protection, and when we reached our quarters, after a long circuit, we had the satisfaction of finding the hero of the day taking his ease in his inn, and, except a few slight cuts, none the worse for his escapade. Those, however, who knew best the danger of his position were much struck by the coolness and address with which he extricated himself from his perilous dilemma.[26]

News of this mishap reached Ruskin's parents and of course Ruskin. Writing in the comfort of the Hôtel de l'Europe, Venice, on 11 September 1845, Ruskin was clearly annoyed by what he considered to be his friend's stupidity and recklessness. "I quite shuddered at Gordon's adventure", he wrote to his father, "which I have never heard of before, but he ought to have had more sense". He added somewhat arrogantly: "I knew better than that at 14."[27]

Responsibility for the missed appointments must rest in almost equal measure with both parties. In his relations with Ruskin – in Britain at least – Gordon does not seem to be an uncertain travelling companion, or someone who arrived for an appointment at the very last minute. However, in Marshall's memoirs published in 1885, he is portrayed quite differently:

> Mr Gordon was not good company for weak nerves. He was constantly on the verge of a catastrophe *de voyage*, which kept his fellow-travellers in a lively state of uncertainty as to his movements. It seemed utterly hopeless, when he was strolling somewhere about, leaving his effects in utter confusion, that he could be ready for boat or train, or any conveyance dependent on time or tide. But at the last possible moment he sauntered in to the place of starting with his usual abstracted air and leisurely gait and look of surprise at any symptom of impatience, though how

chaos had been reduced to order was a secret known only to himself.[28]

Gordon's relationship with the Ruskin family was unharmed and he was a guest, along with Mr and Mrs Pritchard, the dealer Thomas Griffith and wine merchant Robert Cockburn at 163 Denmark Hill on 12 December 1845.[29] This would appear to be the first time that John Pritchard was invited, and would be the first of many such occasions.

In late March 1846, at a small party at Denmark Hill, guests listed in John James's diary were Lady Colquhoun and [Robert?] Monro (both close friends of John James) and "Gordon & Brother".[30] Gordon had two brothers, Alexander and William.

Modern Painters, II, was published on 24 April 1846 and generally favourable reviews followed. Perhaps apprehensive about public reactions to the work, Ruskin and his parents left England before its publication, and did not return until late September. This was yet another long continental tour. Ruskin was now turning his attention to architecture, to the churches and cathedrals of France and Italy.

Gordon's academic career progressed. In 1846 he was appointed University Reader in Greek, and Proctor in the University and Censor of Christ Church in succession to the Rev. Henry George Liddell who left Oxford to become Headmaster of Westminster School. The following year the degree of Bachelor in Divinity was conferred upon him.

But the year ended with personal sadness. Gordon's mother, Elizabeth, died at Linley Hall during the Christmas vacation on 27 December 1846. She was aged 64. Her burial took place on New Year's Day 1847, at Broseley: the ceremony was performed by the Rev. Orlando Forester.[31] Her spinster sister, Martha Onions, took over many of her responsibilities: she is listed as the head of the household at Linley Hall in the census of 30 March 1851.

*   *   *

When the headship of King Edward VI School, Birmingham, became vacant in 1847, Gordon, then aged thirty-four, applied for the post. It would have meant severing his links with Christ Church and he was uncertain about his decision. His weekend stay at the Ruskin family home Saturday to Monday 22-24 January[32] provided him with a much-needed opportunity to discuss the consequences of his action. He may have been invited with this express purpose in mind: John James and Margaret Ruskin would have been ready to give advice. He shared his concerns with Ruskin who then informed his fiancée Effie Gray that Gordon was "anxious about this Birmingham affair".[33] Gordon was unsuccessful in spite of at least twenty-eight testimonials by Oxonions (including John Ruskin) in support of his application.[34] He was rejected on the grounds of his lack of experience of leading a school as Mrs Ruskin explained to her husband in a letter of 3 February 1848: "Gordon does not go to Birmingham, they want one who has kept school before."[35] But such a post of responsibility would nevertheless have suited Gordon and given him the chance to shape young people's lives.

He took a keen interest in education at all levels. Before the Long Vacation in 1847 he published a pamphlet entitled "Considerations on the Improvement of the Present Examination Statute and the Admission of Poor Scholars to the University" (slightly revised and reprinted in the same year).[36] One of his suggestions was that a " much freer play would be given to the genius of individual minds, and to talent of all sorts, *within the system* [Gordon's emphasis], both in respect of matter and of time". In this plea for respect for the individual, Gordon was thinking not only of himself but more likely his student, John Ruskin. As one who had received a scholarship, he was aware of the large numbers of poorer scholars whose parents could not afford an Oxbridge education for their sons. So Gordon proposed a scheme for existing Oxford Colleges to take "300 poor scholars" to reside in "an affiliated Hall to be governed by a Resident Fellow". He also proposed links with National Schools and Grammar Schools to Oxford. At the back of his mind was the Careswell Scholarship that fed into Christ Church. He believed and argued that such a system would revitalise Oxford and give the Church more power over more people and would consequently flourish as a tree "that is planted by the river's side".

But that January weekend at Denmark Hill was not entirely laden with anxiety about the Birmingham post. Gordon delighted in entertaining Ruskin with "nice stories" and gossip about Oxford, much of which was relayed to Effie. One such story was about Dr William Buckland (1784-1856), Professor of Geology at Oxford and since 1845 also Dean of Westminster. Buckland was considered to be an extreme eccentric. The state of his house, more like an untidy and dusty museum of natural history, led John Ruskin in his early days at Christ Church to describe the scene in a letter to his father: "not a chair fit to sit down upon – all covered with dust – broken alabaster candlesticks – withered flower leaves – frogs cut out of serpentine – broken models of fallen temples, torn papers – old manuscripts – stuffed reptiles ... stuffed hyena's [sic], crocodiles and cats."[37]

Things did not seem to have changed much in 1848 and the state of his house was still a subject of discussion, curiosity and amazement. Ruskin wrote to Effie, relaying the gossip and the flavour of Gordon's humour:

> The Dean of Westminster's house came under discussion – dirty
> – or not dirty? I said it was not strictly speaking *dirty* – but only
> mellowed and toned. Well – said Gordon – 'there was a Rats nest
> behind the sideboard in the dining-room that filled a barrow!'[38]

Another of Gordon's stories (also communicated to Effie) was about rowdy students:

> One of the Tutors had been disturbed by a party making a noise
> over his head at 12 o'clock. He went up to them – they were
> rather rude, and he brought them up before the Dean the fol-

lowing morning, who asked 'how they came to be making a noise, – 'Why – Sir,' said one of them – 'we *couldn't* be making much of a noise – for there were but twelve of us, and we were only singing!'[39]

In another letter to Effie, preoccupied with wedding preparations, Ruskin quotes one of Gordon's sayings indirectly (through his mother) and directly: "My mother [...] says not to mind what you finish or what you don't. Pray recollect Gordon's – 'It don't matter how much you have to do if you don't do it.'"[40] This is an echo of Gordon's earlier advice to young Ruskin: "When you have got too much to do, don't do it."

*   *   *

The marriage ceremony took place on 10 April 1848, in the drawing-room of the family home Bowerswell House, Perth, in Scotland. Ruskin's parents did not wish to attend for Bowerswell was associated with too many unhappy memories. The house had originally belonged to Ruskin's ill-fated and debt-ridden grandfather, John Thomas, who had committed suicide there in 1817 by slitting his throat. Margaret Cox's marriage to John James Ruskin was postponed for many years during which time her fiancé worked hard to pay off his father's debts. None of Ruskin's friends attended the wedding, either. Seven years later, Effie and Millais would be married in that same house.

Euphemia Chalmers Gray, usually called Effie, was a pretty, vivacious, nineteen-year-old when she married John Ruskin, aged twenty-nine. She loved parties, fashionable clothes and socialising, in stark contrast to the rather dour man to whom she had pledged lifelong fidelity and who preferred stones to sex. F. J. Furnivall, a Christian Socialist lawyer and vegetarian who was a devotee of Ruskin, described Effie at a party soon after her marriage as a "handsome, tall woman, with a high colour, brown wavy hair, a Scotch woman evidently, dressed in a pink moiré dress".[41] The couple were ill suited and incompatible: the marriage was doomed from the start. After a short honeymoon in the Highlands and Keswick, the couple returned to Ruskin's parental home at Denmark Hill and the constant vigilance and increasing control of the older Ruskins.

Owing to political turmoil and revolutions in continental Europe, Ruskin changed his travel plans from honeymooning abroad and remained in England for several months until calm was restored. After spending two weeks in Dover, and prior to joining Ruskin's parents for a proposed tour of English cathedrals, John and Effie were invited to stay for two weeks in early July with the Aclands at their house in Broad Street, Oxford.

It was the time of Commemoration, the great festival of the Oxford academic year. Effie enjoyed immensely the "continual round of festivities", the endless parties and social whirl. She made the acquaintance of Gordon whom she quoted as saying that this was a time when "every two people meeting on the street exchange invitations".[42] She described the ceremony that took place on 3 July in the packed theatre with much verve in a letter to her parents:

> We went in at ten o'clock, the Ladies being all separated from the gentlemen had a very gay appearance, and the place was crammed full. Then above was the underGraduates gallery and, after the rest of the Theatre was full, all the young men, the doors being opened, rushed in and filled the place just like savages. Then they called out names and shouted or hissed as the person was popular or not, first the Queen and Royal family, then Guizot – tremendous cheering, then Dr. Pusey followed by Jenny Lind, then the Ladies in white gowns, ditto in Pink bonnets and ditto in black which met with no approval, then 'the men that got the Prizes' followed by the 'men that didn't get them', then Mr. Gladstone, who had come to have his degree, was cheered and hissed for seven minutes till both parties were quite exhausted. The Organ then played God save the Queen when every person joined which was very impressive. Then the Chancellor Dr. Plumtree conferred the degrees on Baron Hugel, Mr. Gladstone,

Mr. Hallam, Mr. Cotton etc.[43]

Within a very short time she had made the acquaintance of many titled people ... Mr and Lady Anna Gore Langton, Sir Thomas Dyke Acland, Lady Morgan, Lady Brougham, Lady Dunmore, Lady Dufferin, Lady Lansdowne to name but a few. Effie was "overwhelmed with Invitations",[44] and impressed by this kind of society. Naturally she also met many academics, friends and colleagues of her husband: she had a natural rapport with them for her charm never failed.

On the morning of 4 July, Effie and John were invited by the Rev. Edward Hill (Ruskin's former Mathematics tutor) to breakfast in Christ Church Hall. "About 30 sat down" Effie wrote to her parents, "and enjoyed a very nice meal with fine fruit afterwards".[45] Gordon, a close friend of Mr Hill, may also have been present on that occasion. Feiling, in his book *In Christ Church Hall*, mentions an invitation by Gordon to the young couple to have breakfast in the Hall during this period. That marked what Feiling regarded as the beginning of Ruskin's *via dolorosa*.[46] Differences were quickly emerging between the couple: during a performance of Haydn's *Creation*, which Effie "enjoyed very much", John found the "music detestable and [...] read a book the whole time".[47]

Ruskin's mind was on architecture and a book on that subject. On leaving Oxford his planned "pilgrimage to the English Shrines"[48] had to be aborted (apart from a miserable visit to Salisbury Cathedral) due to illness – Ruskin and his mother caught a heavy cold, his father fell ill with a stomach complaint.

The English tour was replaced by an architectural study tour of Northern France, mainly Picardy and Normandy. It lasted almost three months, from 7 August until 25 October. Ruskin and his wife, assisted by Hobbs, their devoted amanuensis and factotum, and accompanied at the beginning by John James Ruskin, set off for Abbeville via Boulogne from where John James returned to England. It is unclear whether he intended accompanying his son and daughter-in-law further. We can only speculate as to his motives in going as far as Boulogne.

Ruskin had planned the route exclusively according to his own wishes, needs and aims. The purpose of the tour was work, non-stop work at his usual pace from very early in the morning until late at night studying, sketching and measuring cathedrals and churches. Ruskin was preparing his first illustrated book *The Seven Lamps of Architecture*. This was the first real experience that Effie had of her husband's capacity for work and the gruelling schedule that he imposed on all around. It was in stark contrast to the social whirl of Commemoration in Oxford. They travelled over hundreds of miles of rough terrain, often by stage-coach and occasionally by train. From Boulogne, they went to Abbeville, then into Normandy, stopping wherever there was an important religious building such as in Rouen, Lisieux, Falaise, Vire, Mortain, Coutances, Saint-Lô, Bayeux, Caen.

Effie's husband was entirely preoccupied with his work, and angry at seeing so many buildings destroyed, often razed to the ground, in the name of restoration. "John is perfectly frantic with the spirit of restoration here", Effie wrote to her parents, "the men actually before our eyes knocking down the time worn black with age pinnacles and sticking up in their place new stone ones to be carved at some future time". So great and uncontrollable was Ruskin's temper that only Effie's "gentle mediation" prevented him from "knocking some of the workmen off the scaffolding" and probably being put in prison.[49] Clearly, Effie was unsuited to this lifestyle and however hard she tried, could not adapt. She was not accustomed to long walks and after half a mile, Ruskin reported to his mother, "is reduced nearly to fainting and comes in with her eyes full of tears".[50] Ruskin was insensitive to her needs and incapable of displaying sympathy. Ruskin maintained his usual high level of correspondence and his almost daily letters to his parents and friends. Among these was Gordon to whom he wrote from Bayeux.[51]

It must have been a great relief to both to return to London, for Ruskin to use his copious notes to write *The Seven Lamps of Architecture* and for Effie to enjoy being a hostess at 31 Park Street, Grosvenor Square. But the fashionable house was not really theirs: it had been acquired for them on a three-year lease by John James Ruskin. There seems to have been no consultation about the house and it may well have been a cunning ruse by John James to appropriate his son. John James would have known that his son would not like it. For although the choice of location was ideal for Effie, her husband disliked the place and sought refuge at his old home at Denmark Hill. In the heart of Mayfair, Effie was able to indulge in her love of parties, high society and entertaining which she did in a grand style. In one letter alone she mentions Lady Chantrey, Lord Gray, Mr Eastlake, Lady Davy, Mr and Mrs Milman. Other letters mention Mr and Mrs Richmond, Lord Eastnor, Earl Somers, Sir Robert Inglis "very agreeable [...] very religious and clever", Lady Inglis, Lord Glenelg, to name but a few. Osborne Gordon "from Oxford" dined with John and Effie on Saturday 2 December (1848) at their new home.[52]

Not surprisingly, Effie became ill – she was suffering from a severe cold and cough and was losing weight. She developed an inflammation of the eye. Nevertheless, she and John were back at the family home on 12 December for a dinner at which Jane and John Pritchard and Charles Woodd, a family friend, were present.[53] Her condition deteriorated over the Christmas period while staying at Denmark Hill (from 25 December to 5 January) under the authority of the older Mr and Mrs Ruskin. Little or no sympathy was shown to her. Mrs Gray came to visit her and at the beginning of February 1849 mother and daughter returned to Perth and Ruskin to Denmark Hill. Nine months elapsed before their reunion.

While Effie stayed in Scotland, Ruskin set off on a continental tour with his parents. They travelled along a familiar route into Burgundy (Sens, Montbard, Dijon) and on to Geneva, Chambéry, Chamonix and many Alpine villages. Ruskin was given permission reluctantly by his parents to spend one month exploring the Higher Alps: with him were Couttet his trusted guide and George Hobbs his valet. The parents remained anxiously in Geneva, awaiting their son's return. Ruskin needed time on his own to gather material for *Modern Painters*, volumes 3 and 4, especially the latter. It proved to be a good investment of his time for several years later Murray's *Handbook for Travellers in Switzerland* recommended *Modern Painters*, IV, as containing "the most eloquent descriptions of alpine scenery yet written".[54] He wanted to familiarise himself with the different mountains and could only do this by absorbing their structure at first hand, by climbing and living among these peaks. Hence, he spent several days sleeping on the Montanvert, or working for three hours "on a peak of barren crag above a glacier [...] at least 9,000 feet above sea"[55] on the Matterhorn. Although Ruskin had spent three months in 1848 sketching detail of Normandy churches and cathedrals, – his rendering of a finial on the south porch of the west façade of the church of Saint-Lô to demonstrate the visual expression of the medieval carver's deep spiritual feelings and relationship with his craft is a fine example – and had published subsequently *The Seven Lamps of Architecture* in May 1849 containing many of those precise observations, he still felt that his ability to see was inadequate. He knew that his eye needed more training as he explained to his father in a letter from Courmayeur, in the Val d'Osta against the backdrop of Mont Blanc, on 29 July 1849:

> I am quite unable to speak with justice, or think with clearness, of this marvellous view. One is so unused to see a mass like that of Mont Blanc without any snow, that all my ideas and modes of estimating size were at fault. I only felt overpowered by it, and that, as with the porch of Rouen Cathedral, look as I would, I could not *see it*. I had not mind enough to grasp it or meet it; I tried in vain to fix some of its main features on my memory [...].[56]

Ruskin was also experimenting with his camera lucida in the Alps in 1849.[57]

As the end of his one-month's "leave" was approaching, Ruskin requested an extension. He needed more time. Although anxious about their son's health, the parents agreed but only on account of the reassuring presence of both Osborne Gordon and John Pritchard who were staying in Chamonix.[58] Thus perhaps unknowingly, both Gordon and Pritchard were instrumental in influencing the course of events and contributing to Ruskin's career.

* * *

When Ruskin was eventually reunited with his wife, another tour was planned but sensibly, without his parents. Effie wanted to go to Venice. She took as her companion Charlotte Ker, a neighbour from Perth: Ruskin was accompanied by his servant George Hobbs and joined *en route* by the ever-faithful Couttet. As always, John James financed the entire trip for everyone. Leaving England in October, the party travelled through France to Chamonix, on through Switzerland, crossing the war-torn Lombardo-Veneto region overrun and occupied by Austrian and Croatian troops under the rule of the Austrian field marshal Count Joseph Radetzky (1766-1858). They eventually arrived at their hotel in central Venice, the Danieli, close to St Mark's Square. That was their headquarters until the end of March 1850 by which time Ruskin had completed much of his work on the first volume of *The Stones of Venice*.

Effie had experienced not inconsiderable discomfort during the three-month delayed honeymoon tour of Normandy in 1848, staying in many cold, flea-infested, dirty hotels or lodging houses and travelling long distances in badly-sprung carriages over rough terrain. But in Venice, established in one place, she organised her own time more or less as she wished with parties, balls, invitations to lunch and dinner, to *soirées* while her husband pored over his "stones". Her serious husband, engrossed in his work, seemed oblivious to her flirtations with the officers, with Prince Troubetzkoi, with Marquis Selvatico, President of the Venetian Academy, and particularly with the Austrian officer, Charles Paulizza. For selfish reasons, Ruskin encouraged Effie to socialise independently: he wanted to have as much time as possible on his own to devote himself to his stones. She thrived on introductions: social life was essential to her happiness.

It was thanks to John Murray, publisher of the series of famous travel *Handbooks*, that Effie received a letter of introduction, in mid-December 1849, to "a Mr Rawdon Brown who had been residing some time in Venice".[59] Rawdon Lubbock Brown (1806-1883) first took up residence in Venice at the age of twenty-seven and stayed there for the remaining fifty years of his life. He was an eccentric English bachelor, a man of exquisite taste and with a passion for collecting. Brown immediately liked Effie, even preferred her to Ruskin, and confidences were soon exchanged. A few weeks later, Brown introduced Effie (and Ruskin) to a close friend of his in Venice, a wealthy Englishman, Edward Cheney. In late March 1850, it was with a heavy heart that Effie left Venice by gondola for the station to begin the return journey to England, clutching a brooch that Brown had given her as a present.[60]

Chapter 6

From the Palazzo Soranzo-Piovene to Badger Hall

When the first volume of *The Stones of Venice* was published in March 1851, presentation copies were sent to some of Ruskin's close friends: among the recipients were his Shropshire friends Osborne Gordon (now Senior Censor at Christ Church), Edward Cheney and Richard Fall.[1] One might wonder why a rather arid book about Venice would be of particular interest to these friends. If they studied it closely, they would find in it echoes of Shropshire. Perhaps Ruskin drew their attention to Plate IX, depicting a series of twenty-one sketches (by Ruskin) of architectural edge decoration and mouldings?[2] All but one of these are examples from Venice and Verona. However, one (no. 10) belongs elsewhere: that is a photogravure, engraved by J. C. Armytage from line drawings by Ruskin, of *Mouldings of Wenlock Abbey*. It is a sketch of some of the Chapter House's distinctive edge decoration, mistakenly identified as being from the refectory in the Index to the Illustrations.[3] In that same volume of *The Stones of Venice* are also his sketches of two types of dripstone from Wenlock Abbey, demonstrating the development of mouldings in the construction of the wall cornice, illustrated as Figure 8 (g) and (h).[4] Ruskin frequently considered art and architecture in a European context – around a Franco-Italian-Swiss-British axis – and was constantly making links and connections. The

Wenlock Abbey dripstones are part of that process and set in relation to others in Salisbury, Lisieux, Milan and Como, demonstrating the differences between architecture in varying climates.

So when and how did Ruskin come again to Shropshire, after that first visit with his parents when he was twelve years old? The answer lies in his Venetian stay of 1850.

> A nice Venetian servant received us and we found the Palace in most beautiful order for us to see. It was fitted up so splendidly, a mixture of Italian taste & English comforts. There were cabinets of gems, fine pictures, statues and I don't know what all. The marble floors were all covered with fine crimson cloth and nice coal fires blazing. I am quite astonished he, Col. C., was not terrified to leave such valuable property so open and the place so insecure but to see the cleanliness & propriety of everything you would have thought that the Master intended to be back to dinner.[5]

These were Effie's first impressions, in a letter to her father, of her visit to the Palazzo Soranzo-Piovene on the Grand Canal, near the Palazzo Vendramin Calergi. It was on a bitterly cold winter's day when John and Effie Ruskin were taken by Rawdon Brown to see the Palazzo during the absence of the tenant, Colonel Edward Cheney (1803-1884). It was greatly under-used for Cheney resided in it only occasionally, sometimes just once a year. His main residence was elsewhere.

But this was not the first time that Ruskin had met Cheney. In Ruskin's diary of 3 May 1844, he noted a visit from Cheney and his brother: "Cheney came out with his brother; he is a fine fellow, the brother quiet and commonplace. Didn't seem to like Turner."[6]

Edward Cheney and his two other bachelor brothers, Robert-Henry Cheney (1799-1866) and Ralph Cheney (1809-1869) formed a close-knit family unit and were devoted to each other. There were also two sisters: Harriet Margaret Cheney (died aged forty-six years in 1852) who married Robert Pigot, and

Frederica Cheney who, on 27 February 1822, married Mr Capel Cure of Blake Hall, Essex. Frederica and Capel Cure produced four sons and two daughters. The Cheneys' London home was at 4 Audley Square, in the heart of Mayfair: their country residence was Badger Hall, in the tiny village of Badger, in Shropshire. On the death of their father, Lieutenant-General Robert Cheney in 1820, the property had passed to his eldest son Robert-Henry: on his death in 1866 it was inherited by Edward. Badger Hall subsequently passed to Colonel Alfred Capel Cure (1826-1896), the second son of Frederica and Capel Cure.

The Cheneys were a cultured family, more interested in collecting and practising art than in fox-hunting and shooting. Their passion for art was fostered by Harriet Cheney (mother of the five Cheney children) who, as Miss Harriet Carr, had had lessons in watercolour painting from John 'Warwick' Smith (1749-1831). She worked with Smith in Italy, acquiring skills in portrait and landscape painting, as well as an enduring love of Italy and its culture. So successful was Harriet Cheney that she is honoured in her own right as a painter in Bénézit's famous *Dictionnaire critique et documentaire des peintres, sculpteurs, dessinateurs et graveurs de tous les temps et de tous les pays.*

Staffordshire-born landscape painter Peter de Wint (1784-1849) enjoyed the patronage of the Cheneys (as well as other Shropshire/Staffordshire families such as the Clives of Oakley Park, Ludlow, and the Powis family). He often stayed with them during the summer as their private drawing master. The Cheneys also frequented other leading British artists of the day, including Edward Lear, Henry Bright, William Leighton Leitch (1804-1883) and Thomas Henry Cromek (1809-1873).

The catalyst for the development of the artistic propensities of Robert-Henry and Edward Cheney was the untimely death of their father. Robert-Henry had to abandon his studies at Oriel College, Oxford, and return to Badger to assume responsibility for the estate he had inherited. Harriet Cheney asserted to a much greater extent her influence. She transmitted her taste for

Italy and art to her eldest sons in particular and all three shared closely her artistic interests. Mother and two sons visited Naples in 1823 and shortly after settled in the Palazzo Sciarra, on the elegant and fashionable Via del Corso, in Rome.

Although Edward Cheney, after studying at Sandhurst, 'flirted' with army life, he quickly found his vocation in the world of eccentric, literary and artistic people. In Naples, he found members of the Dilettanti Society, a society of wealthy gentlemen and patrons of the arts, particularly classical archae-ology. Most prominent was Sir William Gell (1778-1836), the distinguished antiquary, archaeologist and travel writer. At the time, Sir William was living in Naples in the Villa Anspach, a palace on the Chiatamone overlooking the bay. But not alone. His intimate and colourful companions were the Hon. Keppel Craven, thought to be the illegitimate son of Lady Craven who had left England in a hurry and a flurry of scandal, and Sir William Drummond, a diplomat and scholar. To what extent the three men enjoyed "the closest bonds of friendship" can be surmised from their burial in a single tomb in the Protestant cemetery in Naples.[7]

This powerful engagement with Italy continued and the Cheneys became well established in Anglo-Italian society, in Naples, Rome, Forence and Venice. It was at the Palazzo Barbarini in Rome, at the invitation of Lady Coventry and her daughter Lady Augusta, that Edward Cheney first met Richard Monckton Milnes (later Lord Houghton) in 1834: the two became lifelong friends.[8] The widowed Cheney mother and sons were received in the great Roman houses such as the Sermoneta/Caetani family. Another solid and lifelong friendship was established with the former Christ Church student and diarist Charles Greville (1794-1865).

But it would be wrong to convey the impression that the Cheneys spent all their time in society. Edward, (Robert) Henry and Harriet Cheney painted and sketched the villas, palaces and landscapes of Italy. The two brothers worked together so closely that individual attributions are not always easy to ascertain, such as their fine watercolours of the *Villa Albani* and the *Villa Conti* in Rome in the early nineteenth century.

A few years prior to the death of his mother in 1848, Edward acquired the rambling Palazzo Soranzo-Piovene in Venice, the place that became to him, in the words of R. Monckton Milnes, "a homeland of antiquity and art".[9]

* * *

In mid-August 1850, John and Effie Ruskin were invited to spend a few days in Shropshire with John and Jane Pritchard, and (with some reluctance on Ruskin's part) with the Cheneys at Badger Hall.[10] Badger, a small rural parish with approximately 160 inhabitants, was about ten miles from the Pritchard family home and bank in Broseley.

In the nineteenth century, Badger was a small settlement with a church, rectory, Hall, a few houses and farms. Unlike many villages, there was no public house in the parish. It would be difficult to imagine Ruskin at ease in Badger Hall which had been refashioned, by the famous architect James Wyatt, in the late eighteenth century in the neo-classical style on the orders of the wealthy art connoisseur Isaac Hawkins Browne. It was a rather austere building, isolated from the village, and set in extensive parkland. Wyatt retained the service buildings dating from the late seventeenth century that stood to the south: he added a block of eight bays and three storeys, mainly of brick, on the north end of the old Hall. A conservatory was also built. Fine plasterwork by Joseph Rose of London included a frieze depicting classical gods, heroes and Shakespearean characters. Inside were treasures that had been collected by the Cheneys from (mainly) Italy. One room, full of classical busts, bronzes, Old Master paintings, Tiepolo drawings and sketches and furniture, was designed specifically as a museum. In the Hall were *objets d'art*, coins, medals, faïence, prints and Rembrandt etchings, not forgetting a huge library decorated – as was also the dining room – with chiaroscuro paintings by Robert Smirke (1752-1845).[11]

About one mile away was Badger Dingle, the Cheneys' private forty-acre picturesque landscaped hollow or dell, park, wood and pleasure ground. It was far more elaborate than anything previously seen and was much admired and envied. It was not until 1851 that Badger Dingle was open to the public and became a popular attraction for the town dwellers of Wolverhampton and Birmingham on their workers' outings. The Dingle had been cut through deep, steep, red sandstone: a sheer drop of several yards, down the cliff face, led to the pools that had been created for boating, bathing and recreation. There were waterfalls, along with caves and gateways, and a mill near one of the dams. Reminiscent of Turner's impressive *St Gothard's Pass* was a rock cut path, with a bridge, that led down a steep gorge from the road. The Dingle was planted with exotic shrubs and trees, with Alpine plants, colourful American rhododendrons and azaleas, some protruding from the rock faces. Down in the cool of the Dingle was an ice house, hewn into the perpendicular rock. Inside, along a passage, was an enormous egg-shaped cavity used for storing ice taken from a nearby pool in midwinter. The sophisticated ice house – the equivalent of a modern day freezer – was constructed in such a way as to be insulated against temperature changes and ensured that the ice remained solid for an entire year. This was a necessary feature for any great house of the day. Ruskin may have been inspired by the Badger ice house when he created his own on his Brantwood estate more than two decades later. Collingwood recalled how Ruskin's ice house "was tunnelled at vast expense into the rock and filled at more expense with the best ice".[12] As well as providing ice for the Brantwood household, it was intended for charitable purposes, "to supply invalids in the neighbourhood". But to what extent it was successful seems dubious, for Collingwood relates that the result of Ruskin's efforts was "nothing but a puddle of dirty water".

A classical folly known as The Temple, built in 1783, was also designed by Wyatt. It was placed at the end of a long, tree-lined, private carriageway, a striking vista linking Badger Hall with the folly. The rotunda-shaped Doric Temple, comprising ground floor and first floor linked by a spiral staircase and overlooking a private lake within Badger Dingle, was used as a summer-house, teahouse and architectural ornament. The Temple was in use by the Cheney family and their descendents until the 1930s: it was given a new lease of life when it was splendidly refurbished as a holiday cottage by The Vivat Trust in the late twentieth century. Ruskin would have visited and perhaps disapproved of the little church of St Giles, most of which was rebuilt in 1833-1834: in Pevsner's opinion "in a poor Gothic style".[13]

Effie enjoyed her visit immensely and she consolidated her friendship with Edward Cheney in particular.[14] He would become a loyal friend to her over the years and an ally in her troubles with Ruskin and his parents.

It was during this visit to Shropshire that Ruskin worked in the grounds of Wenlock Abbey sketching material for *The Stones of Venice* and writing "some notes of Wenlock".[15] In the steps of Turner, he also explored towns in the heart of the Industrial Revolution: Coalbrookdale and Ironbridge in the Severn Gorge that provided a stark contrast to the rural life of Much Wenlock and Badger. Ruskin spoke with local people and asked questions about the social conditions. At Coalbrookdale, he learnt about the heavy work and remuneration of the workers. Under his diary heading of "Manufactures", he wrote: "I was told by master of ironworks at Coalbrooke dale that the men employed in the severe work got about £2 a week, and that he had known a family in the receipt of £40 a year: but they were improvident."[16]

* * *

Later in the year, Ruskin returned to Oxford for a baptism. In spite of Ruskin's strong dislike, even hatred of babies and very young children (Effie revealed to Rawdon Brown that her husband "hate[d] children and d[id] not wish any children to interfere with his plans of studies"),[17] he attended the baptism on 2 October 1850 of the son of Henry Acland. It must have been an ordeal for Ruskin and it is difficult to imagine him showing any interest whatsoever in the baby, let alone holding it. He would have tolerated the occasion out of deference to Acland, one of his closest Oxford friends who had qualified as a doctor in 1846 and at the time of this baptism had a flourishing medical practice in Oxford. In 1851, he became Radcliffe Librarian: in 1857, Regius Professor of Medicine.

Ruskin took advantage of the occasion to meet Gordon, discussing at length "the religious state of the University". It was not a theological question that was preoccupying Gordon. The problem was the dull English Sunday and the difficulties undergraduates experienced in coping with it. Gordon "did not know what to do with the young men on Sunday". He "could not recommend them to go to church", he told Ruskin. After early morning prayers, the students went to breakfast and "sat over it for three hours". Gordon wanted the Sunday timetable to be modified to help the students cope with the boredom of the day. His suggestion was pragmatic: "If the Dean would have a cathedral service at 10 o'clock, it would lift them over so much of the day."[18] The very use of "lift them over the day" suggests the seriousness of the problem. It is likely that Ruskin sympathised, for he was obliged to conform to a strict Sunday regime when he was with his parents. His evangelical mother would have been horrified, had she known of Gordon's views: she had already expressed strong disapproval of what she perceived to be his Catholic tendencies in her letter of 12 June 1843, to which we referred earlier.

An Act of Parliament in 1829 had accorded Catholics greater rights to participate more fully in public life: numbers were increasing steadily. But the direct involvement – or interference – of the Italian Pope Pius IX (1846-1878) in the appointment of

Dr Nicholas Wiseman on 29 September 1850 as Cardinal Archbishop of Westminster, with twelve English Bishops under his authority, thus re-establishing a Catholic hierarchy in England, was a catalyst that infuriated many senior churchmen and inflamed an already tense situation. Oxbridge was at the centre of the debate on the march of Catholicism. Ruskin and Effie discussed the situation with Dr Whewell, Master of Trinity College, Cambridge, who told them that his students were "violent about the Papal aggressions".[19] Gordon, although a moderate High Churchman, was part of an Oxford deputation to Queen Victoria opposing "papal aggression". They did not, however, manage to effect change.

Chapter 7

Another continental tour: destination Venice

At the beginning of August 1851 Effie and John Ruskin set off for another continental tour: Venice was their destination. They crossed France fairly rapidly, a journey facilitated by the developing rail network. From Paris they took the recently opened railroad to Sens, then further into Burgundy as far as Dijon, stopping *en route* to examine churches and cathedrals. They were heading for the mountains. From Dijon they posted approximately seventy miles to Champagnole, the small town at the foot of the Jura hills heralding the approach of the real mountains beyond. It provided a fairly gentle terrain for walking, a practice area for the challenges of the High Alps.

Jane and John Pritchard had travelled independently and met the young Ruskins at Champagnole. To what extent this encounter was planned or simply coincidence we do not know, but Ruskin was delighted with their company and that of his other friends. It seems to have been a thoroughly happy time for everyone, especially without the domineering presence of Ruskin's parents. The Pritchards (Jane aged thirty-five, John aged fifty-five) stayed with the party for nearly ten days (10-19 August) in the Jura and Alps. The Rev. Daniel Moore, incumbent of Camden Chapel, Peckham Road, Camberwell, and his wife had joined the Ruskins in Paris and accompanied them on the tour for a fortnight. It was a period of challenging walks and climbs, fresh air, breathtaking views and much uncomfortable and rudimentary accommodation. From Champagnole, where Ruskin's diary entry for Sunday 10 August 1851 records, "Walk at Champagnole with Mr Moore and Mr and Mrs Pritchard",[1] they continued on a route well known to Ruskin – "the old road" as he affectionately called it. Higher and higher they went along twisting, narrow tracks, often with deep ravines on both sides and reached the remote mountain hamlet of Les Rousses with its lake, on the High Jura plateau, close to the Swiss border. Les Rousses – like Chamonix – developed into a fashionable ski and leisure complex in the twentieth century. After dining at Les Rousses, the party continued up more narrow winding roads before the steep descent into Geneva. At Geneva, they were joined, as agreed, by Charles Newton, former Christ Church student three years Ruskin's senior. Newton was a jovial person and twenty-three-year-old Effie delighted in his company. It is fascinating to speculate how she would have interacted with John Everett Millais, had he not declined an invitation to join the party, ostensibly because he was spending the summer painting with Holman Hunt.[2] They left Geneva "with horse" at two o'clock in the afternoon of Tuesday 12 August 1851 to get to Bonneville, "walking the last four miles with Newton and Mr Moore." Effie's long letter of Friday 15 August 1851 to her mother Mrs Gray in Scotland bubbled with excitement. From Effie, we learn much more about the journey "with horse" to which Ruskin laconically refers in his diary![3] It was Effie who rode "a very nice English mare" from Geneva to Bonneville, a distance of approximately eighteen miles, following behind the carriage transporting Ruskin and his guests. They were taking the valley road following the course of the river Arve all the way to Chamonix.

After an overnight stop at Bonneville, they left early the next morning at seven o'clock for the village of Saint-Martin: Ruskin's servant George rode the horse, then Newton took over as far as Cluses. But the horse was suffering – "the saddle had skinned all its back" – and had to be sent back to Geneva. They travelled through lovely countryside "with the vines at their brightest green", with "flowers in every garden, Hops & every kind of fruit getting ripe".[4] Between Cluses and Saint-Martin, on their right rose the lofty and jagged mountain range of the Reposoir that they decided to climb.[5] To reach these mountains, they had to cross, near Saint-Martin, the single-arched bridge over the Arve "clearing some sixty feet of strongly-rushing water with a leap of lovely elliptic curve"[6] to the left bank and to the little town of Sallanches. Sallanches, that Ruskin had first visited in 1833, had been totally destroyed by fire on Good Friday, 1840, thus exacerbating the physical distress that Ruskin observed almost everywhere in Sardinian-ruled Savoy. The town was gradually rebuilt and by the late nineteenth century had risen from the ashes. Cluses suffered a similar catastrophe in 1844 and the village was rebuilt away from the mouth of the gorge where it originally stood: the intention was to shield it from the powerful winds in the gorge that had fuelled the conflagration. Wooden chalets caught fire easily.

They stayed overnight in Saint-Martin at the Hôtel du Mont-Blanc, an inn to which Ruskin was very attached and recalled in *Praeterita* as "the most eventful, pathetic, and sacred" of all his "inn houses".[7] By 1882, the little hotel was deserted and for sale and Ruskin was considering purchasing it.[8] The party continued along the Arve valley on the approach road to Chamonix arriving in time for lunch, for the "Table D'Hote at two" at Ruskin's usual hotel, the Hôtel de l'Union.[9]

There was no respite! More mountain walking followed. No sooner had they had lunch than Ruskin exhorted the more willing members of his party to tackle the mountain range of the Montanvert (variously spelt as Montenvers), north-east of Chamonix. After a short, leisurely stroll following the Arve northwards, they soon turned in an easterly direction, at the point where the river Arveyron joins the Arve, through woods to the village of Les Bois (appropriately named) from where a zigzag path rises rapidly through thick forests. Ruskin wanted to show his friends the source of the Arveyron which issued from beneath an ice-cavern up in the mountains. The vault was concealed at the extremity of the huge glacier, the *Mer de Glace* (Sea of Ice): more precisely at the tip of the much smaller *Glacier des Bois* (Glacier of the Woods). Ruskin was concerned about erosion and glacial recession and the effects were visible during his lifetime. He sketched the *Glacier des Bois* on a previous visit some ten years before: the drawing had captured the giratory effect of sunlight on the ice contained within the hollow cavern.[10] By 1863, Ruskin was extremely concerned and wrote to his father: "The glaciers below have sunk and retired to a point at which I never saw them till this year; if they continue to retire thus, another summer or two will melt the lower extremity of the Glacier des Bois quite off the rocks:"[11] by 1891, the *Glacier des Bois* had retreated so far that Murray's *Handbook for the Alps of Savoy and Piedmont* stated that it was "scarcely worth a visit". How accurate Ruskin's observation and premonition had been for by the twentieth century, the *Glacier des Bois* had disappeared completely and was not even indicated on the official map of Chamonix and the *Massif du Mont Blanc* published by the Institut Géographique National in 1990.

Effie did not share the visit to the *Glacier des Bois*. Instead, she left Chamonix by mule accompanied by Judith Couttet, the daughter of Ruskin's trusted guide, Joseph Couttet and went straight to the refuge, a tiny hut at the top of Mount Montanvert (approximately 6000 feet high) where the party was spending the night. She arrived rested and refreshed after her two-and-a-half-hour journey by mule, in contrast to the state of exhaustion in which she found her husband's friends. Ruskin had been fanatical (*enragé*) about climbing, insisting that his friends followed his pace. In a letter to her mother, Effie described the scene: "I found John had nearly killed with fatigue his friends who were drinking Brandy & water and Mr Newton calling him an enragé. We slept here all night and were only disturbed by a storm of thunder & lightning very fine indeed."[12]

A sheer drop of 280 feet separates the Montanvert refuge (east) from the *Mer de Glace*, the five-mile long, tongue-like glacier joined by two affluents of ice and snow, the *Glacier du Géant* and the *Glacier de Leschaux* (also spelt Léchaud), all with ridged surfaces and blue crevasses. According to Effie's letter to her mother, Jane and John Pritchard joined the party on the Montanvert on Friday 15 August 1851 and then went on the *Mer de Glace*.[13] There were other walks and climbs to the icy peaks and needles of the *Aiguilles des Charmoz* (11,293 feet high), the *Glacier des Bossons* and the *Glacier des Pèlerins*.

What is surprising is not only the degree of mountain walking, some quite hazardous, packed into a short stay, but the fact that Ruskin and his party did not have an official guide – other than Ruskin himself. Judith Couttet took care of Effie. Ruskin's favourite guide, Joseph Couttet, was away on a climb with Sir Robert Peel (eldest son of the famous Peel). However, Ruskin may have decided to dispense with a guide because he felt he knew the area extremely well. He had already stayed in Chamonix in 1833, 1835, 1842, 1844, 1846 and 1849.

Few women ventured high into the mountains, one of the obstacles being of a very practical nature, their cumbersome long skirts. On 2 September 1860, on a visit to mark the incorporation of Savoy into France, Empress Eugénie, wife of Napoleon III, is pictured riding sidesaddle on a mule on her way up to the *Mer de Glace*: she is wearing a long flowing dress and a hat with a veil more suited to Paris.[14] Ladies did not wear trousers. One wonders how Effie Ruskin and Jane Pritchard were attired. John James Ruskin, writing to Elizabeth Fall (sister of Richard) from Paris on 16 September 1856 – the Ruskin family were on their way back from Chamonix – observed with some distaste the apparel of ladies wearing "a man's hat queerly turned up at the sides and a few disfigurations of this kind at Chamouni upon mules".[15] One of the few women climbers at the time was Emma Forman, another of Ruskin's friends, who attracted much attention.

Chamonix in 1851 was at a turning point, on the point of changing from a remote, tranquil village to becoming a "tourist rendezvous".[16] In *Modern Painters*, IV, published in 1856, Ruskin wrote: "The valley of Chamouni, another spot also unique in its way, is rapidly being turned into a kind of Cremorne Gardens."[17] The delights of Chamonix and its glaciers were being vigorously promoted. The following advertisement in *Galignani's Messenger*, the European English-language newspaper read mainly by British tourists abroad, appeared on 21 August 1851, under the heading GLACIERS OF CHAMOUNI:

> A casino is open for the season at this favourite summer resort. Music, refreshments, and reading-rooms. N.B. – Every kind of amusements, as at Baden-Baden, Hombourg, etc. Branch establishment at the Spa of Evian, on the Lake of Geneva.[18]

Ruskin had left behind the Great Exhibition in London that he decried only to find himself in the centre of another kind of commercialisation underway in Chamonix and brought about by one of his compatriots. The exploits of Albert Smith (1816-1860), a doctor turned climber and showman, coincided exactly with the summer stay of Ruskin and his party. "There has been a cockney ascent of Mont Blanc", Ruskin announced to his father on 16 August 1851, "of which I believe you are soon to hear in London".[19]

Smith orchestrated his ascent of the highest peak in Europe to give him maximum publicity. He was not climbing to study or appreciate the mountain but to use it as a stunt, an act of blasphemy in Ruskin's eyes. From his base at the Hôtel de Londres, he made sure that news of his elaborate preparations and date of his ascent (12 August) reached far and wide. His was the largest climbing party ever to leave Chamonix. It consisted of sixteen guides, lead by Jean Tairraz, followed by eighteen porters carrying the most sophisticated of provisions – sixty bottles of *vin ordinaire*, thirty-one bottles of vintage claret and burgundy, cognac, champagne, chocolate, dried fruit, four legs and four shoulders of mutton, six pieces of veal, one piece of beef, eleven large and thirty-five small fowls, bread, salt and candles. Smith was accompanied by three Oxford undergraduates whom he had met, rather casually, at his hotel: they were Francis Philips, George Charles Floyd and William Edward Sackville West.[20] All were "in light boating attire".[21] The ascent was dangerous but successful. Smith and his men eventually reached the summit at nine o'clock the following morning. They had bivouacked for a few hours at the *Grands Mulets*, opened some of their food and wine, lit a fire and rested until midnight when they continued their climb by means of the reflected moonlight. The ascent provided Smith with material to entertain and hold audiences spellbound at his series of dioramas at the Egyptian Hall in Piccadilly: Henry James was among those who found them fascinating. Smith also made a great deal of money from his shows.

Sir Robert Peel, an amateur climber, had arrived in Chamonix just after Smith's party set off. He too was fascinated by the ascent and all night long, in moonlight, watched their every move through a telescope, willing them to succeed and merrily drinking their health.[22]

A trend had been set and the character of Chamonix had changed forever. More and more visitors were arriving – "an immense number of people here", commented Ruskin. The peaks around were becoming popular and crowded attractions for tourists: at one time, Effie Ruskin counted forty mules on the Montanvert.[23] But business was booming for hoteliers such as the landlord of the Hôtel de l'Union.

In the summer of 1856 both Albert Smith and Emma Forman were enjoying their exploits and the surrounding publicity. In a perverse way and in spite of their criticisms, the Ruskin family encouraged the crowds by their participation in the events. John James Ruskin's lively account is most revealing:

Albert Smith has sent half the travellers abroad straight to Chamouni & a few up Mont Blanc. We saw Miss Foreman go off

for the ascent & return none the worse being the fourth lady only
who has yet ascended the Mountain. She gave my son a full
account of her adventure – of visitors to Chamouni we counted
coming up one evening 17 carriages full & the Landlord of
Union said he had dispatched same morning 23 carriages.[24]

Ruskin himself was not immune to the thrills and wrote in his
diary of 1 August 1856: "Yesterday to Les Ouches […] up to
Aiguille Blaitière, & then to meet Emma Forman coming down
from Mont Blanc at the Pelerin wood."[25]

The trend was unstoppable. By 2006, Mont Blanc had become
so polluted by huge numbers of climbers and walkers (about
30,000 each summer) that an attempt was made to limit the
number of people scaling it. Jean-Marc Peillex, mayor of Saint-
Gervais, on the French side of the mountain, attempted to address
the ecological problem by proposing curbs on the numbers of
climbers and a system of permits. He faced strong opposition.

In this stimulating company (in 1851) with compatible companions of his own choice, away from his overbearing parents
who fretted and were frightened if their son was even five
minutes late for tea,[26] striding among the rocks in the bracing
Alpine air – without the constraints of authoritarian adults –,
picnicking in the woods, Ruskin was enjoying some of his
happiest moments. He felt "refreshed", he wrote to his father[27]
and was harnessing his strength for the challenge that lay ahead
– the huge volume of work he intended to do in Venice during
the long winter of 1851-1852.

The Pritchards returned with the party to Geneva on 19
August and then went on their own way.

* * *

Effie and John Ruskin arrived in Venice in early September 1851.
They set up home at the Casa Wetzlar – Palazzo Wetzlar according to Effie – (later part of the Gritti Palace Hotel) instead of in
their usual hotel, the Danieli. The Wetzlar was in a convenient

location in the *sestiere* of San Marco, close to the church of Santa Maria Zobenigo and only a few steps from La Fenice opera house. Ruskin enjoyed a short period of comparative calm thanks to the immense practical support afforded by Brown (who helped to find the new lodgings) and Cheney. By mid-September, Ruskin wrote of his happiness to his father:

> I am now settled more quietly than I have ever been since I was at college – and it certainly will be nobody's fault but my own if I do not write well – besides that I have St Mark's library open to me, and Mr. Cheney's: who has just at this moment sent his servant through a tremendous thundershower with two books which help me in something I was looking for.[28]

Ruskin made much use of Cheney's library as the reading room in Venice had closed down.[29]

Effie was overjoyed to be mistress of the house, to invite and be invited. Among the first guests invited for tea (on 8 September) were Edward Cheney and one of his nephews (one of four sons of Frederica, Edward's elder sister). Henry Hart Milman, Dean of St Paul's Cathedral, London, and his wife were also present.[30] This was a potentially explosive mixture – and an occasion for which Rawdon Brown had sent his apologies – for Ruskin did not see eye to eye on many issues with Milman and Cheney.

The Ruskins spent considerable time in the company of Brown and Cheney. They walked together two or three times a week in St Mark's Square. Invitations to tea were exchanged although Ruskin was embarrassed to receive Cheney and Brown in the relative poverty of the Casa Wetzlar: "their own houses are much more luxurious that ours", he informed his father, "so it is a small compliment to ask either of them to come here".[31]

But the promised calm did not last. Ruskin began, ungraciously and ungratefully, to be critical of Brown and Cheney. "They are both as good-natured as can be," he explained to his father, "but of a different Species from me – men of the world –

caring very little about anything but Men".[32] It was an unfair and unjust assessment of two well-educated men who provided Ruskin with invaluable practical assistance during his Venetian sojourns. He made little attempt to enter their spiritual and aesthetic worlds. By distancing himself from Cheney, Ruskin also missed a unique opportunity to discover, at first hand, Sir Walter Scott (1771-1832). Ruskin greatly admired Scott and his writings, was much influenced by his style and even promised to write a biography of his Scottish hero. Cheney had been Scott's cicerone in Italy during the last years of his life and would have had many stories to tell, even being able to contribute to the biography.

As work continued unabated on the second and third volumes of *The Stones of Venice*, Effie spent more and more time without her husband. She longed to socialise more, to go to the theatre to see the great tragic actress Rachel (1821-1858) playing the central roles in Racine's *Phèdre* and Corneille's *Horace* at the Teatro San Benedetto. As Phèdre and Camille she was unrivalled in Europe. Cheney and Brown thought Rachel "very grand" and went to four of her performances.[33] Although Ruskin was an avid theatre-goer, he declined to go to the theatre on this occasion, perhaps on account of his heavy work schedule. Cheney and Brown wanted to take Effie with them but she hesitated and eventually refused on the grounds of Rachel's immoral reputation. It was a missed opportunity, for Rachel, although only thirty years of age, was reaching the end of her life and like Dumas' heroine of *La Dame aux camélias* (1848) and Verdi's *La Traviata* (1853) would die of consumption in her prime. Effie's coy refusal may have been motivated by her fear of being reprimanded, even ostracised, by her severe, critical and cantankerous parents-in-law at Denmark Hill.

Cheney was a meticulous host and organised his receptions and dinners to perfection. He entertained frequently, so frequently that Ruskin was obliged, on occasions, to refuse invitations. He accepted out of politeness as Effie explained to her parents in a letter of 17 November 1851: "The other day [we] dined at Mr Cheney's where John went as he did not wish to offend Mr Cheney by refusing so often."[34] Guests at the "elegant little dinner" included Cheney's companion Rawdon Brown (as was to be expected), and an assortment of aristocrats and *émigrés*.

Ruskin's eccentricities and egoistical, opinionated behaviour did not go unnoticed by Cheney and Brown who found his company awkward. This led to a temporary cooling of relationships but one that Effie's great charm, sociability and tact managed to overcome. In spite of sensing a problem that she could not quite identify, and not wishing to lose their friendship, she persisted in calling on both men regularly. The relationship was repaired and so on Christmas Day 1851 the young Ruskins were invited, along with Edward Cheney, to dinner in the Palazzo Barbaro by the pro-Austrian English Consul-General, Clinton Dawkins and his wife. Mr and Mrs Dawkins, whom Effie had only met in early October, resided in a spacious and "most beautiful apartment" in the Barbaro with a ballroom with "frescoed and stuccoed walls and [Tiepolo] ceiling"[35] capable of accommodating over two hundred dancers. In spite of the presence of potentially interesting guests, Ruskin did not enter into the spirit of the occasion and conducted himself in an embarrassingly anti-social manner as Effie reported to her parents: "I left at half past nine as John looked bored as he sat in a corner reading by himself, but he never talks to any body and he says his great object is to talk as little and go through a dinner with the smallest possible trouble to himself – and I suppose it is best just to let him do so although I think it is a great pity that he does not exert himself to speak more as he speaks so well."[36] At Marshall Radetzky's prestigious January Ball (1852), Ruskin found a "quiet seat – and a book of natural history".[37] He was, Effie recognised, "very peculiar"[38] … and increasingly so.

As the year drew to a close, Ruskin's attention was focussed again on Turner on learning of his death in late December. The possibility of purchasing more Turners might arise if they were released onto the art market and Ruskin discussed the matter with his father. He recalled a Turner drawing from Cheney's collection that he had bought "on account of the pig in it".[39] It was an original of one in the *Liber Studiorum*: Bradley suggests it was a first study of Turner's *Farmyard and Cock*.[40] Ruskin had a strange fascination with pigs – in art and as farm animals. Presents of home produced pork were often sent by Ruskin's mother: Turner was a recipient of such a gift in 1845.[41]

Ruskin did not share Edward Cheney's passion for classical art. In 1851, when Cheney became an unofficial consultant to the trustees of the National Gallery, London, advising about the purchase of Italian paintings, clashes with Ruskin were inevitable. On one occasion, a dispute arose about the colours of some mosaics. Ruskin wrote to his father: "I got into a little dispute with Mr Cheney about some mosaics one day – and was quite nervous the whole day after – merely a question whether the colours were faded or not [...]."[42]

Ruskin was horrified to find so many paintings in Venice in danger, as was Henry James two decades later.[43] He campaigned to persuade the National Gallery to enrich their collections with great Venetian paintings, thereby also rescuing them from neglect in their own country. In March 1852, he approached one of the trustees, Lord Lansdowne, about the perilous state of many of the precious works of art in Venice: "It is a piteous thing to see the marks and channels made down them by the currents of rain, like those of a portmanteau after a wet journey of twelve hours; and to see the rents, when the bombshells came through them, still unstopped [...]."[44]

Two Tintorettos were of particular importance to Ruskin: the *Crucifixion* that he considered to be "among the finest in Europe",[45] hanging in the church of San Cassiano, and the immense *Marriage at Cana* in the church of Santa Maria della Salute. Both paintings were fulsomely praised by Ruskin in his Venetian Index to *The Stones of Venice*.[46] Ruskin knew the commercial (as well as the aesthetic) value of works of art: he had been buying and selling for decades. He informed the painter Sir Charles Locke Eastlake (1793-1865), then one of the prominent trustees of the National Gallery (its Director in 1855), that he could purchase, for the National Gallery, the *Crucifixion* for £7000, and the *Marriage at Cana* for £5000. That was a considerable sum of money.

Ruskin sensed potential difficulties with powerful, influential Cheney. He knew that the matter was extremely sensitive and had discussed it with him at great length and in such a way, so he thought, as to avoid making him jealous, for a "word that piqued him might have spoiled all".[47] For many years Cheney had enjoyed a certain hegemony in matters of art and probably felt susceptible to being usurped by a now famous and controversial art critic sixteen years younger (Cheney was forty-nine years old: Ruskin thirty-three). However, Ruskin believed he had convinced Cheney to agree to the purchase. The two men were extremely different and viewed each other with a degree of disdain, suspicion and dislike, yet distant respect. Cheney revealed his opinion about Ruskin and Effie in a letter to his friend Lord Holland:

> Mrs Ruskin is a very pretty woman and is a good deal neglected by her husband, not for other women but for what he calls literature. I am willing to suppose he has more talent than I give him credit for – indeed he could not well have less – but I cannot see that he has either talent or knowledge and I am surprised that he should have succeeded in forming the sort of reputation that he has acquired. He has so little taste that I am surprised he admired Holland House.[48]

Effie perceptively recognised that Cheney's (and Rawdon Brown's) satirical manner and anger towards her husband was a façade to conceal their acknowledgement that "he knew much better about art here than themselves".[49] Ruskin, on the other hand, felt that Cheney was a man of great talent and "excellent judgment"[50] in matters of Venetian art but who did not apply himself. An undated letter from Ruskin to Rawdon Brown refers to Cheney's caustic yet kind temperament: "Mr Cheney's sayings are very sweet and kind. Who would ever think there was such a salt satire in the make of him! [...] What a lazy boy he is; why doesn't he write a history of Venice?"[51] In another letter of 1877 addressed to Brown as "My dear Papa", Ruskin was preoccupied with Cheney's satire: "His satire, surely is one of his chief gifts – he seldom speaks without a sparkle of it in his eyes."[52]

Eastlake contacted other Trustees who in turn consulted Cheney, the final arbiter who, Ruskin believed, put "a spoke in the wheel for pure spite".[53] Ruskin's powers of persuasion had not worked. Effie too had tried hard and had taken several initiatives to try and ensure a successful outcome. She enlisted the help of Lord Lansdowne[54] and discussed the matter with Cheney and Rawdon Brown. According to Effie, Cheney wrote "a capital letter" of support to the Treasury in London: but this may not have been entirely true for Cheney and Rawdon Brown were doing their best to discourage and dissuade Ruskin from the project because they believed that it would be "quite impossible to get Church property".[55] One of the official reasons for refusing to proceed with the purchase was that "Mr. Cheney [did] not entirely concur with [Mr. Ruskin] in his valuation of the works".[56]

*   *   *

Innumerable invitations to balls, parties, *soirées* continued and Effie became more and more accustomed to this kind of life. It was a shock for her to realise that the end of this enjoyable Venetian existence was in sight and that she would soon have to return to England and face the realities of being in close proximity to the old Ruskins. She learnt that Mr Ruskin, without consulting his son and daughter-in-law, had taken a seven-year-lease on No. 30 Herne Hill, immediately next to No. 28, the house still owned by Mr Ruskin and let on a lease. Effie craved Belgravia, not this secluded spot in a quiet rural setting. Since Mr Ruskin financed everything, he expected to take decisions, usually unilaterally. Her dislike of Mr and Mrs Ruskin had increased during the two long Venetian stays when confidential letters, sometimes critical of her lifestyle and expenditure, were passed around between the Grays and the old Ruskins. Effie revealed her feelings in a letter of 17 April to her parents: "I have found it equally impossible to be fond of Mrs R[uskin] or to trust Mr R[uskin]. I always get on with them very well but it is at a great loss of temper and comfort, for the subjection I am obliged to keep myself in while with them renders me perfectly spiritless for any thing else. One of the things that distress me perhaps most is hearing them all railing against people behind their backs and then letting themselves be toadied and flattered by the Artistic canaille by whom they are surrounded." She added: "I am quite of Mr Cheney's opinion that of all canaille they are the lowest with very few exceptions."[57]

In late April Cheney too was preparing to leave Venice. "He is", Effie reported to her parents, "going to give up his beautiful rooms here and return to England, selling most of his furniture and taking all his pictures and articles of vertu with him. His departure will be a great loss to Mr Brown & Mr Dawkins, who are great enemies but curiously enough are both great friends of Mr Cheney's."[58]

*   *   *

On 15 May Effie and John Ruskin took new lodgings on the Piazza San Marco. Effie, seemingly without her husband, went to Cheney's *palazzo* for a farewell dinner: Rawdon Brown was also invited. Cheney was preparing to leave and the house looked "very dismantled but all concerning the dinner was perfect", Effie wrote to her parents.[59] But it was a sad occasion for close friends were about to disperse. Rawdon Brown was unusually quiet, apprehensive about being alone in Venice. "He is really very fond of us I think", wrote Effie, "and the idea of us all going and leaving him alone, for he has literally no one else, made him I thought very dull for he generally talks so much".[60] For a short while, Cheney lived with Brown as his own house was being emptied. It is not clear why Cheney sold the contents of his *palazzo* and left Venice, apparently against his wishes. Cheney was "much out of humour at having to go back to England".[61] His sister Harriet, wife of Robert Pigot, had died on 25 March 1852, "after a long and wasting illness", aged forty-six years.[62] Perhaps Cheney felt the need to be closer to his existing siblings and to take a greater role in the management of Badger Hall.

*　*　*

The Ruskins' departure from Venice was delayed by what Effie called an "unfortunate affair"[63] – the theft of her best jewels including a diamond bird and a heart, her blue enamel earrings and a chain of pearls, and several items such as diamond studs belonging to her husband. Suspicion fell on "a gentleman, an *Englishman*, and an Officer serving in the Emperor's own Regiment", a friend whom Effie trusted implicitly – Mr Foster.[64] Foster was a confidant of Radetzky and of Count Thun, Radetzky's aide-de-camp. Thun seemed to think that Ruskin had accused his friend of the theft. Unsubtantiated rumours easily inflamed an already tense political situation: honour was at stake and Ruskin was challenged to a duel. Effie and her husband were the subject of suspicion and much unpleasant gossip. Once again, Cheney and Brown came to their rescue: they were "exceedingly kind",[65] helping them to cope with the Venetian authorities and police methods, and advising them to leave Venice as quickly as possible. Ruskin wrote to his father: "Mr Brown and Mr Cheney, both men of the world, are my advisors in anything requiring advice."[66] Cheney wrote a letter of explanation on behalf of the Ruskins, to Dawkings, the English

Consul, requesting that all possible help be given in the circum-stances.[67] Cheney and Brown thought that the Ruskins should have applied to Radetzky for an escort to conduct them out of the Territory.[68]

Ruskin himself appears to have taken a detached, and self-righteous, view of events. He considered that Effie had been taught a lesson about being careless with her jewels.[69] The affair, Ruskin informed his father, had brought out the very best in Cheney: "One thing I am very glad of among the other good con-sequences of a misfortune, it has brought out Mr Cheney's char-acter; I believed him to be a man like Mr Beckford. I have found him active – kind – and right-minded, in the highest degree, and he has been my chief adviser and support in this affair in which not only single words – but *tones* of words, were of great impor-tance."[70] Although doubtless preoccupied with his imminent departure, Cheney had gone to great trouble to help the Ruskins out of a potentially dangerous situation – imprisonment and a duel – and one wonders to what extent he was appropriately rewarded. It was Effie alone who appreciated his totally indis-pensable role: "Mr Cheney has also left now and gone home by Vienna. Nothing could exceed his good nature in this business of ours and the respect I have for his great probity and knowledge of the world and what ought to be said & done. Although John and myself wished to do every thing that was right, also the Consul & Mr Brown, Mr Cheney advised us all, and without him we should I think have committed some bêtise or other."[71]

As they journeyed back to England, Effie's thoughts were of Venice and of Cheney and Brown. From Airolo, north of Locarno, in the Italian-speaking Swiss canton of Ticino (Tessin), she wrote a sensitive and kindly letter to Rawdon Brown, alone in the Serenissima:

I am afraid you will now be feeling Mr Cheney's absence very much but you are sure to see him very soon again. He said to me that he would return to see you and I don't think England will hold him very long. He is so good and perfect in every way that I think you are favoured in having had such a friend so many years. I never ceased admiring both he & you in this late affair of ours and without you both I am sure I do not know what we should have done. We very likely might have committed some bêtise which would have kept us in Venice till now and weeks longer.[72]

Cheney stayed on for a while in Vienna from where he reassured Effie that news of the theft had not reached that city.[73] However, British newspapers reported the affair and eventually Ruskin was obliged to write a letter to *The Times* in his defence.

*   *   *

From Venice, Ruskin had maintained regular contact with Gordon, who earlier in the year, on 5 February 1852, had been nominated as a Moderator under the New Examination Statute for Greek and Latin.[74] Ruskin often shared letters with his father as was his custom. It was an irritating habit that denied correspondents any confidentiality or privacy. "I will enclose a line for Gordon tomorrow", he informed his father on 8 May 1852.[75] But it was not a sealed letter for Ruskin was under an obligation to show the contents to his father. Hence he wrote the next day: "Please enclose the enclosed to Gordon. There is not much in it to interest you, but you would be disappointed perhaps if you had it not to look over."[76] In a letter of 7 June 1852 to his father, he discussed Gordon's religious tendencies: "The letters of Gordon and Colquhoun are interesting – but Gordon is quite a Gladstone man himself, now. I mean very high church, and not knowing exactly what he would be at."[77]

*   *   *

The death of the eighty-three-year-old Duke of Wellington, on 14 September, followed by a State funeral on 18 November, gave

Gordon an opportunity to be on centre stage, at least in Oxford.

The then Dean of St Paul's was the Oxford scholar and former Professor of Poetry (erstwhile winner, like Ruskin, of the Newdigate prize for poetry), Henry Hart Milman (1791-1868). Milman and his wife were particularly friendly with Effie, but less at ease with Ruskin with whom there had been strong disagreements about architecture. On a tour of Murano Cathedral in September 1851, Ruskin hardly endeared himself to Milman by making offensive remarks about St Paul's Cathedral. "I showed the Dean of St Paul's over the Duomo of Murano yesterday," he informed his father, "abusing St Paul's all the time, and making him observe the great superiority of the old church and the abomination of its Renaissance additions, and the Dean was much disgusted".[78] Effie was given two coveted tickets, by Dean Milman, to attend the Iron Duke's elaborate funeral in St Paul's Cathedral, London.[79] Since Ruskin refused to go to the funeral, a "ridiculous and tiresome pageant",[80] Effie asked her father to accompany her. Ruskin had mixed feelings about being replaced by Mr Gray and expressed them to him: "I am partly happy – partly sorry that Effie has persuaded you to come up to the Duke's funeral."[81]

The Duke of Wellington had been Chancellor of Oxford University since 1834, and was also a member of Christ Church. Gordon gave the Censor's speech, in Latin, at Oxford, on the loss of the Duke. It was an impressive *tour de force*, "cast in an heroic mould; [...] classical in form and sentiment; and hardly [bore] translation from the Latin, in which Mr Gordon thought as he wrote".[82] In churches and cathedrals throughout the land, there were polished orations commemorating the Duke's life and heroic deeds.

Chapter 8

The divorce

On Tuesday 22 March 1853, John Pritchard achieved his political ambition and was elected Member of Parliament for the Borough of Bridgnorth.[1] He had taken the seat occupied by Sir Robert Pigot who had been unseated "on the ground of bribery and treating by agents".[2] Pritchard, "of the firm of Messrs. J. and G. Pritchard, bankers, of Broseley and Bridgnorth", had been proposed by Mr. T. Pardoe Purton, banker, and seconded by Mr. H. S. Richards, a magistrate. A meeting of Pritchard and his friends was held at Cross Lane Head, a hamlet about two miles north of Bridgnorth on the main road to Broseley, at ten o'clock on the Tuesday morning, followed by a more formal meeting at the town hall in Bridgnorth where Pritchard's reception "was very flattering".[3] He was declared unanimously elected.

Pritchard held the position until 1868 when the Bridgnorth became a single-seat constituency. His fellow MP was Henry Whitmore (1814-1876) who represented the Borough from 1852 to 1870. Pritchard's political leanings were summarised in the *Who's Who of British Members of Parliament* in which he was described as a "Liberal-Conservative, in favour of national education being extended by voluntary exertion, aided by public grants; of a reduction of the qualification in counties and boroughs; of Dissenters being relieved from the payment of church-rates; but opposed to the ballot".[4] In his acceptance

speech in Bridgnorth town hall, he described his political principles as being "Conservative". Pritchard and his wife took an
active part in the life of his constituency. He was President of the
Bridgnorth Literary & Scientific Institution, and Patron of many
amateur dramatic performances in aid of funds for the
Bridgnorth Infirmary.

As befitted his rising status and needs, Pritchard acquired
extensive lands and property around the Broseley/Bridgnorth
area, as well as a prestigious London address at 89 Eaton Square.
On the death of his childless brother George in 1861, he inherited Stanmore Grove, a country property near Bridgnorth. It
was described unflatteringly by one of Pritchard's opponents as
"a very mean-looking square-built brick house, the front facing
due east, the north overgrown by closely approximating fir trees
. . . the south with a tolerable view towards Bridgnorth, and the
west, or back door, opening immediately upon the mixens of
Mr. S. Ridley's farm-yard".[5] It appears that John Pritchard never
lived at Stanmore Grove, partly because it was in such a dilapidated state. It was described as "unlettable" and its only
occupant being Mr. Richard Boycott, son of John Pritchard's late
partner, and "a domestic". The house was known locally as
"Gitton's Folly", before John Pritchard came to own it because of
a mortgage of the Bridgnorth solicitor Gitton.

The encroachment of the developing railway network
through the countryside in the nineteenth century was as
familiar to Ruskin as it was to Pritchard who found himself in
the midst of a dispute. He had at first publicly supported the
development of the Bridgnorth, Wolverhampton &
Staffordshire Railway at a public meeting in Bridgnorth in May
1865. But, much to the anger of local people, he changed his
mind and became known and mocked as "chameleon" John
Pritchard. He alleged that the railway would pass within 100
yards of Stanmore Grove, destroying "its beauty, comfort, and
privacy" and so unfitting it for his habitation.[6] Perhaps realising
that he would be in a stronger position to resist any further

attempts to encroach on his estate if he resided there, Pritchard decided to radically transform Stanmore Grove into a most desirable residence in the heart of his constituency.

Pritchard engaged John West Hugall, architect and author of historical guides of York Cathedral (1850) and churches in Scarborough and district (1848), to direct the new project. The mainly Georgian Stanmore Grove was extensively altered, refurbished and extended in 1868-1870 to become Stanmore Hall, with advice from Ruskin.[7] Hugall was essentially a church architect and the domestic, secular architecture of Stanmore presented a different kind of challenge. He accepted the commission soon after completing the church of St Michael and St Mary Magdalene at Easthampstead to the satisfaction of Pritchard's brother-in-law the Rev. Osborne Gordon.

The completed building featured in *The Builder* of 1 October 1870. An illustration by John W. Hallam, engraved by W. E. Hodgkin, shows Stanmore Hall resplendent as a French Renaissance *château* with roofs surmounted by wrought iron cresting and finials, dormer windows and roof lanterns, decorated parapets and balustrades, turrets, and a symmetry that is associated with the *châteaux* in the Loire Valley. The windows on the ground and first floors have features of Venetian Gothic. It was strikingly polychromatic, constructed of red brick and covered with red and blue tiles, arranged in lines. Specialist companies were engaged from all over England to provide the finest materials and fittings. As well as aesthetic considerations, comfort was paramount. Modern conveniences were installed – mains water and gas, a central heating system by means of hot water, a luggage lift reaching from the basement to the attics, a bathroom and three separate toilets on the first floor, together with two more toilets on the ground floor. There were nine bedrooms, three dresssing-rooms, a nursery (a surprising inclusion for the Pritchards were childless), an upper hall and Jane Pritchard's own south-facing sitting-room on the first floor. Downstairs were the servants' quarters, housekeeper's room, hall, drawing-room, dining-room, morning-room and a library. Eric Mercer regarded Hugall's design as "adventurous" and "eccentric"[8] because of an unusual feature – the ground floor butterfly wings on the northwest side extending off the servants' hall and a scullery. Standing in front of the main triple portalled entrance in Hallam's illustration is perhaps the *châtelain* himself, John Pritchard with his black horse and dog, about to go riding on his 1,300-acre estate.

Here is a description of Stanmore Hall in *The Builder*:

This house, of which we give an illustration, has recently been erected on the estate of Mr. John Pritchard, near to the picturesque town of Bridgnorth, Shropshire, under the direction of Mr. J. W. Hugall, of Oxford.

The site selected is very high, and the grounds are beautifully varied with an extensive view across the Severn valley, along which the river is seen to flow at various points.

The house is built of pressed red brick from Broseley, with Bath stone dressings, and is covered with red and blue tiles, arranged in lines. The flats are covered with Vieille Montagne zinc, by Fox; and the cresting and finials, of wrought iron, surmounting the roofs, together with the gas-fittings, balustrading, and coil cases, are from the works of Messrs. Thomson & Co., of Birmingham; Messrs. Edwards, of Great Marlborough-street, fitted up the hot-water apparatus, the culinary arrangements, and the laundry; Mr. Coalman, of St. Mary Church, near Torquay, supplied the marble mantel-pieces, slabs, inlays, and columns; Mr. Steinitz laid down the parquetry in the entrance-hall; Messrs. Jackson executed the very elaborate ceilings in their fibrous plaster; and the general contractors, Messrs. Wall & Hook, of Brimscombe, have carried out their various works with care. Water and gas have been laid on from the town of Bridgnorth, a distance of two miles.

The principal and some subsidiary rooms have a line of hot-water pipes passing through them, and coils are placed in the halls, covered by wrought iron and brass cases with marble slabs. A lift for luggage reaches from the basement to the attics. The

principal staircase is of oak and enclosed beneath, to form a
serving passage to the dining-room.
The house being erected on a slope of the ground to the north,
advantage has been taken of it to form a basement for laundry,
larders, cellarage, and so on.
A considerable quantity of stone carving is executed both externally and internally.[9]

* * *

A few weeks after his electoral success, John Pritchard MP and
his wife Jane were guests at a dinner hosted by John James and
Margaret Ruskin at the family home at Denmark Hill. At the
table were John and Effie Ruskin, Effie's lover (or lover-to-be),
twenty-three-year-old John Everett Millais (1829-1896), Sir
Walter Trevelyan and his wife Pauline (1816-1866), a wealthy,
sensitive and talented patron of the arts and friend of the Pre-
Raphaelite Brotherhood. Lockhart and Cheney are also listed as
being guests at dinner in John James Ruskin's diary.[10] Lady
Trevelyan described the dinner party as "heavenly"[11] and the old
Ruskins as "very kind and pleasant & Effie very nice".[12] The com-
position of the guest list ensured that it would be interesting and
stimulating. Millais, proud of being a successful and controversial artist at an early age – "only 24 in June" – provided insights
into the workings of the art world, "the mean way the Academy
treated him", his anger at Windus's refusal to buy paintings
direct from him. Lady Trevelyan, although three years younger
than Ruskin, was not afraid to criticise him for what she considered to be his "savage" treatment of people in his books: he naturally disagreed and suggested that he "ought to be ten times
more so".[13] In spite of her forthright manner, Pauline Trevelyan
and Ruskin were to become and remain close friends and as she
lay dying from ovarian cancer in a hotel in Neuchâtel, it was
Ruskin who was invited to be at her deathbed.[14] The chemistry
and flirtation between Effie and Millais at that April dinner
party would have been difficult to conceal. Three months later,

the young lovers, with Ruskin, would endure a tense situation in a small rented Highland cottage at remote Glenfinlas for the month of July 1853. Millais' task was, he informed William Holman Hunt, to "paint Ruskin's portrait by one of these rocky streams".[15] The weather was cold and wet, and made the *huis clos* situation even more intolerable. Effie's escape from her loveless, sexless marriage would take place nine months later.

Jane and John Pritchard were again guests at Denmark Hill on 1 June.[16] The company included thirty-one-year-old Scottish landowner William Macdonald (1822-1893) described in *Praeterita* as "a thin, dark Highlander" and "the son of an old friend, perhaps flame, of my father's, Mrs Farquharson".[17] Macdonald had been best man at John Ruskin's wedding.[18] John James's business partner Henry Telford and the artist brothers George and Thomas Richmond were also present. Another invitation was accepted by Jane and John Pritchard on 25 June.[19]

Events moved swiftly between the summer of 1853 and April 1854. As Effie became increasingly estranged from the Ruskin family, so her closeness to her own family and to Cheney and Brown increased. Secrecy in planning her release and divorce from Ruskin was paramount. Cheney proved to be a loyal friend to her. On the surface, things appeared normal. In late November 1853, Effie and John were invited to stay again at Badger Hall with the Cheneys. Effie wanted to accept but John refused as she explained to Rawdon Brown: "I would have very much enjoyed a couple of days with our kind friends at Badger, and they wished it, but John is not inclined."[20]

*   *   *

Dinner parties continued as normal at Denmark Hill. In mid-January, John James noted in his list of guests John and Effie, Gordon, George and Thomas Richmond and others.[21] The older Ruskins continued to consolidate their relationship with the Pritchards, especially since the election, and had invited them to their home for dinner on Tuesday February 28th along with Gordon and Charles Newton, but seemingly without Ruskin.[22] On learning of this arrangement, Ruskin immediately and high handedly cancelled an invitation he and Effie had accepted to dine with Lady James, informing Lady James that Effie would go alone. Ruskin wanted to be with his parents, the Pritchards and his two Christ Church friends. He did not consult Effie: she refused to go on her own to Lady James's.[23] In retaliation for what Ruskin considered to be Effie's unacceptable behaviour, he ordered her in a most dictatorial way to either "stay here all the summer alone or go to Perth", for he was planning another long continental tour with his parents.

On 5 April 1854, the Pritchards dined again with Mr and Mrs Ruskin at Denmark Hill.[24] Other guests were the Rev. Thomas Dale (Ruskin's former tutor), evangelical vicar of St Pancras, London, and his son Lawford. Effie, her eleven-year old sister Sophie (a shrewd observer of the Ruskin household), and Effie's devoted Scottish friend Jane Boswell were also present. It must have been a strange and strained occasion. Effie was in a nervous state and suffering from terrible pain throughout her body. Wine flowed freely, to such an extent that "old Madam" (Mrs Ruskin) became inebriated and descended into vulgar conversation. Effie provides a fascinating insight into a little-known aspect of Mrs Ruskin's personality: "Jane is perfectly rabid on the subject of the R's, especially Mrs R. She was so disgusted with her conversation last night that she thinks she must have been quite drunk."[25]

Tension was increasing between Effie and her husband. She confided fully in Rawdon Brown and Cheney who did not betray her secrets. Ruskin insisted on working and dining with his parents at Denmark Hill: it was, he told Effie, "absolutely necessary". Life was "a perpetual struggle",[26] a battle of the wills between the incompatible couple.

Effie could no longer tolerate Ruskin's hypocrisy, and that of his parents. She revealed to Rawdon Brown Ruskin's true feelings about the "kind friends" the Cheneys: "As for John, he is as hypocritical about the *Cheneys* as in other things. He says they are intensely worldly, know nothing about Art etc, but as he thinks everybody who does not flatter him mad or bad – this is not singular."[27] Ruskin was becoming more and more selfish and intolerant – that was Millais' opinion.[28]

Plans were being put in place for Effie's departure. Her parents arrived in London on 14 April, took legal advice and made appropriate arrangements for the divorce.

Almost on the eve of the continental journey from which Effie was excluded, Ruskin said goodbye to her at King's Cross railway station, London, on 25 April 1854. He had, seemingly, no suspicion that she was planning to leave him and would never return. She left for Scotland and the home and care of her own family. Later that day, a citation was served on John Ruskin. Effie returned her wedding ring, keys and accounts book to Mrs Ruskin and enclosed a letter informing her of the impending divorce and the reasons for it. Effie severed all relations with the Ruskins and decisively signed the letter "Euphemia C. Gray".[29]

Ruskin's marriage was annulled on the grounds of non-con-summation on 15 July 1854. He was conveniently in Chamonix at the time with his parents and was to remain abroad, spending much of his time in the Alps, until the beginning of October. Liberated from the strain of his marital situation, and back in the familiar family triangle, Ruskin pursued his work with renewed vigour, preparing materials for the third and fourth volumes of *Modern Painters*.

* * *

Meanwhile, Gordon was preoccupied with other things, in par-ticular the constitution of Christ Church. He argued his case for change with W. E. Gladstone, who, in 1854, was both Chancellor of the Exchequer and MP for Oxford University.[30] Gladstone had also been educated at Christ Church. Gordon believed strongly that Fellowships at the College should be earned and based on merit and achievements. He explained his strong personal feelings to Gladstone: "I was appointed by the Dean unasked and without any knowledge – and I felt at the time and ever since that the college had acquired a right to my services, such as they are. But if I had been appointed, for instance, after I obtained the Ireland scholarship, I should have considered that I had earned it by fair examination, and felt under no obligation to any one."[31] The correspondence to hand on the matter of scholarships and studentships begins on 21 March 1854 and demonstrates Gordon's commitment to his principles and his relentless pursuit of the matter in the face of opposition, and some criticism from Gladstone who had accused him of being too negative. Gordon demonstrates an overriding concern for the welfare of Christ Church undergraduates and staff. At one point Gordon only pauses to take "a week's tour in Normandy" just after Easter in April 1854.[32]

That same year marked the marriage of Gordon's brother William Pierson Gordon, a solicitor, to Anne Hunt. John and Jane Pritchard, who remained childless, were close to William and his family, and particularly fond of his only son (their nephew) William Pritchard Gordon[33] who inherited much of their estate on their death. A word of explanation is called for as there is a potentially confusing clash of names. William's middle name of Pritchard is both an acknowledgement of his grand-mother's maiden name and his uncle's family.

Shortly before Christmas Jane and John Pritchard celebrated the festive season at a small party at the old Ruskins' house to which the Rev. Daniel Moore and his wife – travelling compan-ions abroad in 1851 – the two Richmond brothers and Mr and Mrs Fall were invited.[34]

* * *

Ruskin did not go abroad in 1855. Work was paramount and

unnecessary social invitations were refused. In a letter to
Rossetti Ruskin explained: "I am deep in difficult chapters of
Modern Painters. I cannot be disturbed even by my best friends
or greatest pleasures."[35] However, the winner of the Newdigate
prize for poetry in 1839 now displayed a renewed interest in
poetry and contemporary poets. The Poet Laureate, Tennyson –
successor to Wordsworth – was invited to Denmark Hill.[36] On 14
April Gordon was introduced to Coventry Patmore (1823-
1896), whose book of verse *The Betrayal* had been published the
previous autumn. Ruskin's own feelings at the time may have
been in harmony with the title, an uncomfortable reminder of
his recent divorce. Patmore was also a critic, a reviewer of
Modern Painters, II, and *The Stones of Venice,* and had written
articles on architecture with views at times opposed to Ruskin's.
In February 1854 he had praised the new style of railway architecture and wrote: "What can be more pleasing [...] than the
light iron roof, with its simple, yet intricate supports of span-
drels, rods, and circles, at Euston square, or the vast transparent
vault and appropriate masses of brickwork at King's Cross?"[37]
Along with Gordon and Patmore were George Richmond and
Edmund Oldfield[38] with whom Ruskin had collaborated on the
stained-glass windows for St Giles's Church, Camberwell. In this
stimulating company, against the background of the Turner collection, the conversation ranged from art, religion, architecture
and the battle of the styles, to poetry and church windows.

Although Liddell's temporary departure had facilitated
Gordon's career in 1846, it was his return to Christ Church as
Dean in 1855 that precipitated Gordon's leaving. Liddell's hasty
appointment as Dean was not without controversy. Dodgson
recorded in his diary of 7 June 1855: "The *Times* announces that
Liddell of Westminster is to be the new Dean: the selection does
not seem to have given much satisfaction in the college."[39] The
previous incumbent Thomas Gaisford (1779-1855), Regius
Professor of Greek, had been Dean since 1831. For Ruskin,
whose undergraduate drawings had been so admired by

Gaisford,[40] he was England's "greatest scholar".[41] John James Ruskin had shown his gratitude to Gaisford for helping his son by sending him a hamper of thirty-six bottles of rare vintage sherry of 1823.[42] Gordon was particularly close to Gaisford, his "chiefly trusted aid".[43] His sudden and unexpected death at the age of seventy-seven caused much sorrow. Dodgson wrote in his diary of Saturday 2 June 1855:

> This day died our old Dean, respected by all, and I believe regretted by very many – only Saturday last he was with Mr Gordon and myself in the Library, putting away the new books, and apparently in perfect health: little did I suppose that was the last time I should ever see him – all this morning they have been issuing bulletins hour by hour: the one announcing that all was over came out about half past 11.[44]

On the death of Dean Thomas Gaisford in 1855, Gordon delivered a lengthy funeral oration, in Latin, that was "worthy of the best days of Roman eloquence".[45]

John Pritchard MP was now on Royal guest lists and was invited by Queen Victoria to a "Drawing-room" – a court reception – in St James's Palace on the afternoon of Thursday 14 June 1855.[46] Similar invitations were received in subsequent years (on 29 May 1856, and again in 1858). Gordon too was on the Royal guest list of the Prince of Wales (whom he tutored at Christ Church in 1859) and was invited to several all male receptions, called levees, at St James's Palace on 26 June 1868, 1 June 1869, 11 March 1878, and on 3 May 1879 with his brother-in-law John Pritchard. On another occasion in July 1872, Gordon was invited by the Prince and Princess of Wales to a garden party at Chiswick.

* * *

Ruskin wanted to introduce the Pritchards to his own circle of friends away from Denmark Hill, so he arranged for Jane and

John Pritchard to meet his new (to be lifelong) friends John Simon (1816-1904) and his Irish wife Jane (*née* O'Meara). Dr Simon (later Sir John in 1887) was a medical doctor who, in 1855 (the year before Ruskin and his parents met him) had been appointed to the new post of Medical Officer to the Privy Council. He was also the first Medical Officer of Health for the City of London, appointed in 1848, and had a particular responsibility for the prevention of cholera and other public health issues.

Ruskin was concerned that the threatened dissolution of Parliament – it was dissolved in March 1857 – would thwart his plans. At first he thought that Pritchard would have to be out of London, campaigning in his Bridgnorth constituency, at the time of the proposed meeting with the Simons. But all was eventually arranged and the meeting eagerly anticipated as Ruskin confirmed in his letter to Mrs Simon: "I did not answer your kind note, because the threatened dissolution of Parliament might have sent Mr Pritchard and his wife, whom we wanted you to meet, into the country again, – but as matters are now arranged, they are coming, and if you can come too, it will give us all very great pleasure."[47]

The voice of the leading art critic of the day was eagerly awaited in the annual review of the Royal Academy Exhibition that opened in early May. Within a few days, Ruskin's *Notes on some of the Principal Pictures Exhibited in the Rooms of the Royal Academy and the Society of Painters in Water-Colours, Etc.* had to be completed, published and made available to the public. Budding art collector and connoisseur John Pritchard attended, along with John James Ruskin on 5 May 1857.[48] There they saw works by Millais (about whom Ruskin was uncomplimentary), Naftel (whose *Paestum* Pritchard would purchase a few years later), Stanfield, E. W. Cooke, J. D. Harding (Ruskin's former drawing master), Pierre Édouard Frère and many, many others.

In June, Ruskin's *Elements of Drawing* was published. It was a manual and practical guide, a kind of *Teach Yourself Drawing* book, made up of much of the material that Ruskin used in his classes at the Working Men's College, London. On 8 December 1857, John and Jane Pritchard were invited to John James Ruskin's home along with Dr Grant, Harrison and artist Tom Richmond.[49]

*   *   *

Towards the end of 1858, Ruskin became an Honorary Student of Christ Church. This was a great honour – he was only one of ten elected at the time – and due to the influence of Gordon who put his name forward, seconded by the Dean. Other Honorary Students elected at the same time were Gladstone, Sir George Cornewall Lewis, Sir Frederick Ouseley (Professor of Music), Dr Acland, Henry Hallam, Lords Stanhope, Elgin, Dalhousie and Canning.[50]

Chapter 9

The Rev. Osborne Gordon, a not-so-ordinary country parson

In spite of Gordon's outstanding contribution to Christ Church, there seems to have been some disagreement with the then Dean Henry George Liddell, the great classical scholar renowned for his *Greek-English Lexicon* (1843). It was tactfully recorded that Gordon's views were "not quite in accordance" with Liddell's and so Gordon left the world of academia in 1860. It cannot have been an entirely happy turn of events for Gordon was through and through a Christ Church man. As Ruskin remarked: "His ambition was restricted to the walls of Christ Church."[1]

Gordon, at the age of forty-seven, became rector of the church of St Michael and St Mary Magdalene, Easthampstead, Berkshire in 1860, succeeding the Rev. Abraham Boyle Townsend. It was not an unusual career change. Gordon's own headmaster Thomas Rowley at Bridgnorth School left to take the living at Willey Church and even died there in November 1877, aged eighty years, "in the performance of his sacred office" as the inscription on a quatrefoiled plaque marking the spot where he died reminds us.[2] Easthampstead, situated half way between Oxford and London, proved to be the ideal place for Gordon. He enjoyed country life and would have been ill at ease in or near an industrial city in mid- or late-Victorian Britain.

Gordon shunned the outskirts of London disfigured by slipshod houses and the railways. In one of his Oxford lectures as Slade Professor of Fine Art, "The Relation of Art to Use" (delivered on 3 March, 1870), Ruskin, deliberating on the need for quality dwellings and good town planning, invoked Gordon, "an English clergyman", to support his argument:

> Not many weeks ago an English clergyman, a master of this University, a man not given to sentiment, but of middle age, and great practical sense, told me, by accident, and wholly without reference to the subject now before us, that he never could enter London from his country parsonage but with closed eyes, lest the sight of the blocks of houses which the railroad intersected in the suburbs should unfit him, by the horror of it, for his day's work.[3]

Gordon, who had obtained his BD in 1847, had gained a reputation for being a talented, eloquent preacher and speaker. At Easthampstead he had his own fiefdom, away from university tensions yet he remained in touch with his *alma mater* – for his church was a living within the jurisdiction of Christ Church. On Easter Day 1861, he returned to Oxford to preach, in Christ Church Cathedral, a sermon, later published by Parker, based on Psalm VIII, 1: "O Lord our Governor, how excellent is Thy Name in all the World!"[4]

The village and parish of Easthampstead included extensive woodlands – pines were prevalent – and heaths: some of the land was training terrain for officer cadets from the Royal Military Academy at Sandhurst, a few miles to the south. Also in the parish was Bracknell, in 1860 nothing more than "a long village of one street, containing a graceful modern church of flint and chalk".[5] Murray's *Handbook* was referring to the new church of Holy Trinity built in 1851, close to Priestwood Common. With the coming of the railway in the 1850s, Bracknell (on the Waterloo to Reading line) began to expand as a market town: from 1949 it developed rapidly, acquired a new identity as Bracknell New Town and eventually totally eclipsed

Easthampstead. When Gordon arrived in Easthampstead, the population was "about 720":[6] twenty years later it had increased to 888.

In the first edition of Murray's *Handbook for Travellers in Berks, Bucks, and Oxfordshire* of 1860, literary critic and travel writer Augustus John Cuthbert Hare (1834-1903), under cover of anonymity in the tradition of the series,[7] had little to say about the church other than it had "a thick red-brick tower, and a fine old yew-tree in its churchyard".[8] He was more interested in the monuments inside, not for their artistic qualities but as memorials to Sir William Trumbull and the poet Elija Fenton, both friends of Alexander Pope (1688-1744). No mention was made of the fine box pews that lined both sides of the central aisle.

The move to village life was no sinecure. Gordon faced many challenges, one of the most serious being the church building itself. Neglected over many years, it was in need of repair and restoration. Previous bachelor rectors, Thomas Pettingal (in office 1783-1826) and Abraham Boyle Townsend (in office 1826-1860), had presided over a deteriorating, rundown rectory, outbuildings and church. In 1836 the parsonage was pulled down and not rebuilt. Townsend, renowned for his sharp tongue, had been largely unsuccessful in his attempts to persuade patrons to undertake maintenance and repairs. His relations with his neighbour and wealthy landowner the 4th Marquis of Downshire were at a low ebb and there was considerable hostility between them. The Marquis had tried unsuccessfully to oust Townsend and buy the living (the advowson) from Christ Church. Townsend stood firm, but consequently he lost the confidence of his most powerful financial backer.

Murray's description of Easthampstead in 1860 as "a pretty rural village"[9] belied the undercurrent of tension into which Gordon was plunged. All his charm, sensitivity, diplomacy and common sense were needed to diffuse the situation. This he did and achieved results beyond any expectations. His major task was that of a fund-raiser: his parish church was falling down and there was no rectory. In 1863, he alerted his Christ Church patrons to the extent of the problem: "The church is of the worst character. I have had it surveyed and estimate sent in for its enlargement & repair which is virtually rebuilding it at a cost of £3000."[10] Two years later, a decision had been reached that the parish church "should be taken down and rebuilt as far as may be found practicable".[11] This was a drastic measure and one that Ruskin would have opposed. Challenges appealed to Gordon and soon he succeeded in charming and winning over local landowner and church patron the Marchioness of Downshire (Caroline, wife of Arthur Hill, fourth Marquis of Downshire) who contributed in full the money required. Thanks to this generous benefactor, work commenced in 1865 according to designs by the architect John West Hugall. Hugall, who hailed from Sutton Courtenay, had already established a reputation in Berkshire: he had been responsible for St James's Church, Bourton, completed in 1860.[12]

Gordon had been at Oxford during the controversial building of the Oxford Museum (later the University Museum), con-structed in the late 1850s, designed by Dublin architect Benjamin Woodward. He was well aware of the debate and heated argument surrounding the choice of style and materials. The initiative for a science building and museum of natural history came from Henry Acland, and the architectural initiative from Ruskin. But Ruskin was not in charge of the project and remained ambivalent and never satisfied with it: that was his nature. He was critical of some of O'Shea's carving as "not yet perfect Gothic sculpture": although a wrought-iron spandrel on the roof depicting horse-chestnut leaves produced "a more agreeable effect than convolutions of the iron could have given", he did "not call it an absolutely good design".[13] Nevertheless, whatever reservations Ruskin harboured, he contributed an undisclosed amount for decoration for "Completing the Doorway and the Sculptures of the West Front" – along with twenty-five named individuals and some unnamed architects.[14] He also donated £300 "towards carving the windows of the Front".[15] Ruskin's father sponsored the statue of Hippocrates, the 'father of medicine', sculpted by Alexander Munro, at a cost of between £70-£100:[16] John James's name appears next to that of Queen Victoria who funded statues of the scientists Bacon, Galileo, Newton, Leibnitz and Oersted. Gordon is listed as one of the "Donors of Shafts costing £5 and upwards".[17]

To what extent was Gordon influenced by the Gothic Revival, by the furore over the University Museum and of course by Ruskin in the choice of his architect for his church? And to what extent did his wealthy donor influence decisions?

The new church was rebuilt in 1866-1867 in the neo-Gothic style but vestiges of the previous church were retained. A small slab mounted within the red brick on the exterior west wall is inscribed "Henry Boyer, 1664". The pulpit dates from 1631. There is an octagonal font with an oak lid elaborately and finely carved with leaves, flowers and various symbols: in one of the segments two doves facing each other (a symbol of Concord) are partly separated and framed by a Greek cross and foliage. In the second, revised edition of Murray's *Handbook for Travellers in Berks, Bucks and Oxfordshire* published in 1872, the travel writer Augustus Hare described the new church as being "in a mixed Byzantine and Early English style". Mention is made of a "noble yew-tree, 63ft in circumference" growing in the churchyard.[18] Murray's *Architectural Guide to Berkshire* of 1949 was critical:

> the church was rebuilt in 1866-7 in a style that combines late thirteenth century English and Byzantine characteristics from designs by J. W. Hugall. The result is (as Meade Falkner's version of Murray's Handbook rightly calls it) 'pretentious' rather than original or successful. No doubt it shows an attempt on the architect's part to think in an impressive, personal style but he surely thought too much and felt too little. Much Italian marble and carved oak are used in the heavy fittings […].[19]

In 1869, an organ built by J. W. Walker and Sons was installed in the church. The same famous Suffolk firm was also responsible for the organ in newly restored St Leonard's Church, Bridgnorth.

Gordon enhanced and embellished his church with quality ornament, sculpture, furniture and stained-glass windows. He was absolutely determined to have the finest possible glass, design and craftsmanship, particularly for the great East Window. He informed Ruskin of the outcome of his negotiations in a letter of 11 June 1874: "Morris & Co. are going to do the East Window in my Church and I have no doubt it will be a success."[20] The project had been the subject of previous correspondence in which Ruskin had challenged Gordon about his expenditure on works of art. Gordon defended himself and wrote to Ruskin: "I must undeceive you as to what you said about my 'spending my money on bad art'. I spend none on art good or bad – but only on things necessary – £5 is all that windows have cost me – and I have never asked any one for a farthing. But I have not refused to allow other people to do what they offered – and have only done the best according to my light – which is perhaps very like darkness."[21]

The East Window was financed by the lady of the manor, Georgiana (*née* Balfour), Marchioness of Downshire, in memory of her husband, Arthur, fifth Marquis of Downshire who had died in 1874. The foremost artist of the day, Edward Burne-Jones (1833-1898), produced designs for the subject, *The Last Judgment*, presented in a trio of windows surmounted by a sexfoil rose window *Dies Domini*, the Day of the Lord. The central window shows the warrior Michael, Archangel and Saint (an appropriate subject for a church dedicated to him) dressed in a short tunic and holding in his left hand a balance scale in which the souls of the departed will be weighed in judgment, and a spear in his right hand. Angels blowing straight trumpets are depicted in the panels on each side.

Two windows depicting the *Resurrection and St Mary*

Magdalene, also the work of the Burne-Jones and William Morris (1834-1896) partnership, were placed above the altar in the Resurrection Chapel in the north aisle. The left light shows Mary Magdalene, clutching her robe in an attempt to find comfort, and an angel seated on the slabs pointing to the empty tomb. In the right-hand light, Mary Magdalene kneels, holds her hands with her palms upwards and gazes at the risen Christ standing before her. The story is told in St John 20:11-18. Above the two lights is a quatrefoil framing two angels blowing straight trumpets (a favourite motif of Burne-Jones and one which echoes *The Last Judgment* window). The white and pale yellow robes of the six figures predominate against a background of shades of green in the rocks and foliage. These windows were commissioned as a memorial to W. J. Scott of Wick Hill House, Bracknell, who died in 1875. They date from 1878.

Several other stained-glass windows were commissioned during Gordon's incumbency, including works by William Wailes of Newcastle-upon-Tyne and Nathaniel Hubert J. Westlake. Westlake's windows were the gift of local resident John Thaddeus Delane, former editor of *The Times* who died in 1879. At Delane's funeral in November, Gordon made a particular reference to his generous gift in his homily.[22] By the end of the nineteenth century the church of St Michael and St Mary Magdalene was endowed with some of the finest stained glass in the country, mainly due to the efforts of Gordon.

We do not know where Gordon lived in the very first few years of his incumbency. He addressed this urgent problem immediately and by 1863 he had achieved this goal. "I have built a house here –", he informed the Christ Church Censors, "and any number who will favour me with a visit will I hope be satisfied that it is suited to the Parish".[23] There appears to be no extant pictorial record of the house save an amateur twentieth-century oil painting by W. R. Newson entitled and dated *The Rectory 1950s*. In the distance the rectory, although indistinct, appears to have a red roof, gabled windows and a tall chimney.

It was reached along a drive through established grounds with old trees that protected its privacy. Outhouses and sheds are positioned on both sides of the approach. This Victorian rectory, situated about a mile from the church, was demolished in the late 1950s. On the site a hexagonal seventeen-storey tower block of accommodation for single people or couples without children was constructed by Arup Associates in 1960-1964. It remains in the twenty-first century a prominent landmark visible from afar – one could think of it affectionately as "Gordon's tower". However, some of the old trees that Gordon and Ruskin would have known have been preserved and soften the effect of the reinforced concrete. An echo of the previous building is found in the address of the tower – Rectory Road.

Not only did Gordon have responsibility for the church but also for some ninety-three acres (approximately thirty-eight hectares) of glebe, the land granted to a clergyman as part of his benefice. A competent farmer and manager, Gordon improved the wild, neglected glebe so skilfully that it "was before long", Marshall reported, "in a state of high cultivation".[24] Stressing his success to his Christ Church patrons, he wrote: "the Rectorial farm of 93 acres when I took it was fast going out of cultivation but I have reclaimed it, and in another year or two it will be in good order." He added confidently: "I think it will prove a very excellent tithe farm and should I at any time wish to give it up I have no doubt it would fetch a much higher rent than it did when I took to it."[25] So renowned a farmer did he become that he "soon became quoted as an authority on agricultural matters".[26] His agricultural projects were far more successful than Ruskin's experiments. The entrepreneurial Gordon worked immensely hard and directed his energies to making the glebe profitable and fruitful and a source of income for Christ Church. He gave financial details to his patrons in his account of his living:

The gross value on an average of the last three years I have returned to the bishop of Oxford at £653 15 0 including glebe at an estimated rent of £97/a. the net value I have returned at £506 5 5 but this does not include fees which are insignificant, the tithe is commuted at £516 – I think – but this includes the tithe on the glebe which I have the pleasure of paying myself with greater punctuality than I am able to enforce on the rest of the tithe payers.[27]

There was a shortage of good labourers and Gordon's solution, at least to his own immediate problem, was to provide accommodation for them. By this means, he could attract and keep under his supervision the quality staff he required. He sought permission from his patrons to borrow £200 in order to build the tied cottages.[28] Here is the letter, August 26, but of uncertain year, that he wrote:

Dear Sir

I do not know which of the Canons may be in residence now so I write to you. I wish to borrow £200 from Queen Anne's Bounty for building one or more cottages on the glebe. At present there is not one and it is consequently impossible to obtain good labourers. The approval of the Chapter is required for this and I hope there will be no obligation as I have hitherto laid no charge on the living and spent large sums upon it – I should wish to begin at once but fear I shall have to wait for a chapter – will you have the kindness to show this to the resident canon and believe me

Sincerely yours, O. Gordon[29]

But in the year prior to the Marchioness of Downshire's benevolence, John James Ruskin made an even larger gift of £5000 as a personal tribute to Gordon. In John James's account book, in his own hand, under the heading "Charities and Gifts 1862", can be found the following entry: "July 1st Rev. O. Gordon for poor livings Ch[rist] Church Oxford £5000."[30] The money was given directly to Gordon in person rather than to the college authorities. When the munificent gift was presented, John James stressed the key role of Gordon when he pronounced: "I give it to *you*, Mr Gordon, as Representative of the College, for the College."[31] According to G. W. Kitchin, – Gordon's successor as Censor at Christ Church and later Dean of Durham Cathedral – so completely did John James trust Gordon that in order to "express his gratitude for the good his John had got from Christ Church, he sent Gordon a cheque for £5000 to be given at the tutor's discretion for the augmentation of poor and needy parishes in the gift of the House".[32] This was a huge sum of money. To put this in perspective, in 1855 Dodgson, as a master at Christ Church, received an annual salary of £300.[33] It represented the esteem in which Gordon was held and the gratitude owed to him by John James Ruskin for his indispensable help and friendship to his son. In a letter written from Venice ten years earlier, Ruskin advises his father on a presentation the latter intends making to Christ Church: "Pray offer the presentation at Christs to Mr Snow – or anyone whom you think best."[34] Although John Lewis Bradley, editor of *Ruskin's Letters from Venice, 1851-1852*, suggests this refers to the above-mentioned gift of £5000, it would seem more likely that John James was intending to make an earlier gift to the College. Who was "Mr Snow"?

In November 1862, John James gave £2 to an unnamed Shropshire Church.[35] This was a minute sum in comparison with his generosity to Christ Church livings.

Gordon was concerned about the poverty of his parishioners, their increasing numbers and the lack of a proper school and facilities. He explained the situation to the Christ Church Censors:

> The population is about 720 and likely to increase. I think all the people are well disposed and there is nothing like organized dissent if there are dissenters in the place, but the parish is very badly supplied with everything that a parish requires for its well being. There is no school & I have hitherto failed in establishing

one – though if established it would be supported at little or no cost to the clergyman. There are two dames schools and I get about 40 children together on a Sunday and I have had an evening school attended by an average of 20 during the winter months. This is the only provision for education in the Parish.[36]

It was not until 1870 that the Elementary Education Act was passed, mainly due to the work and drive of William Edward Forster (1819-1886), Liberal MP for Bradford who rose to cabinet rank and was placed in charge of education in Gladstone's first period of office as Prime Minister (1868-1874). The Act instituted a State system of compulsory, basic education: Forster argued that since householders had been given political power – the right to vote since 1867– they needed to be educated in order to exercise that right. There was much debate about the compulsory nature of the Act and the right to freedom. Ruskin, of course, had strong views. He favoured the acquisition of manual skills, an apprenticeship system in which "wholesome and useful work" was the first condition of education.[37] He challenged and questioned the meaning of the word "education" as used by Forster and initiated a debate, via his public letters published monthly as *Fors Clavigera*, on the curriculum and what skills and knowledge were needed to produce good, useful, contented citizens who had satisfying jobs.[38] Ruskin opposed compelling children to undergo the kind of "education" Forster proposed that was totally at odds with his own views. As late as 1886 Ruskin was still vehemently opposing Forster's bill as a kind of theft and angrily wrote a letter to the *Pall Mall Gazette*:

I do extremely object to Mr Forster's breaking into my own Irish servant's house, robbing him of thirteen pence weekly out of his poor wages, and, besides, carrying off his four children for slaves half the day to play tunes on Wandering Willie's fiddle, instead of being about their father's business.[39]

Although Gordon supported the general principles of the Bill, he was opposed to a system that only allowed a modicum of religious instruction, by which he meant the Established Church: he believed that the State had a duty to include that subject. In this, Ruskin agreed with him in so far as a child should be taught a "religious faith".[40] Gordon made repeated references to the importance of religious education in his sermons, one of which, entitled "The Great Commandment and Education", was published in 1870.[41] In it he warned his rural congregation of the danger of "a design for covering the whole land with a system of schools, from which religious teaching shall be entirely excluded".

In contrast to the poor dwellings of the villagers stood the Downshire family country house of Easthampstead Park, a large mansion set in over sixty acres of parkland. Easthamstead Park had many royal and historical connections: Richard III had a hunting lodge in the Park; Queen Catherine of Aragon, the estranged wife of Henry VIII, stayed there in 1531; James 1 resided there in 1622 and 1628. Like the little parish church, over the centuries it had suffered from neglect and had become dilapidated. This fine building, apart from the stable block, was demolished in 1860 and work commenced on a new mansion almost immediately. So demolition and rebuilding were already in operation when Gordon arrived – another reason why there was a shortage of workmen for the glebe – and his decision to act similarly as regards his church may have been influenced by these ongoing works and prevailing ethos. The idea of preserving and repairing these monuments was not considered. In later years, the new Easthampstead Park was described as a "building of historic and architectural interest, in Jacobean style with curved gables, pierced stone parapet and stone frontispiece of naive classicism".[42]

* * *

Ruskin's spirit was restless and disturbed. In an effort to separate himself physically and psychologically from the tyranny of his parents, he spent substantial periods of time abroad in 1862 and 1863.[43] He never really succeeded for, as James Spates has pointed out, Ruskin had a "negative" symbiotic relationship with them.[44] Ruskin left London, without his parents, on 15 May 1862, primarily for Milan: however, in defiance of parental wishes, and unknown to them, he had invited Edward and Georgiana Burne-Jones to accompany him as his guests. John James Ruskin was, as usual, paying all the bills. The simmering resentment and tension between father and son would increase crescendo-like, culminating in the Brezon *débâcle* and ultimately the death of John James Ruskin. It was a struggle to find just equilibrium and a *modus vivendi* between a dutiful son and a head of family.

Recently discovered correspondence – the work of Helen Viljoen brought to light by Van Akin Burd and James Spates[45] – shows the extent of the tension and struggle and the degree to which the parents, instead of feeling proud, contrived to make their son feel guilty and insecure with their almost constant criticisms, nagging and jealousy. When Ruskin preferred not to spend Christmas of 1862 with them – he chose to be in Mornex, in Savoy – John James, writing on 15 December, the very day of his son's departure, emphasised the bleakness and their loneliness: "Mama was dull. I was dull – the house very dull, the Servants were dull. The Candles were dull. The lamps burnt blue."[46] This attempt at pathos and guilt induction did not have the desired effect. Ruskin remained abroad, for he had serious projects to address and bring to fruition.

He had already taken steps to secure plots of land at Chamonix and near Mornex. The little isolated alpine village of Mornex, two or three miles south-east of Geneva, at the northern tip of the Salève mountain range, and close to the river Arve, was at the centre of Ruskin's preoccupations. He first discovered this beautiful spot in August 1862: it seemed to offer him the peace and tranquillity he needed, as well as being ideally situated for his geological studies. The mountain scenery was inspirational and breathtakingly beautiful. "The broad summit of the Salève lay, a league long", he wrote to his father in mid-winter, "in white ripples of drifted snow, just like the creaming foam from a steamer's wheels, stretched infinitely on the sea, and all the plain of Geneva showed through its gorges in gold: the winter grass, in sunshine, being nearly pure gold-colour when opposed to snow".[47]

As well as mountain walking and writing, Ruskin was busy sketching the winter foliage and bleak scenes. At least two of his works from this period were destined for the Gordon/Pritchard families – a juniper bough with leaves and berries,[48] and a view from the Brezon.[49] Ruskin despatched his "first juniper bough" to his father with precise instructions that it be framed by Richard Williams of Messrs Foord's (frame-makers), on a "white mount about 2 inches or 2½ inches wide" and on "a light frame".[50] Ruskin's gift to Gordon, his *View from the Base of the Brezon above Bonneville, Looking towards Geneva: the Jura in the Distance; Salève on the Left*, was inherited by William Pritchard Gordon who lent the painting to E. T. Cook for reproduction in the Library Edition of *The Works of John Ruskin*.[51]

At this time, John James Ruskin was becoming increasingly jealous of the influence of some of his son's friends: the Pritchards and Gordon are mentioned. He felt excluded and a "nonentity". In his defence, Ruskin told his father: "you have cut me out with half my friends. The Richmonds – Dr. Brown – Bayne – Gordon – the Pritchards – think twice as much of you as they do of me."[52] Perhaps John James was jealous of the paint-ings and drawings that his son was making for his friends' col-lections instead of devoting all his time to writing as the father wished. Ruskin shaped the artistic taste of John and Jane Pritchard and Osborne Gordon through the kinds of paintings he generously gave them and the way in which he influenced some of their art purchases. At the Old Water Colour Society's

Exhibition in 1861, it was Ruskin who advised Pritchard to purchase Paul Naftel's large watercolour of *Paestum*.[53] Other works that the Pritchard/Gordon families acquired were Ruskin's *Walls of Lucerne*, his *Square at Cologne* (1842) one of "the last drawings ever executed in my old manner"[54] (i.e. in Proutesque style), his fine watercolour *The Valley of Chamouni* (1844) in a Turnerian style, and Samuel Prout's *Old Street in Lisieux*.[55]

Ruskin wanted to settle in Savoy and planned to build a house for himself among the mountains: he even investigated purchasing an entire mountain. He eventually decided to build his chalet on Mont Brezon,[56] in the Pointe d'Andey, south of Bonneville, close to his beloved Chamonix and Geneva. The land he chose was isolated and bleak, "about 5000 feet above the sea". Ruskin seemed totally committed to a foolhardy project, almost an escape from his father to whom he wrote, from Mornex:

> I mean to have the summit with two or three acres round it, and the cliff below: this is all barren rock, and should cost almost nothing – there is only a little goat browsing on it in summer [...]. But from the flank of it slopes down a pasturage to the south; the ridge of which is entirely secure from avalanche or falling rocks, and from the north wind: it looks south and west – over one of the grandest grouped ranges of jagged blue mountain I know in Savoy. It is accessible on that side only by a footpath, but the summit is accessible to within a quarter of an hour of the top, by a bridle path (leaving only a quarter of an hour's walk for any indolent friend who won't come up but on horseback).[57]

As regards the proposed dwelling:

> I think it would be foolish to build a mere wooden châlet in which I should be afraid of fire – especially as I should often want large fires. I mean to build a small stone house, which will keep anything I want to keep there in perfect safety, and will not give one the idea of likelihood to be blown away.[58]

Ruskin had taken the project further by formalising it: he arranged for the Mayor of Bonneville (Bonneville local council owned the site) and the Mayor's lawyer to go up the Brezon to be shown the land, then for a surveyor to prepare a plan and for an offer to be made to purchase it. One can imagine the chill that went through his father's veins on receipt of this information. John James would have been even more anxious on learning a few days later that his son had impetuously bought, beneath the *Aiguille de Blaitière*, in a rugged area south-east of Chamonix close to the *Glacier de Blaitière*, some "splendid rock and wood, the space of ground being altogether about 100 times as large as the village of Chamouni", for the sum of "£720 (18,000 francs)".[59]

* * *

Ruskin returned to the parental home at Denmark Hill on 1 June (1863). John James Ruskin reflected on how best to cope with his headstrong son's projects: his powers of persuasion were ineffectual. So he decided on a strategy of harnessing the help of friends likely to exert some influence and make Ruskin change his mind. Foremost among these was Gordon, renowned for his cool, common sense, and a man respected by John James. Georgiana Burne-Jones, wife of painter Edward, was also one of the concerned friends and had written to John James expressing her worries about the scheme. His reply to her reveals his anxiety and his hopes that Gordon will be able to exert some sound influence, indeed he suggests that he is the only person capable of this:

I am happy to think of my Son possessing so much of your and Mr Jones' regard, and to hear of so many excellent people desiring to keep him at home; [...] my hopes are, that my Son may ultimately settle in England; but these hopes would not be strengthened by his too suddenly changing his mind, throwing up his Engagements, breaking his Appointments, or at all acting on the whim of the moment. He so far proceeded towards a settlement in Savoy as to have begun treating with a Commune about a purchase of Land. His duty is, therefore, to go to Savoy and honourably withdraw from the Affair, by paying for all Trouble occasioned, and I fully expect the Savoyards will afford him some ground for declining a purchase by the exorbitant prices they will ask for their Land. As for the ground he has bought at Chamouni, it will be a pleasure to him to keep it though he saw it not once in seven years. It is the Building Plan near Bonneville that I should rejoice to see resigned [...]. He has made a short engagement to go to Switzerland with the Rev. Osborne Gordon, which I hope he will keep, and I shall endeavour to hope that his Engagements abroad may in future be confined to a Tour with a friend, and that Home Influences may in the end prevail [...].

My Son's fellow Traveller now is the best he could possibly go with. Being rather cynical in his views generally, and not over enthusiastic upon Alps, he is not likely to much approve of the middle heights of the Brezon for a Building Site.[60]

Towards the end of this three-month summer interlude in England in 1863, Ruskin spent a few days in Cheshire. His destination was Winnington Hall, a girls' boarding school near Northwich, run by Miss Margaret Alexis Bell. He enjoyed participating in the life of the school, and directing the students in areas of dance, art and music. In spite of Ruskin's professed dislike of children – by which he really meant babies and infants – he was in many ways a born teacher but liked to dictate his own curriculum according to his beliefs, at the centre of which was art education or the education of the eye. But even in the relaxed environment of Winnington, Ruskin was preoccupied with the purchase of land and property in Savoy, as his daily letters to his father testify. At times he tries to reassure his father that he is behaving in a responsible and business-like manner and consulting with sound friends (of whom one was Gordon): "I shall examine the ground well with Dr Gosse, Coutet, Gordon & perhaps Henry Acland, and fix my price, and require an answer in a week at most – yes or no, I don't care which. I can find plenty other places."[61] Ruskin also discussed the purchase with Headmistress Miss Bell, who opposed the plan. He could not stay at Winnington as long as he would have liked as he had fixed a date with Gordon for their departure for Mornex. That could not be changed for Gordon did not have the flexibility to alter his schedule owing to the requirements of his regular priestly duties at Easthampstead.

*   *   *

So the country parson and the famous writer, walking companions, intellectual companions and true friends travelled together through France, leaving England on Tuesday 8 September 1863. They breakfasted with the Richmonds at Boulogne on the Wednesday morning and left that same day at 12.20, arriving at Bonneville at six o'clock the next day.[62] Nothing but the Brezon occupied Ruskin's mind: "Red light comes out on Brezon crags", was his diary entry of 10 September.[63] "Up Brezon", was his only entry on Friday 11 September. Five days were then spent in Chamonix, from Saturday 12 until Wednesday 16 September, the day that Gordon left.[64]

On the first working day of their Chamonix stay, Monday 14 September, and immediately after breakfast, Ruskin "sent for the notary and Couttet to take counsel with". The plan was to formalise as quickly as possible the purchase of a plot of land near Chamonix. They "got the act drawn up in form": it was, Ruskin continued to inform his father, "very simple and unmistakable".[65] Couttet had made enquiries during Ruskin's absence in England relating to the titles of the property, "and f[ound] them all right". Couttet, a local guide descended from a long line of Chamonix guides, had excellent knowledge of Mont Blanc and the Alps, but how competent was he to do the property and land search and come to the conclusion that the titles were "all right"? An example of misplaced confidence by Ruskin and another foolhardy act. Then Ruskin proceeded to inform his father about extra costs in the form of a purchase tax: "There is a Government duty on purchases of land which is either 6 or 6½ per cent., which will add £50 nearly to the price. But, on the other hand, being proprietor in the Valley gives me the right to a share of all the common pasture and wood, which is much more than £50 worth." This information was followed immediately by a request for money, the substantial sum of £1000: "You had better now send me a credit to Geneva for £1000 – the odd £200 I shall want for travelling, for Allen, etc."[66] Ruskin also conveyed to his father the strong impression that Gordon, in whom John James Ruskin had so much confidence, supported the scheme: "Gordon likes the look of this place very much – nobody seems to approve of the Brezon."[67]

Gordon did exert the beneficial influence so desired by John James Ruskin and dissuaded Ruskin from embarking on the Brezon "Building Plan". Gordon broached the delicate subject with his stubborn, determined friend in a pragmatic way: they both walked up the Brezon and there they discussed the practicality, or rather impracticality, of the scheme. From a height of several thousand feet, "a waste of barren rock, with pasturage only for a few goats in the summer",[68] the sheer folly of the plan was obvious as Ruskin conceded: "Osborne Gordon [...] also walked up with me to my proposed hermitage, and, with his usual sagacity, calculated the daily expense of getting anything to eat, up those 4000 feet from the plain."[69] Water too would have to be carried up the mountain. Gordon used convincing arguments, highlighting Ruskin's isolation and how deterred his friends would be from visiting. "If you ask your friends to dinner, it will be a nice walk home for them, at night", Gordon remarked with sarcasm.[70] In response to Ruskin's anxiety that unexpected visitors might arrive at the isolated chalet and, finding no-one at home, might not come again, Gordon added simply, "and I don't think they would come again anyhow".[71] Ruskin stayed on in Alps and reflected.

The day after Gordon left, and soon after receiving John

James's letter "with various objections to the Brezon", Ruskin
wrote to his father that the "wisdom of Gordon" was one of the
reasons – others included "the persuasion of Winnington [...]
and affectionate sense of John Simon – and chiefly, your & my
mothers wishes" – why he was considering withdrawing from
"the Brezon business".[72] But he understood that his negotiations
about the plot of land at Chamonix had reached a point of no
return and that he must pay for the land as promised.

On his way back to Easthampstead, Gordon called in to see
Ruskin's parents and to report on the Brezon affair and the
"Savoy news". He was due at Denmark Hill on 22 September.
Ruskin had enclosed a note for him in a letter to his father. This
was a happy and reassuring occasion for the Ruskins and the
success and influence of Gordon a cause for celebration with the
best wines and spirits brought up from John James's cellar.
Ruskin, in Chamonix, sensed the sparkling scene and advised
his father about Gordon's tastes in wine: "I have very improper-
ly and wickedly forgotten to give you warning in time that he
doesn't like champagne – drinks it merely out of compliment,
when it is drawn. He enjoys his claret – but I have no doubt he
will have courage to say so himself on the occasion of his
bringing you his Savoy news."[73]

But on the very day of the celebration with Gordon at
Denmark Hill, Ruskin had further doubts and thought he "*may*
have to pay something for Brezon". This was followed by an
urgent request, to his father, for £500 or rather £774 to be transferred to a Geneva bank by 1 October at the latest.

A diary entry by John James Ruskin on 26 September 1863
appears to be a summary of a letter from his son about these
events: "Miss Bells letter led to further reflection – In case of
illness – no Dr nor surgeon – Delicate no stamina ... Jones ill of
cold now I like Chamouni & Mornex only for a pilgrimage in
June & July – agrees with Gordon – impossible & unpracticable
to build – unwise to throw away money –."[74]

After peregrinations into Germany (Baden), Switzerland

(Schaffhausen, Basle) Ruskin eventually returned, via Paris and Abbeville, to England on 14 November 1863.

Ruskin was struggling to be independent, to own his own property and home for the first time. But he was thwarted and stifled by his father. Not surprisingly, simmering resentment built up and angry words of indictment were expressed to his parents. John James Ruskin controlled the purse and consequently controlled his son. It was an angry and embittered son who unleashed his pent-up feelings in a letter of 16 December 1863 to his father. He accused his parents of treating him so effeminately and luxuriously that he had been rendered incapable of travelling "in rough countries without taking a cook with [him]". But the most cutting criticism followed: "you thwarted me in all the earnest fire of passion and life."[75] It was hardly appropriate for the seventy-eight-year-old patriarch to be canvassing support (from Edward and Georgiana Burne-Jones and others) behind the back of his forty-four-year-old son.

Parental pressure was becoming more and more unbearable and by New Year 1864 Ruskin had abandoned his Savoy plans. This had made him feel "unsettled and vexed" and very uncertain of his future.[76] John James Ruskin had undermined his son's authority and masculinity.

John James Ruskin died a few months later on 3 March 1864, ten weeks before his seventy-ninth birthday. John Pritchard and John Champley Rutter, a senior partner in the law firm of that name, (a "gentleman",[77]) were his trusted executors for his will. In some ways, Pritchard had had greater affinity with John James: both were born in the late eighteenth century and there was only eleven years' difference in their ages (Pritchard was the younger). Pritchard, however, was twenty-three years older than Ruskin.

Chapter 10

The years of change

At the beginning of 1866, Ruskin was planning, or at least hoping, to remarry. He had become deeply attached to a young Irish girl, Rose La Touche (1848-1875) whom he had first met in 1858: she was then aged ten, he was thirty-nine. His proposal of marriage was neither accepted nor rejected by the eighteen-year-old: she kept him in suspense, asking him to wait three years for an answer. Rose's parents vehemently opposed the marriage: at one point, Effie Millais intervened and objected on the grounds that her former husband was not free to remarry under the terms of the annulment of 1854. In any case, Ruskin himself agonised over what Rose's decision would eventually be. He became more and more distraught. Rose's feelings oscillated between obsession and hatred. At a casual meeting in the Royal Academy on 7 January 1870, she rebuffed him: her ostensible reason was religious incompatibility.

Ruskin had had unrealistic expectations from the relationship. It was almost a kind of imaginary, phantom love. Virginal Rose was inaccessible most of the time, and he projected his feelings upon her and created an idealised couple, not unlike the way in which he reacted to Effie before their marriage. The relationship was flimsy, yet troubled, and it haunted Ruskin for the rest of his life. It destabilised him and at times he reverted to infantile behaviour and language, almost a kind of protection as he expressed his need to be cared for and loved by a female. Rose withdrew from Ruskin emotionally and physically: she was suffering from symptoms of anorexia and had psychiatric problems. She was also excessively pious.

On Ruskin's return from a three-month continental tour in France and Switzerland, Gordon was at Denmark Hill for dinner "unexpectedly" on 26 July.[1] In late August, he was invited to dinner where he made the acquaintance of William Henry Harrison, Ruskin's "first editor" (of the magazine *Friendship's Offering*) who had published many of the aspiring writer's poems.[2] Gordon also came to know Joan (Joanna) Agnew who was now living at Denmark Hill as a companion for Margaret Ruskin. Gordon and Joan became good friends and frequently corresponded over many years. Another visit by Gordon was noted in Ruskin's diary on 8 November.[3]

Ruskin's physical and emotional health continued to be poor. "Frightfully tormented in various ways", he wrote in his diary in January 1867.[4] His mother's health was also poor – her sight was failing and her son thought she would not live beyond the spring.[5] But a suggestion he received from Thomas Dixon, a cork-cutter from Sunderland in the industrial north-east of England, asking for copies of his writings on political economy, prompted him to commence a regular series of public letters or pamphlets on a range of socio-economic issues. This was to become *Time and Tide* and provided Ruskin with a focus for his work.

Meanwhile, during the bitter frost and snow in the first months of 1867, Ruskin devoted time to Gordon and the Pritchards. Gordon was invited to dinner on several occasions at Denmark Hill and Ruskin made a point of visiting the Pritchards at their London home. The relevant diary entries are as follows:

15 January Tuesday "Browning called. Gordon at dinner."[6]
13 March Wednesday "Called on Mrs Pritchard."[7]
18 March Monday "Bitter frost and snow. Sent off conclusion

letter on prodigal son to Dixon. Gordon at dinner with Joan and me alone."[8]

2 April Tuesday "Drove in with Joanna, to call on Mrs. Pritchard. Waited in vain."[9]

15 April Monday "Gordon dines with us."[10]

26 April Friday "Gordon and T. Richmond in evening."[11]

9 May "Into town. Call at Mr. Pritchard's – found riding school! (Con and Mrs. H[illiard] at lunch)."[12]

28 May Tuesday "Mrs. Pritchard called."[13]

Ruskin spent the Whitsun weekend, 8-10 June 1867, *chez* Gordon at Easthampstead, no doubt hoping to have some moments of calm and respite from his anxiety about Rose. Before setting off on Saturday 8 June he "read 10th Psalm in R[ose]'s book [and] planned [a] commentary on it. [Then] down to Gordon's."[14] After the main church services on Whitsunday, Gordon and Ruskin "drove through pine woods to Sandhurst",[15] a few miles to the south. This relaxing ride and Gordon's reassuring company and wise counsel about Rose contributed a little to his recovery. He returned to Denmark Hill on Monday 10 June "in lovely day, but sad in evening".[16]

In early autumn (on 9 October 1867), Gordon travelled to Ireland for the wedding of his neighbour Lady Alice Hill (daughter of the Marquis of Downshire) and Lord Kenlis at Hillsborough (County Down). He was invited not only as a guest but he had a religious role. Along with the Venerable the Archdeacon of Down and the Rev. St. George, he assisted the Lord Bishop of Down and Connor in the performance of the marriage ceremony. It was a glittering occasion and in the evening the town was illuminated and bonfires blazed on the surrounding hills. *The Times* reported that the festivities would continue on the Downshire estates "for some days".[17]

1868 continued to be a time of emotional turmoil with strain and uncertainties surrounding his relationship with Rose La Touche. In early March Ruskin consulted with his medical friend Dr John Simon about the nature of Rose's mysterious illness(es), suggesting to him that she might have some kind of "fatty degeneration" or heart disease. The reply was not particularly reassuring:

> [...] the 'fatty degeneration' is something in which I should ask you not to believe except of first-rate medical authority. [...] My knowledge of your will-o'-the-wisp is neither much nor recent; but such impression of it as I have leads me to extreme a priori scepticism as to have her having any true signs of the disease. [...] Fearfully and wonderfully made are the insides of hysterically-minded young women. [...] If there is really anything beyond co-feminising twaddle to justify a *suspicion* of organic heart-disease of any kind, by all means get a conclusive medical opinion.[18]

Ruskin's tortured sexuality and suppressed sexual desire for Rose, transferred to Joan Agnew, manifest themselves at this time in a snake dream charged with sexual overtones:

> Dreamed of walk with Joan and Connie [Hilliard], in which I took all the short cuts over the fields, and sent them round by the road, and then came back with them jumping up and down banks of earth, which I saw at last were washed away below by a stream. Then of showing Joanna a beautiful snake, which I told her was an innocent one; it had a slender neck and a green ring round it, and I made her feel its scales. Then she made me feel it, and it became a fat thing, like a leech, and adhered to my hand, so that I could hardly pull it off – and so I woke.[19]

Gordon's visit to Ruskin very soon after receiving that letter from Dr Simon, and after the snake dream, may have been to provide his friend with comfort and advice. The diary entry of 10 March Tuesday reads: "[...] Gordon in evening. [...]."[20]

Margaret Ruskin presided as a martinet at Denmark Hill, but she was kindly towards Gordon whom she considered to have a beneficial influence on her son. They also found common ground: Gordon and Margaret Ruskin shared an interest in farming. Margaret Ruskin's seven acres of land were tiny compared to Gordon's ninety-three acres. In *Praeterita*, Ruskin described the land – a small farm – behind the house at Denmark Hill and his mother's enjoyment in gardening and her pleasure and pride in managing the estate: "My mother *did* like arranging the rows of pots in the big greenhouse; [...] And we bought three cows, and skimmed our own cream, and churned our own butter. And there was a stable, and a farmyard, and a haystack, and a pigstye, and a porter's lodge."[21] There were also orchards, vegetable and flower gardens, chickens and hens. The Ruskin family were almost, if not entirely, self-sufficient in food (perhaps apart from flour?) – and plentiful supplies of wine were in the cellars. The cows were particularly dear to Margaret Ruskin, and as early as 1845 she was extolling their virtues and writing to her son that "the white of our Cows is so purely white".[22] So when Gordon lost one of his calves at Easthampstead in May 1868, she immediately offered to replace it with one of her own. Joan Agnew, who had developed a close relationship with Gordon through his frequent visits to Denmark Hill, relayed his delight and acceptance to Margaret Ruskin: "I have had a note from Mr. Gordon saying how delight-ed he will be to have the calf *any day*, especially as one of *his* cows has lost hers and I am to thank you very *very* much."[23]

Ruskin's decision to work in Abbeville in late summer/early autumn was a wise one. Abbeville was one of his favourite places. He had found immense joy and happiness there on his very first visit as a boy in 1835. On this 1868 visit, he experi-enced again that sense of elation and deep satisfaction among the Flamboyant Gothic of St Wulfran's and in the little town of Rue. This two-month stay in Abbeville was the longest and most prolific he ever made: he accomplished "a good spell of work".[24] The purpose of the visit was to prepare a lecture entitled "The Flamboyant Architecture of the Valley of the Somme" to be given at the Royal Institution, London, on the evening of 29 January 1869. Ruskin prepared over fifty illustrations, many of which were his own drawings. Ruskin also enjoyed the stimulating company, among others, of his American friends Charles Eliot Norton and the poet Henry Wadsworth Longfellow. It was a temporary respite during which he regained his strength and zest for life and work and his delight in travelling abroad.

In the days leading up to his fiftieth birthday, Ruskin was depressed. Even an invitation to dinner at John Pritchard's did not dispel his gloom. He wrote in his diary on 2 February, 1869: "Did duty at the evening dinner – sick and weary beyond all word – at Mr. Pritchard's."[25] Henry James observed a strangeness and sense of disorientation about Ruskin when he visited him in the spring of that year.

Ruskin left London on 27 April, with his assistant Arthur Burgess, for the continent: to Verona, where he was gathering information on tombs and to Venice, his first visit since 1852. From Verona, he sent twelve books, unnamed, to various friends including Froude and Gordon.[26] Whilst abroad, Ruskin learnt that he had been unanimously elected first Slade Professor of Fine Art at Oxford University. Preparation for the task and a series of important lectures began in early autumn.

Gordon decided to go to Denmark Hill for a short break 4-5 October 1869 soon after Ruskin's return from abroad. Such was their degree of friendship and so relaxed was their relationship that it was understood that Gordon could visit and stay any time he wished. This is exactly what he did! On this occasion Ruskin was obliged to explain, in advance to Mrs Cowper-Temple, Gordon's presence at the very special private dinner, on 5 October. The letter reveals much about Gordon's character and the absolute trust between the two men:

Today – by chance – not, I hope – mischance – it happens that my dear old Oxford private tutor – afterwards Censor of Christchurch – now Rector of East Hampstead – (on the moors of Ascot –), a farming – squire loving – conservative – thoroughly sensible – except for a little (rosy!) edge of Ritualism on the softest leaves of his mind, clergyman of the old school –

having always leave to come here whenever he likes, has chosen to come yesterday – and stays until dessert – to-day – leaving about seven oclock – I warn you – that you may not think I asked any one to meet you – and that you may not be checked in anything that might otherwise have been talked about – even at dinner – by Osborne Gordon's seemingly light or somewhat careless manner – which is indeed the veil that this kind of Englishman always manages to throw over what is best in him – complicated in Gordon with a curious sort of cheerful despair about old Toryism, which he intensely worships in the spirit of it – without seeing his way to do it in the letter – (or motto) also, as we do – because his farmer's 'commonsense' trips him up always, the moment he feels himself becoming romantic.[27]

Also present at this special dinner, arranged at Denmark Hill perhaps at the instigation of Mr and Mrs Cowper-Temple, were Laurence Oliphant (1829-1888) and seventeen-year-old Connie Hilliard (1852-1915). It must have been an interesting encounter for Gordon. Oliphant was something of a mystic: he was a colourful character, wealthy, possibly a homosexual and the author of several travel books. He was a keen supporter of the fraudulent English-born American spiritualist medium Thomas Lake Harris (1823-1906), founder of a sect called the Brotherhood of the New Life. Connie Hilliard was the daughter of the Rev. J. C. Hilliard and his wife Mary, of Cowley, near Uxbridge. She was the niece of Lady Trevelyan, Ruskin's loyal friend who had died in Neuchâtel whilst on holiday with him in 1866. Ruskin had first met Connie in 1863 at a tea party the eleven-year-old girl had organised.[28] The conversation turned to spiritualism and perhaps to Rose, for Ruskin derived immense satisfaction from it. He wrote in his diary of 6 October 1869: "Heard marvellous things – Breath of Heaven."[29]

Ruskin extended Gordon's circle of friends. At the beginning of November, he took him to dinner at the home of John and Jane Simon, probably at their London home in Great Cumberland Street, where he also met Mr and Mrs

Hutchinson.[30] Mr Hutchinson was most likely Dr (later Sir) Jonathan Hutchinson (1828-1913) who became a surgeon at the London Hospital (1863-1883) in the East End and Hunterian professor of surgery at the Royal College of Surgeons. One of his great discoveries was the identification of three symptoms of congenital syphilis, known as "Hutchinson's triad". The day after the dinner, Ruskin made a strange comment in his diary: "Had to talk at the Simons'; felt as if silent Mr. Hutchinson thought me conceited."[31]

The promotion to Professor of Fine Art at Oxford did not alleviate Ruskin's sorrow and highly charged emotional state. His unrealistic hopes of being united with Rose La Touche were dashed by her refusal to speak to him or have anything to do with him at a chance encounter at the Royal Academy in Burlington House on 7 January 1870.[32] Rose had either categorically rejected him or was playing games with him. Ruskin sought to assuage his pain by surrounding himself with a number of interesting and supportive friends. Among these were Edward Burne-Jones and William Morris – both were frequent visitors – invited to dinner on Wednesday 12 January. Consoling and loyal friend Gordon came on Friday 14 January. Perhaps some light entertainment would alleviate Ruskin's distress? That evening, Gordon and Ruskin went to the Haymarket Theatre in central London for a performance of *New Men and Old Acres*, a comedy by Tom Taylor and A. W. Dubourg.[33]

But it was not simply to relieve some of his despondency that this play was chosen. Ruskin had a very special interest in it: he knew both the leading lady, his "much-regarded friend" Mrs Madge Kendal (*née* Robertson) and the co-playwright Tom Taylor, his erstwhile rival for the Slade Professorship at Oxford and a witness on his behalf at the Whistler trial in 1878. Madge Kendal, playing Lilian Vavasour, was already the leading lady at this grand theatre at the age of twenty-one: Jeffrey Richards has described her as "an actress of great verve and charm".[34] But there were other reasons for his interest. The word "Ruskinism" had been coined (perhaps for the first time by Taylor) and became a catchword. Ruskin more than anyone would have been amused to hear Lilian say of another girl in the play that "in spite of her Ruskinism-run-mad she isn't half a bad sort".[35] We know of Ruskin's fascination with reptiles: snakes and serpents were often present in his dreams along with an attractive female presence.[36] *New Men and Old Acres* provided a memorable example compressed in the short line, "And his wife – well, she's a caution for snakes!" uttered by Lilian Vavasour. It was not quite a dream, but not quite reality, for here on stage was a beautiful inaccessible woman being linked with venomous reptiles. Ten years later, Ruskin's lecture at the Royal Institution on 17 March 1880 was entitled "A Caution to Snakes": he explained to his audience that he had chosen the title "partly in play, and partly in affectionate remembrance of the scene in *New Men and Old Acres*, in which the phrase became at once so startling and so charming, on the lips of my much-regarded friend, Mrs Kendal".[37]

*   *   *

After delivering his Inaugural lecture in Oxford on his fifty-first birthday and successive lectures on art until 23 March, Ruskin soon embarked on another long continental tour – 27 April to 29 July 1870 – mainly in Italy. He generously invited six guests at his expense – or rather at his late father's expense – for three months: Joan Agnew, Mary Hilliard and her daughter Connie: there were servants as well– Lucy, the Hilliards' maid, Frederick Crawley, Ruskin's valet and his gardener, David Downs.[38] The party journeyed from Boulogne to Paris, Geneva, Vevey, Martigny, Brieg and on over the Alps to Milan, Verona and Venice where they spent three weeks.

In Venice, while Ruskin worked on Carpaccio, Brown and Cheney helped to entertain Joan Agnew and the Hilliards with visits to see glass-blowing and gondola building. Ruskin wrote a note of thanks to Brown on 30 May 1870: "My people [...] very happy with you & Mr Cheney today."[39] In that same letter, Ruskin revealed his continuing feelings of ambivalence towards Cheney, affection tempered by fear: " I am always terribly afraid of him – & yet very fond of him though he may not believe it."[40] Ruskin was delighted with an arrangement that left him free to carry on with his own work.

On the return journey, they stopped at several other towns in Italy – sometimes zigzagging from one to another – including Florence, Siena (to visit Charles Eliot Norton), Pisa, Padua, Como, then through Switzerland – Bellinzona, Airolo – to Geneva before going back via Paris to Boulogne and England.[41]

These were the dying days of the Second Empire, of the dwindling megalomaniacal power of Napoleon III. His fate was to be sealed on 1 September at the battle of Sedan, a small border town, close to Belgium, on the river Meuse in the French Ardennes, at which his army was defeated and he was captured. Ruskin returned to safety only a few weeks before the commencement of the Franco-Prussian war in which France suffered severe humiliation and the loss of some of her territories in Alsace and parts of Lorraine. Ruskin was far from indifferent to this war.

About two weeks after Ruskin's return from the continent, Gordon came to dinner at Denmark Hill on Friday 12 August: this was a moment of welcome respite and "pleasant rest".[42] He was invited again for dinner on Wednesday 12 October 1870 and was "delightful"[43] with Joan Agnew and Lily Armstrong, the attractive young Irish girl whom Henry James met in 1869. Lily Armstrong (later Mrs Kevill-Davis) was a former pupil of Winnington School and she remained a lifelong friend of Ruskin. Ruskin had a short overnight stay at Gordon's rectory in Easthampstead on the night of Thursday 27 October 1870, returning home on the Friday and experiencing a "various quarrel on the way".[44] For whatever reason, Ruskin was concerned that he had not written to Gordon, perhaps to thank him for his hospitality on 27-28 October. He notes in his diary of 3 November: "*Must* write to Gordon."[45]

Ruskin gave a series of lectures in November and December at Oxford on "The Elements of Sculpture", published later under the title *Aratra Penteleci* ("The Ploughs of Pentelicus").[46] Instead of residing in the centre of Oxford, he often preferred to stay in the picturesque market town of Abingdon, about eight miles away. He usually stayed at the "Crown and Thistle", a fine seventeenth-century coaching inn with cobbled courtyard, stables and garden, on Bridge Street, close to the river Thames. Several of his letters in *Fors* were composed at the window of this "quiet English inn".[47] From there, he enjoyed the walk into Oxford, admiring the view that Turner had painted, chatting to local people on the way and helping anyone in need. On one of his walks, he came across a little girl in extreme poverty and saved her from being sent to the "Union" – a workhouse such as the one Henry James visited in Yorkshire at Christmas 1878 – by financing her apprenticeship as a shepherdess on a farm belonging to his friends near Arundel.[48] That satisfied Ruskin's deep need to have opportunities to change the world.

Gordon was one of Ruskin's guests at Abingdon where, as Ruskin reported to Joan Agnew, "Gordon enjoyed himself" but "found when he came to Oxford, he could'nt come to lectures at all. So like things always –".[49] He initiated Gordon into the delights of this rural English town, whose charms Gordon seemed to prefer to attending Ruskin's lectures in Oxford!

* * *

1871 was a year of many changes for Ruskin. On 20 April, Joan Agnew, his mother's companion for over a decade, married the painter Arthur Severn, son of Joseph Severn, British Consul in Rome. This was not an unexpected event for Ruskin had exercised his authority over Joan and Arthur and insisted on their waiting for three years, a trial period of separation, before marrying.[50] Perhaps he hoped the marriage would not take place, for it would disrupt the family dynamics. Ruskin had no choice but to adapt if he wished to remain within this new orbit.

Ruskin's not entirely altruistic wedding present to them was his own childhood home, 28 Herne Hill, with an agreement that he could have use of his old nursery on the top floor. That would be Ruskin's London base until 1888. The domestic arrangements of the Severns and John Ruskin would remain inextricably linked (at Herne Hill and at Brantwood) until his death. It was a mutually advantageous situation. The ageing, increasingly sick Sage would be looked after by a mother substitute and the Severns had financial security and desirable, free accommodation for life.

In the summer of 1871, Ruskin purchased, unseen, for the sum of £1500, a property known as Brantwood, comprising a house and fellside grounds above Coniston Water, in the heart of the English Lake District. It was to be his country residence from 1872 and more and more his home as he became increasingly infirm until his death in 1900. It was Ruskin's only home that was ever saved for the Nation, thanks to the intervention of John Howard Whitehouse in 1932. 54 Hunter Street, his birthplace, was demolished to make way for the Brunswick Centre, near Russell Square underground station. 163 Denmark Hill was razed to the ground in 1947 and the land used for the building of a large, high-density council estate.

But Brantwood, as Ruskin discovered when he went there for the first time in the autumn of 1871, was in a state of disrepair: it was a huge challenge, responsibility and a constant preoccupation for the new owner. But the location was superb. "I've bought a small place here" he wrote to Charles Eliot Norton in September 1871, "with five acres of rock and moor, a streamlet, and I think on the whole the finest view I know in Cumberland or Lancashire, with the sunset visible over the same".[51] It was so dilapidated, perhaps more so than Ruskin imagined: "The house

– small, old, damp, and smoky-chimneyed – somebody must help me get to rights."[52] But owning his very own home, chosen by himself without parental interference, was paramount. He wrote again to Norton of his joy: "Here I have rocks, streams, fresh air, and, for the first time in my life, the rest of the purposed *home*."[53]

The year ended with the death of Ruskin's mother at the age of ninety on 5 December 1871. It had been a slow, lingering decline as he explained to W. H. Harrison: "My Mother has been merely asleep – speaking sometimes in the sleep – these last three weeks. It is not to be called paralysis, nor apoplexy – it is numbness and weakness of all faculty – declining to the grave. Very woeful: and the worst possible sort of death for *me* to see."[54] For the very first time, and at the age of fifty-three, Ruskin was free of parental control.

* * *

Ruskin had the task of preparing the Denmark Hill house for sale. But he was plagued by fits of depression and general illness.[55] At the same time he was finalising his next series of lectures for Oxford. To relieve his ill health and sadness, Ruskin invited Gordon to dine with him at Denmark Hill on 16 January 1872. It was a happy occasion confirmed by the diary entry: "Enjoyed ourselves."[56] It was Gordon's last opportunity to enjoy the elegant house and gardens. Ruskin sold the property shortly after and on Thursday 28 March he vacated it for ever.

But the end of one life marked the beginning of another. One of Ruskin's first visitors to Brantwood was Gordon who stayed there from Tuesday 8 October until Friday 11 October. It was usual for visitors to Brantwood to be met by carriage off the train at Ulverston, on the West Coast, and then driven approximately thirteen miles inland to Coniston. This was often quicker than taking the train to Coniston on a much longer circuitous route via Barrow and Foxfield. The under-used little Coniston station, the terminus of a branch line from Foxfield Station, was eventually closed, partly due to the decline of the mines, whereas Ulverston remained functional throughout the twentieth and into the twenty-first centuries. Gordon was a special guest and Ruskin went in person to meet him at Ulverston. On the way back to Brantwood, they crossed Spark Bridge, then on to Low Nibthwaite approaching the southern tip of Coniston Water. They took the narrow valley road, a stretch of five miles along the eastern shore of the lake with the fells and forests on their right. Almost at the northern tip of the lake, nestling in the hills, was Brantwood, in splendid isolation. From the house, across the lake and soaring beyond the little village (with about the same population as Easthampstead) were the Coniston Fells and immediately opposite was Ruskin's favourite peak, *The Old Man*, that he called affectionately the *Vecchio*.

The early autumn Lakeland scenery was intensely beautiful with brown and golden hues. The Lake District lived up to its reputation for rain during Gordon's stay. The diary entries confirm this: 10 October. Thursday. "Y[esterday] […] pretty showery day"; 11 October. Friday. "Y[esterday] pouring all day long."[57]

Also staying at Brantwood was Lily Armstrong (the attractive Irish girl whom Gordon had first met in 1870), who had been there since 18 September. Ruskin showed Gordon some of the surrounding area and went to Langdale on Wednesday 9 October, accompanied by Lily Armstrong and Laurence Hilliard ("Lollie") (1855?-1887), his much-loved friend, secretary, painter and Brantwood neighbour and brother of Connie.

Ruskin was an able, enthusiastic guide who knew the area well. The most likely route to Langdale would have been through the village of Coniston, then in a northerly direction to Yewdale and Skelwith Bridge, skirting Elter Water, through Elterwater village and on to Langdale, in the direction of Ambleside. They were in a part of the country that had been the inspiration for much of Wordsworth's poetry – the Lakeland

scenery had "haunted him like a passion" – and Dorothy
Wordsworth's lyrical *Journals*. Wordsworth had made his home
at Dove Cottage, in Grasmere, only a few miles from Langdale.
Ruskin too had been haunted by this landscape from an early
age: he had composed *Iteriad*, a verse travelogue on the Lakes,
on a visit in 1830. He had a deep admiration for Wordsworth
and his belief in nature's role as educator, not forgetting his
campaigns for the protection and preservation of the landscape.
His first book *Modern Painters* was a homage not only to Turner
but to the Lakeland poet with a quotation from *The Excursion* as
its motto.

In 1860, Gordon at Easthampstead had faced not dissimilar
challenges to those that confronted Ruskin in 1871: dilapidated
buildings and acres of land to cultivate and tame. Both men
shared a mission – to improve people's living conditions and the
moral fabric of society. By the time of his visit to Brantwood,
Gordon had twelve years' practical experience of managing
ninety-three acres of glebe, numerous staff, rebuilding a church
and rectory. He was already a successful, much-respected
farmer. Ruskin, on the other hand, lacked practical experience.
He tended to indulge in schemes and projects that he was not
able to sustain for any length of time: he called them experiments. Nevertheless, he had many ideas, was extremely creative
and had much enthusiasm.

Ruskin had a particular purpose in taking Gordon to
Langdale, a quiet, unspoiled spot, untouched by industrialisation. The aim was to show him its system of waterworks and
sluices, powerful cascades and forces that could be used to
provide natural energy for the villagers. On the Brantwood
estate, a "deep and steep water-course, a succession of cascades
[...] over hard slate rock"[58] served as a laboratory for Ruskin's
geological observations concerning erosion and riverbeds.
Clean, bacteria-free water was a most precious commodity and
Ruskin gave considerable thought to a distribution system.

In Switzerland in 1869, harnessing the snow waters of the

Alps for humanitarian purposes had been one of his preoccupations. From Brieg, on 4 May 1869, he wrote of his concerns:

> I have been forming some plans as I came up the valley from
> Martigny. I never saw it so miserable, and all might be cured if
> they would only make reservoirs for the snow waters and use
> them for agriculture, instead of letting them run down into the
> Rhone, and I think it is in my power to show this.[59]

Ruskin was also instrumental in a scheme to provide a
fountain with fresh drinking water in the village of Fulking, in
Sussex:[60] similarly, Pritchard's fountain was equally important to
the people of Broseley.

It was at Langdale also that Ruskin initiated his scheme for the
spinning of linen and the development of what would be known
as the Langdale Linen Industry, thus providing work for the villagers.[61]

Ruskin spent much of the following year (1873) at
Brantwood, interspersed with lectures at Oxford.

*   *   *

Ruskin's next continental tour took place between late March
and the end of October 1874. Apart from the Alps, much of the
time was spent in Italy, in Rome (where he worked for over two
weeks in the Sistine Chapel copying Botticelli's *Scenes from the
Life of Moses*), in Assisi (spending several weeks copying works
by Giotto and Cimabue), in Florence, in Lucca (sketching the
tomb of Ilaria di Caretto) and other places. At some point
during the tour he was joined by Jane Pritchard and as her
brother informed Ruskin: "My sister was much pleased at
meeting you abroad. She did not return very well, and I think
got a touch of fever which she has not quite shaken off."[62]

Architecture and preservation of buildings remained at the
foremost of his mind. His refusal of the prestigious Royal Gold
Medal of the Royal Institute of British Architects (RIBA) pro-

pelled Ruskin once again into the centre of controversy. From Rome, on 20 May, he wrote to the Secretary, Charles Eastlake, explaining the reasons for his refusal. A further exchange of correspondence ensued.[63]

While in Italy, Ruskin received an invitation from Mr Chapman of the Glasgow Athenæum Lecture Committee to speak at one of their meetings during the winter. He declined. His letter of refusal (26 May 1874), although addressed privately to Mr Chapman, quickly became public and was published first in *The Glasgow Herald* of 5 June 1874, and reprinted in *The Times* of 6 June. Professor Ruskin's letters were much sought after and of such originality that they were guaranteed to increase newspaper sales. The question of copyright and confidentiality does not seem to have been considered. His refusal to speak in Glasgow was, he explained, not only due to an "increase in work" but to the types of audiences who attended solely for entertainment:

> I find the desire of audiences to be *audiences only* becoming an entirely pestilent character of the age. Everyone wants to *hear* – nobody to read – nobody to think; to be excited for an hour – and, if possible, amused; to get the knowledge it has cost a man half his life to gather, first sweetened up to make it palatable, and then kneaded into the smallest possible pills – and to swallow it homœopathically and be wise – this is the passionate desire and hope of the multitude of the day.[64]

Ruskin recommended: "A living comment quietly given to a class on a book they are earnestly reading – this kind of lecture is eternally necessary and wholesome."[65] But he denounced, intentionally in popular language, "your modern fire-worky, smooth-downy-curry-and-strawberry-ice-and-milk-punch-altogether lecture [as] an entirely pestilent and abominable vanity".[66] He invoked Charles Dickens (1812-1870) whose continual round of speaking engagements and epic tours in America in 1867-1868 had contributed to his death and reminded readers of his demise: "the miserable death of poor

Dickens, when he might have been writing blessed books till he was eighty, but for the pestiferous demand of the mob, is a very solemn warning to us all, if we would take it."[67]

Gordon read the letter, almost certainly in *The Times*, and was prompted to respond not only to Ruskin but also to Joan Severn. In his letter to "My dear Ruskin" he expressed his approval:

> I wrote to her [i.e. Joan Severn] to say how glad I was that you had declined to waste your strength on public lecturing – All you say on that subject is perfectly true. People go simply (at least the mass of them) to be amused and many of them come away with the idea that they have done you a compliment by attending. It is perfectly monstrous to expect any man to waste his strength and shorten his life, for what not one in 100 is able to value, or cares for, one hour after the lecture is over. I believe too that lecturing has a bad effect on the performer himself. You will do well to confine your lecturing to workers and students who will value it [.] When I used to attend lectures, I used to find that I knew part before that I could not understand and there part – and that the residuary quantity did not always agree with me.[68]

Ruskin shared this letter with Joan Severn, his "Darling Pussie", and he was highly amused by Gordon's own reaction to lectures. "The bit about the three parts of lectures is very funny", he wrote at the top of the letter.[69]

Gordon kept Ruskin, then staying in a Sacristan's Cell in a Roman Catholic monastery in Assisi, informed about his private and social life. There had been a gap in their relationship. Gordon, seemingly not knowing that Ruskin was abroad, had gone to see him in Oxford but learned that he "had departed the day before".[70] He was planning to go to Shropshire the following day, 12 June, to visit his sister Jane at her country mansion Stanmore Hall, near Bridgnorth.[71] He also wrote about his invitation, two weeks before, to dine with "Mr Ritchie" at Highgate, in north London: it was his first visit and he was "quite charmed with the view". "The house", he continued, "is about on the level of the Cross of St Pauls".[72] Henry Ritchie had been John James Ruskin's trusted clerk in his Billiter Street office.

* * *

On his return, Ruskin delivered a series of lectures in Oxford on science and geology, published later as part of *Deucalion*. He was working hard and feeling overwhelmed: "Greatly oppressed by impossibility of doing what I plan, and by failing strength."[73]

But his personal life was far from happy and on 28 May he received news he was dreading but knew to be inevitable: Rose La Touche had died on 25 May 1875 at seven o'clock in the morning. He wrote to his Coniston friend Susan Beever: "I've just heard that my poor little Rose is gone where the hawthorn blossoms go."[74] In January 1875 he informed his readers in Letter 49 of *Fors Clavigera*: "The woman I hoped would have been my wife is dying."[75] If any letters were sent in response to this *cri de cœur*, they were not published by Cook and Wedderburn the editors so protective of Ruskin's private life. Ruskin saw Rose for the last time on 25 February 1875 and recalled, in a letter to the artist Francesca Alexander twelve years later, the poignant scene:

> Of course she was out of her mind in the end; one evening in London she was raving violently till far into the night; they could not quiet her. At last they let me into her room. She was sitting up in bed; I got her to lie back on the pillow, and lay her head in my arms as I knelt beside it. They left us, and she asked me if she should say a hymn, and she said, 'Jesus, lover of my soul' to the end, and then fell back tired and went to sleep. And I left her.[76]

Ruskin's sketch of Rose on her deathbed encapsulates the wasted life of the young woman, her hysteria and the demise of his longed-for happiness with her.

In December 1875, Ruskin was invited to stay at Broadlands, the spacious Hampshire home of his close and sympathetic friends Georgiana and William Cowper-Temple. They took spiritualism seriously and in the stillness of the winter countryside conducive to such activity – tapping and faint voices could be distinctly heard – organised regular *séances*. Several spiritualists had been invited as house-guests.[77] Thus on 14 December, Ruskin learnt from a medium "the most overwhelming evidence of the other state of the world that has ever come to me".[78] In his extremely fragile state, he was predisposed to believe that Rose was communicating with him.

Ruskin wrote to Gordon about his spiritual contact with Rose. Knowing his friend's mental anguish, Gordon was extremely supportive, sympathetic and understanding. His reply was pragmatic and kindly: "I feel sure that that Presence was permitted to make itself known on purpose to cheer and comfort you."[79] Gordon stressed that it was not a figment of the imagination since a complete stranger witnessed the vision: "If you only or even Mrs Temple who knew the hearts of both of you had been witnesses it might be supposed to have been fancy making to itself a reality – but the evidence of a stranger staying in the house disposes of that presumption."[80]

The apparition was meant to be beneficial, Gordon argued: "I am sure you think rightly that this was not designed for your evil but for your good – and you connect her visit with her prayers."[81] Gordon gave Ruskin further consolation in stating his firm belief in the power of prayer in alleviating suffering and cited an example of its beneficial effect on one of his very sick friends:

> I was asked two weeks since to offer the prayers of the Church for a dear friend – In answer I said that I certainly would for prayers might be answered in other ways besides miraculous healing – as e.g. by mitigation of pain or peace of mind and that happened in this case for the disease was of the most agonising kind, he had not a throb of pain; and his mind was in perfect peace and clearness till the very last, knowing everything and thinking of everybody[']s good[.][82]

Gordon concludes: "I am a firm believer in spirits and in prayer & in miracles – nor is my belief in the latter at all weakened because I have had no experience of them – I at present expect none – It is a great real power but at present in reserve."[83]

* * *

Gordon was a recipient of *Fors Clavigera*, Ruskin's monthly public pronouncements (letters) on a wide range of issues, often written in a rambling, sometimes incomprehensible manner. They were supposedly addressed to the workmen of England, sometimes more specifically the "Sheffield ironworkers" or "working men of Sheffield". Even Gordon did not read many of them: neither did his friends "except to find the mistakes".[84] However, one of Ruskin's communications attracted his attention – Letter 64 ("The Three Sarcophagi") of April 1876. Just before leaving for Dublin, he found time to comment on this dogmatic letter that commences with a "Bible lesson" – an analysis of Genesis – and an exhortation to learn by heart the fifteenth chapter "with extreme care".[85] Ruskin acknowledged that he was not sure of his interpretation of Psalm 87, but suggested that, "as far as any significance exists in it to our present knowledge, it can only be of the power of the Nativity of Christ to save Rahab the harlot, Philistia the giant, Tyre the trader, and Ethiopia the slave".[86] It so happened that Psalm 87 was fresh in Gordon's mind as he had "expounded it in a sermon some time since, and was talking of it to a very learned Hebraist last Monday".[87] He wrote to correct Ruskin's error about the meaning of Rahab in the context of the Psalm: "Rahab, there, is generally understood to mean 'the monster', and has nothing to do, beyond resemblance of sound, with Rahab the harlot. And the monster is the crocodile, as typical of Egypt. In Psalm lxxxix. 10 (the Bible version, not the Prayer-Book), you will see Rahab explained in the margin, by '*or Egypt*'."[88]

Gordon made a further suggestion: "Perhaps Rahab the harlot was called by the same name from the rapacity of her class, just as in Latin *lupa*."[89] The problem of interpretation was, Gordon believed, due to the bad translation that rendered it "unintelligible", but it remained nevertheless "charged with deep prophetical meaning".[90] In a footnote to his letter, Gordon added: "I hope you will have had a pleasant journey when you receive this. The Greek Septuagint is much better than the English, but not good. As regards the general meaning, you have divined it very correctly."[91]

So in the June letter of *Fors Clavigera*, entitled "Miracle", Ruskin acknowledged Gordon's help, but without naming him, in rectifying an error in the April letter: "I've got a letter, not from a jackanapes, but a thoroughly learned and modest clergyman, and old friend, advising me of my mistake in April *Fors*, in supposing that Rahab [...] means the harlot. It is, he tells me, a Hebrew word for the Dragon adversary."[92]

Ruskin remained preoccupied with this Biblical interpretation (and many others) when in Venice the following year.[93] The problem arose again when he was writing *St Mark's Rest*. In chapter two, he returned to "Rahab" and linked the reference to the statue of St Theodore, first patron of Venice, standing on a crocodile, representing his "Dragon-enemy – Egypt and her captivity", at the top of a pillar in the piazzetta. He publicly acknowledged his gratitude to "Mr. Gordon" and seemed to enjoy drawing attention to his own "curious mistake".[94]

During this long Venetian stay, Ruskin was welcomed by many friends, old and new. Rawdon Brown was there: so was Edward Cheney, who, since the death of his brother Robert Henry on 30 December 1866, was *châtelain* of Badger Hall. Ruskin was immensely indebted to Cheney for his learned publications – *Remarks on the Illuminated Manuscripts of the Venetian Republic*, privately published in1868, and his *Original Documents Relating to Venetian Painters and their Pictures in the 16th Century*, privately published in c. 1873. These works assisted Ruskin in the compilation of his *Guide to the Principal Pictures in the Academy of Fine Arts at Venice, arranged for English Travellers*, published in 1877. He acknowledges Cheney's "admirable account" of Titian's fresco of St Christopher over a door in the Ducal Palace.[95] As a homage to Cheney, Ruskin reprinted, as an Appendix to his *Guide*, Cheney's text of the interrogation undergone by Veronese regarding his painting *The Supper in the House of Simon*. Ruskin introduced the Appendix with full recognition of Cheney:

> The little collection of *Documents relating to Venetian Painters* already referred to [...], as made with excellent judgment by Mr. Edward Cheney, is, I regret to say, 'communicated' only to the author's friends, of whom I, being now one of long standing, emboldened also by repeated instances of help received from him, venture to trespass on the modest book so far as to reprint part of the translation which it gives of the questioning of Paul Veronese.[96]

Ruskin also drew on his Shropshire friend's publication for information about the legend of St Theodore that he used in *St Mark's Rest*.[97]

* * *

Ruskin's departure for the continent coincided with Gordon's visit to Bridgnorth. The occasion was the unveiling of a memorial window – the great east window – in St Leonard's Church to his former Headmaster Dr Thomas Rowley on the latter's seventy-ninth birthday on 24 August 1876. St Leonard's Church had been almost completely rebuilt in the 1860s, thanks to the initiative of the Rev. George Bellett (rector from 1835 to 1870) and generous sponsors among whom was John Pritchard. In particular, Pritchard funded the construction of the south aisle – formerly the chantry chapel of Our Lady – in memory of his brother George who had died in 1861. The architect was William Slater (1818/19-1872), a pupil and partner of the

Gothic Revivalist Richard Cromwell Carpenter (1812-1855). This mainly Victorian, red sandstone edifice with its dominating tower was – and so remains in the twenty-first century – an impressive sight in the High Town.

Clayton & Bell were chosen to design and make the memorial window: they had already worked in St Leonard's in 1872 on windows in the south wall. This was a prestigious firm with many commissions throughout England, such as the large Minstrel window of 1874 in St Peter's Church, Bournemouth, nearly all the stained glass in Exeter College, Oxford, from 1859 onwards and much more.[98] The theme chosen for the great east window in St Leonard's was the *Te Deum*, with Christ seated in majesty with the four Evangelists and figures from the Old and New Testaments below.

Gordon was a guest of honour and other students and acquaintances of Rowley were invited to this very special birthday event. How satisfying for Rowley to witness the success of two of his star pupils: the Rev. Osborne Gordon and the Rev. Dr James Fraser (1818-1885), Bishop of Manchester, who took a key role in the proceedings of the day. Fraser delivered an address in the church and presided at a Public Luncheon in the Agricultural Hall at which Gordon proposed his health. Gordon's speech was described in the local paper – *The Bridgnorth Journal* – as "sparkling throughout with bright flashes of the liveliest wit and gayest humour". The praise continued: "his easily flowing, – almost gushing, – and gracefully refined eloquence, charming and really entrancing his audience; who testified their delight by no measured and oft repeated applause."[99]

The town of Bridgnorth was immensely proud of Gordon. On the occasion of the unveiling of the window it was stated that, with Gordon and other scholars, the "town could proudly boast of such an assemblage of literary, learned and scientific men as could not be surpassed by any town in the kingdom".[100]

*   *   *

Within Letter 82, *Fors*, of October 1877, Ruskin quotes large
sections from C. O. Müller's *Dorians* about capital punishment
including a punishment that consists of "throwing the criminal
into the Cæadas". In a footnote, Ruskin expresses his gratitude to
Gordon for explaining the meaning: "I did not know myself
what the Cæadas was; so wrote to my dear old friend, Osborne
Gordon, who tells me it was probably a chasm in the limestone
rock; but his letter is so interesting that I keep it for *Deucalion*."[101]
Ruskin does not seem to have used Gordon's letter.

It was in *Fors* of August 1877 that Ruskin gave a list of his
tried and trusted friends "with their respective belongings of
family circle". Gordon was among the chosen eleven! The
"family" members were Henry Acland, George Richmond, John
Simon, Charles Norton, William Kingsley, Rawdon Brown,
Osborne Gordon, Burne-Jones, "Grannie" (Georgiana Cowper-
Temple), "Mammie" (Mrs Hilliard), and poet Jean Ingelow. His
criterion was "those who will help me in what my heart is set
on".[102] Ruskin was overwhelmed by work and sometimes
annoyed by correspondents who wrote about what he considered to be trivia. A request from a chronophage to see him for
five minutes and show him his little daughter sparked a reply
about friendship.

Chapter 11

Epilogues

Gordon never married. He remained for twenty-three years as rector of St Michael and St Mary Magdalene until his death, at the age of seventy, on Friday 25 May 1883.

His last years were overshadowed by two unpleasant events that took their toll on him. The first was the unresolved death of Gordon's neighbour, Sir William Hayter, retired Judge Advocate General, at his large estate of South Hill Park.

Late morning, on Boxing Day, Thursday 26 December 1878, a hat was seen floating on one of the icy lakes at South Hill Park. "That's my dear master", exclaimed James Dougal the steward as he arrived on the scene. He grabbed a rake and immediately jumped into the water. With the help of John Ayres the butler and other members of staff who had been searching for Sir William since his disappearance earlier in the day, he dragged the cold body out of the water. There was no sign of life and no sign of any struggling near to where the body was found.

An inquest was held on Saturday afternoon, 28 December 1878, chaired by the Reading coroner Mr W. Weedon. Gordon was one of thirteen jurymen who listened to evidence from witnesses including Sir William's steward and butler. Dr Orange, medical superintendent of Broadmoor Asylum, who had known the deceased for the last fifteen years, and who examined the body externally, had no doubt that death was due to drowning, perhaps after an attack of dizziness. The evidence was inconclusive as it was also reported that Sir William had been prone to depression. In summing up, the coroner indicated to the jury that "it might have been an accident and might have been suicide", adding that "to return an open verdict of 'Found drowned' would meet the case".[1] After a short deliberation, that was the verdict of the jury.

For such a sensitive person as Gordon, hearing the harrowing evidence relating to the unexplained loss of a friend and neighbour would have been painful. The whole affair was a shock. Gordon conducted the funeral and Hayter was buried at Easthampstead on 2 January 1879: he was in his eighty-seventh year.

Shortly before he died, Gordon received a terrible shock from which he never seemed to recover. Like Ruskin, he was a devoted, loyal and caring employer. In his household was a young male servant whom most employers would have dismissed when no longer needed or able to do the job satisfactorily. But Gordon, out of the kindness of his heart and sense of protectiveness, kept the boy in his employment when there was no work. Eventually, he was obliged, reluctantly, to dismiss him. Marshall relates what happened next:

> The poor lad left his master's presence, wished his fellow-servants a hurried good-bye, rushed to his own room and shot himself. To Mr. Gordon, the most tender-hearted and considerate of men to all about him, this was a frightful blow from which it is probable he never quite recovered. He did not sleep for three nights; he shrunk from observation: and when he was prevailed upon to keep a long-standing engagement at Milton, was on his arrival utterly prostrate.
> It was plain that his whole system had received a violent shock.[2]

The suicide of his servant as a contributory factor to Gordon's death was mentioned in *The Times* obituary.

Outwardly Gordon continued to exercise his functions and

enjoy his work and social life. He lunched with Ruskin at Herne Hill on 20 December 1882, shortly after Ruskin's return from a long continental journey. His diary entry is brief: "Thursday 21 Dec 82 [...] Y[esterday] Gordon at lunch."[3] After partially recovering from illness, the now bearded Ruskin aged sixty-three had spent late summer, autumn and early winter of 1882 in France (mainly Burgundy), Switzerland and Italy, accompanied by W. G. Collingwood. Ruskin had subjected himself to a gruelling schedule abroad and, unable to relax and engaged in a permanent battle against time, suffered increasingly from depression and mental instability.

At the time of Gordon's death, Ruskin was nearby in Oxford. He had been re-elected as Slade Professor of Fine Art in January 1883 and was heavily involved in the preparation and delivery of a series of lectures on English art. On Wednesday 16 May, the day of his lecture announced in the *University Gazette* as "Mythic Schools (Burne-Jones and G. F. Watts)",[4] Ruskin had enjoyed the company of Gordon (whom he called affectionately "Ozziegogs") and his sister Jane and had reported positively about Gordon's health and happiness. He shared his joy with Joan Severn in a letter the following week:

> It has been hot to day – but I've got a lot of work done, and a pleasant evening walk.
> I never told you that on the day I came up to lecture, and returned – Wednesday last week, I met Osborne Gordon and Jane at Reading and got them into my carriage to Oxford. Ozziegogs looking so well and both so glad to see me![5]

Only a few days later, he learnt of Gordon's death from Jane Pritchard but he delayed informing Joan Severn until the day of the funeral (30 May). He was writing from Oxford, where, on that very afternoon, he had to give another public lecture announced as "Fairy Land (Mrs Allingham and Kate Greenaway)".[6] Although Ruskin had an unmitigated horror of burials and disliked mourning and the wearing of black, on this occasion he had a valid reason for not attending Gordon's funeral. His thoughts were with Gordon and he preferred to grieve inwardly and silently in a very personal way for his dear friend, as he explained to Joan:

> I was extremely grieved this morning to hear of Mr Allen's death: – Mrs Pritchard told me of Gordon's on the day he died, but I had no heart to tell you in your zest of happy excitement. I am thankful to have had strength spared to me to complete at all events one course of lectures rightly, it does not seem to have tired me at all – and I hope that I may still be useful and active as Gordon was, to the last. I wrote a line to Mrs Pritchard at once – and shall take notice of Osborne in a quiet but I hope – just and loving way, the next time I have to speak in Oxford.[7]

The funeral, conducted by Dean Liddell of Christ Church, took place on Wednesday afternoon, in Gordon's own church. Many friends, relations and dignitaries attended, including Lord Arthur Hill, 6th Marquis of Downshire, Sir Arthur Hayter MP (Lord Haversham from 1906) of South Hill Park, Easthampstead (the son of the late Sir William), Colonel Peel, Mr Walter MP, John Pritchard, William Pritchard Gordon and Alexander Gordon.[8]

Gordon was buried in his own churchyard. His grave is marked by a standing tombstone of granite with a Celtic cross at the top. It was sculpted by Marylebone resident James Forsyth (1826-1910) and bears the following inscription with a biblical quotation from Hebrews XI:4:

> TO THE LOVED MEMORY OF
> THE REV. OSBORNE GORDON
> FOR 23 YEARS RECTOR OF THIS
> PARISH WHO DIED MAY 25 1883
> "HE BEING DEAD YET SPEAKETH"

At the base on the right-hand side is the name of the sculptor:

FORSYTH Sc
BAKER STREET
LONDON

A funeral sermon was preached in Easthampstead Church on
Sunday 3 June by Gordon's friend and former pupil, the Rev.
Robert Godfrey Faussett (1827-1908). Faussett was laudatory
about his old teacher:

> I see a man of so happy and genial a nature, that he was ever the
> welcomest of the welcome in the society – even of the youngest,
> towards whom indeed his own fresh sympathies seemed in an
> especial manner to attract him: but who, while he could laugh
> unreservedly with the merriest lad among them, never tolerated
> an excess, or a profanity, in deed or in word.
> I see a man who, apart from his powers of conversation and vast
> range of knowledge of men and things, possessed so keen a sense
> of humour, so sparkling and ready a wit, that his presence in his
> 'common-room', or at the table of his co-evals, was always the
> centre and life of the party, but who was never known to utter an
> ill-natured word, nor do I think he ever harboured an unkind
> thought.[9]

Gordon was greatly respected as a priest and farmer – his pigs
were renowned. He delighted in country life and in observing
the habits and peculiarities of the animal kingdom, particularly
any displays of "high courage".[10] Faussett reminisced: "He had a
favourite black mare, whose vicious tricks were a source of
absolute delight to him, though he was totally devoid of any
conceit as to being able to ride her."[11] Former Christ Church
student, tutor and Censor George William Kitchin (1827-1912)
recalled that at his funeral one of his Berkshire farmers said:
"Well, we have lost a real friend; we've had before parsons who
could preach, and parsons who could varm; but ne'er a one
before who could both preach and varm as Mr Gordon did."[12]
Obituaries to Gordon were published in *The Times* of 29 May

1883 and in *The Telegraph*. *The Times* praised in particular his character, his achievements and the high regard in which he was held: "Among his Christ Church pupils were many men distinguished in after life – Lord Salisbury, Lord Harrowby, Sir Michael Hicks-Beach, Mr. Ward Hunt, Mr. Ruskin. To have distinguished pupils is an accident, but to possess their esteem bespeaks merit."[13] Tribute was paid to him in *The Telegraph*: "Remarkable for his witty and incisive conversation, Mr. Gordon leaves a gap in the circle of those who knew him best which is little likely to be filled. [...] His loss will be lamented far and wide, and by none more than his old and intimate friend, Mr. John Ruskin." His native Shropshire did not forget the local lad and an obituary published in *The Bridgnorth Journal* on 2 June 1883 proudly extolled his academic accomplishments: "By his death the nation has lost one who added lustre to the blaze of learned fame surrounding Oxford University, as one of her most brilliant scholars. [...] In his school days he was surrounded by and closely allied with a phalanx of ripe scholars, – young men of the highest attainments and ability, who in the ranks of learned men and in public life achieved the highest honours and distinction."

His wealth at his death was recorded as £25.572. 11s. 0d: probate was granted on 7 August 1883.[14] He bequeathed all his possessions to his younger brother, Alexander John, who was residing at The Hill, near Bridgnorth, Shropshire. Gordon's goods included "farming goods and livestock including named horses and a black retriever dog and kennel, and [...] books in the library (mostly classical and religious works, including an 88 volume 'library of Anglo Catholic Theology', the works of John Ruskin and Alice in Wonderland)".[15] The total value was £1772, 12s. 6d. Alexander John did not live long enough to enjoy his inheritance and died intestate, a month later on 28 June,[16] aged seventy-one, after being thrown from his carriage. The land that Gordon had owned at Priestwood Common, near Bracknell, subsequently passed to Alexander John's son, Alexander. In his will, Gordon also left £100 for children who were members of the choir of the Parish of Easthampstead.[17] Gordon's successor was the Rev. Herbert Salwey, a former Christ Church student who also hailed from Shropshire.[18]

In Memoriam: Oxford and Easthampstead

On Wednesday 26 September 1883, the following letter was published in *The Times* announcing an Osborne Gordon Memorial:

Sir, – The committee appointed to promote a memorial to the late Osborne Gordon have to request that you, with your usual courtesy, will allow them to make known, through *The Times* to any of Mr. Gordon's friends who have received no direct intimation of the proposed memorial, that if they should wish to take part in it they should communicate with one of the secretaries on the subject before October 10.

Subscriptions (not to exceed £2.2s) can be paid to either of the secretaries, or to the Osborne Gordon Memorial Fund, Messrs. Parsons and Co., Old Bank, Oxford.

A general meeting of subscribers (at present about 120 in number) will be held in the course of the October term, at Christ Church, to determine the form of the memorial.

On behalf of the committee, we have the honour to be, Sir, your obedient servants,

Geo. Marshall

R. Godfrey Faussett Hon. Secs.

Christ Church, Oxford, Sept. 19.

The public responded generously and support, in addition to that of Marshall and Faussett, was given by John Ruskin and many other public figures – the Lord Bishop of Oxford, the Lord Bishop of Manchester (Fraser, Gordon's old school friend), the Very Rev. the Dean of Winchester (Gladstone had appointed George William Kitchin to the deanery of Winchester in April 1883), the Archdeacons of Berkshire and Maidstone, the Rt. Hon.

Sir J. R. Mowbray, the Rt. Hon. Sir Michael Hicks-Beach, Sir R. Harington, Col. H. B. N. Lane, J. G. Talbot MP, H. W. Fisher, the Rev. Canon Hill, Thomas Vere Bayne (1829-1908), H. L. Thompson, E. F. Sampson, the Rev. Richard St John Tyrwhitt (1827-1895) (writer on art, illustrator of the mountain murals in the Oxford Museum and friend of Ruskin).[19] The Dean and Chapter of Christ Church wholeheartedly endorsed the proposal and ensured its successful completion.

The two bournes of Gordon's life were Christ Church and Easthampstead. It is appropriate that these places were chosen for his memorials.

It was decided to commission a bust of Gordon and an inscription in Latin next to it to be placed in the Cathedral cloister of Christ Church.[20] The work was executed by Conrad Dressler (1856-1940), an English sculptor of German descent who had studied at the Royal College of Art with Joseph Edgar Boehm (1834-1890). Boehm's bust of Ruskin had been placed in the Drawing School in Oxford in 1881. Dressler had acquired a reputation for large, portrait-medallions in bronze – of Sir John Mowbray and Henry Morton Stanley (1841-1904), the explorer. He was also a friend of Ruskin who may have suggested him as a suitable sculptor for Gordon's bust. In the spring of 1884, Dressler was a frequent visitor to Brantwood for a series of sittings that took place in an out-house where Ruskin, seated upon a platform, posed. A bust of the bearded Professor was completed later that year.[21]

In his old parish church at Easthampstead, Gordon's memory was perpetuated and honoured by the skills of some of the greatest figures in Victorian England. Of these, three were also Oxonians, who had actively engaged with Gordon in so many different ways during his lifetime: Edward Burne-Jones, William Morris and John Ruskin. A window, a pavement and a tablet were erected. A Celtic tombstone marks Gordon's grave to the north-west of the church tower. His initials O. G. are engraved inside his church.

A two-light, stained-glass memorial window, the collaborative work of Burne-Jones and Morris & Co, was placed at the east end of the north side of the chancel in 1885, depicting *The Adoration of the Magi*. In the left panel of this memorial to Gordon, three Magi, one clad in white, another in yellow and the third in deep blue, with gifts in their hands, look in the direction of the right-hand panel which depicts the nativity scene – Joseph, dressed in dark red, Mary, in luminous blue, and four red-winged figures in white robes paying homage to the Christ child.

Craftsmen from the firm of Farmer and Brindley (who had worked on the University Museum in Oxford) were charged with executing a mosaic pavement placed just inside the altar rails. They worked from designs by Thomas Graham Jackson (1835-1924), the prolific architect and writer on art and architecture who had, in the words of Pevsner, "set his elephantine feet on many places in Oxford".[22] Jackson shot to fame after winning the competition for the design of the New Examination Rooms, and thereafter changed the face of Oxford as he gained more and more contracts for University work (Hertford College, Brasenose). In one of his lectures on art, "The Fireside: John Leech and John Tenniel", delivered during his second tenure as Slade Professor at Oxford on 7 November – and repeated on 10 November – 1883, Ruskin inveighed against Jackson's overuse of Renaissance features, with particular reference to the New Examination Rooms in the High Street, built 1876-1882. Ruskin angrily declaimed to his packed audience:

It is a somewhat characteristic fact, expressive of the tendencies of this age, that Oxford thinks nothing of spending £150,000 for the elevation and ornature, in a style as inherently corrupt as it is un-English, of the rooms for the torture and shame of her scholars […]; but that the only place where her art-workmen can be taught to draw, is the cellar of her old Taylor buildings, and the only place where her art professor can store the cast of a statue, is his own private office in the gallery above.[23]

We do not know what opinions Ruskin held about Jackson's tiles, but it is ironic that the work of a man whose aesthetic principles he abhorred should find a place next to Ruskin's own homage to Gordon at Easthampstead.

It was fitting that Professor Ruskin, one of Gordon's most prestigious, devoted surviving friends, should be asked to compose an epitaph. Here is a diplomatic transcription of Ruskin's original manuscript:

~~The adjacent window~~ and mosaic floor
This window
[are] Is dedicate to God's praise
In loving memory of His servant
~~Beneath this tablet~~
~~is buried~~
Osborne Gordon
*Censor Student and *Tutor of Ch. Ch. Oxford.
Rector of this Parish
From 1860 to 1883
An Englishman of the Olden Time
Humane, without weakness. Learned without ostentation
Witty without malice. Wise without pride
Honest of heart, Lofty of Thought
Dear to his fellowmen, and dutiful to his God
[He spent his pastoral life
In Kindly ministries, Errorless lessons
And Blameless example.
Few lives so little conspicuous
Have been so largely useful as his.
Few minds, as high in power
Like his, serene in activity, – undimmed in rest.]
When his friends shall be also departed
And can no more cherish his memory
Be it yet revered by this stranger.[24]

Ruskin's draft was edited by Rev. Herbert Salwey and the following shortened version, signed John Ruskin, was inscribed on

a brass plaque on the north wall of the chancel, to the left of the
Magi and *Nativity* windows:

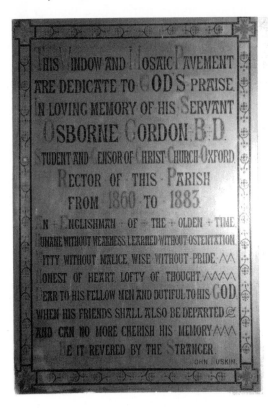

This "Shropshire student",[25] "a man of quite exceptional
power, and there is no saying what he might have done, with any
strong motive",[26] remained in Ruskin's thoughts throughout his
life and is recalled affectionately in *Praeterita*.

In Memoriam: Shropshire

In Shropshire, homages to the Pritchard-Gordon families can be
found in Broseley, Jackfield, Much Wenlock and Bridgnorth.

In Broseley Parish Church, there are tablets on the north transept wall in memory of John Pritchard Senior and son, and their families. One short inscription focuses on the son's status as Member of Parliament:

To the Glory of God and in the memory of John Pritchard of Stanmore Hall, Bridgnorth for fifteen years one of the members of parliament Borough of Bridgnorth who died August 19th 1891 aged 94. Also of Jane his wife who died February 25th 1892, aged 75. Also of Mary Anne Pritchard, sister of above John Pritchard, who died March 5, 1882.

A substantial testimony to John Pritchard Senior's personal qualities and philanthropy is recorded on a nearby tablet:

The esteem in which George Pritchard, brother of John, was held is recorded in the inscription on his memorial, a marble tablet also on the interior north wall in Broseley Church:

GEORGE PRITCHARD

ELDEST SON OF JOHN AND ANN PRITCHARD, DIED THE 24 DEC 1861 IN THE 69 YEAR OF HIS AGE. HE TROD IN THE STEPS OF HIS HONOURED FATHER, AND AS A GOOD NEIGHBOUR AS A PROTECTOR OF THE FATHERLESS, AND WIDOW, AS AN ABLE AND UPRIGHT MAGISTRATE, AND AS A CONSIDERATE GUARDIAN AND BENEFACTOR OF THE POOR, HE SO ENTIRELY GAINED THE AFFECTION AND RESPECT OF ALL AROUND HIM, THAT THE CHURCH AT JACKFIELD, AND THE MONUMENT IN THE PUBLIC STREET OF THIS PLACE, WERE ERECTED BY PUBLIC SUBSCRIPTION TO PERPETUATE HIS MEMORY.

HIS DOMESTIC VIRTUES AND HUMBLE PIETY ARE BEST KNOWN TO HIS WIDOW AND NEAR RELATIVES, WHO ARE LEFT TO MOURN HIS LOSS, AND WHO DESIRE BY THIS TABLET, TO RECORD THEIR FOND REMEMBRANCE OF ONE SO JUSTLY LOVED.

RIGHT DEAR IN THE SIGHT OF THE LORD, IS THE DEATH OF HIS SAINTS. Ps. cxvi.15.

ALSO HARRIOTT PRITCHARD, HIS WIFE, WHO DIED ON JANUARY 23 RD 1887.

AND MARY ANN OSTLER, HER SISTER, WHO DIED ON JUNE 16 TH 1878.

'THESE ALL HAD THE SAME HOPE OF A JOYFUL RESURRECTION.'

A major problem in Broseley was the difficulty of not having access to supplies of water, even though the river Severn was close by. Records of 1811 state that water had to be carried, in winter, from a well, called the Down Well (with a very irregular supply), about one and a half miles outside the town, and in summer, from distant brooks and from a pool called the Delph. The need for fresh and accessible water was urgent and was the subject of much debate, correspondence, and acrimony. Facts are difficult to ascertain, but it appears that George Pritchard agreed to finance a water supply from the property of Frederick

Hartshorne, of Alison House, Church Street, to provide the much-needed water. A reservoir constructed to store water fractured owing to mining subsidence. After George Pritchard's death, an ornate memorial fountain, designed by Robert Griffiths of Quatford, near Bridgnorth, was erected in the Square in Broseley in 1862. Built of Grinshill stone from quarries near Shrewsbury, it was octagonal in shape, with moulded, Gothic arches and ornamental gables, above which were appropriate inscriptions. The memorial looked like a little house: it was high and covered with a sloping roof surmounted by a tower and weather vane. The fountain, intended to provide water for the poor – but the high level of iron rendered it unusable – was demolished in 1947. Only the plinth remains.

In his will, George Pritchard left money to support the Jackfield curacy on condition that Jackfield, about three miles from Broseley, became a separate parish. A Memorandum dated 19 January 1859, found with George Pritchard's will, states his intentions and places the responsibility for executing them on his brother, John:

> I wish my Brother out of my Property to apply such sum as he shall think fit in the better endowment of the Church of Jackfield, on condition that Jackfield be formed into a distinct District. The income should not be less that £150 per annum. And I wish this appropriation to be considered as in memory of our late revered Father, who felt gratefully attached to Broseley Parish & that it should be so expressed in some Parish Record as to show that it arose from his property, & was a provision for the spiritual wants of a portion of our Parish, which we know he would very much approve.[27]

His wishes were respected and a new church, known as St Mary's, was erected by public subscription to perpetuate his memory. It was built at Calcutts in 1863 on land given by Francis Harries of Cruckton, owner of Broseley Hall. The architect was (Sir) Arthur William Blomfield (1829-1899). It was a small church, intended to look rich as Pevsner observed, by the "use of buff, red, yellow and blue bricks, and stone dressings".[28] Local historian John Randall described it as a "handsome little structure" [...] in which "the service is usually [...] bright and cheery, and such as draws good congregations".[29]

The arrangements for continuing financial support – the endowment – were recorded in the Parish Book. The income in 1865 totalled £168. 19s. 4d., of which £20 was charged on the Estate of Francis Harries Esquire in Broseley; £20 from the rent of a farm in Melverly purchased with money from Queen Anne's Bounty; £24. 10s. from tithes of Jackfield District given up by the Rector of Broseley. In addition the annual interest (£104. 9s. 4d.) on the following investments: "£1500 sterling appropriated by John Pritchard Esquire M.P., according to the wish of his Brother, from money which belonged to their late revered Father, & from regard to his memory. £1500 given by the Ecclesiastical Commissioners of England to meet the first named £1500, & the two sums, making together £3000, being invested by the Commissioners, now pay to the Cure annually the sum of £104. 9s. 4d."[30]

George Pritchard was Mayor of Wenlock in 1853: his name is engraved in the oak panelling in the Guildhall. His name is also recorded as a donor and contributor to the Library of the Wenlock Agricultural Society housed in a room above the Corn Exchange in the High Street.

The memory of both Pritchard brothers is commemorated in St Leonard's Church, Bridgnorth. On entering the red sandstone church, through the south door, the visitor is drawn towards an elaborately carved, octagonal, two-tiered, alabaster Italianate font, on a stepped pedestal, elaborately carved by the great Victorian craftsman Thomas Earp of Lambeth. Earp was one of the finest craftsmen of the day and the favourite sculptor of the Gothic revival architect George Edmund Street (1824-1881). In 1862, a magnificent marble pulpit designed by Street and carved by Earp was exhibited at the Great International Exhibition at

South Kensington. It was highly praised in the *Building News*: "No finer work ever came from Mr Street's hands, no better carving ever left Mr Earp's."[31] His font in St Leonard's has eight figures, each standing on a serpent, around the upper tier – a bishop, a king, a mechanic, a maiden, a soldier, a sage, an old woman and a merchant – symbolising Government, Wealth, Progress and Life. At the front of the font is a figure holding a bible in one hand, and a chalice in the other, a symbol of the Church as teacher and priest. This is an impressive memorial to John Pritchard and his wife, with the following inscription on the brass plaque at the base: "To the Glory of God in memory of John and Jane Pritchard, this font, the gift of William Pritchard Gordon, June 24th 1894". The tall, pinnacled font cover, the work of J. Phillips, was added later in 1911.

John Pritchard's obituary was published in *The Shrewsbury Chronicle* of 21 August 1891, page 8:

BRIDGNORTH. Death of Mr. John Pritchard. We regret having to announce the death of Mr. John Pritchard, D.L., J.P., of Stanmore, near this town, which occurred at his residence on Wednesday afternoon last. The deceased gentleman was senior partner in the late banking firm of Pritchard, Gordon, Potts & Shorting, of Broseley and this town; who in 1889 amalgamated with Lloyds Bank. The deceased was within a month of attaining the patriarchal age of 95, and has until a few months ago led a wonderfully active life. Mr. Pritchard was ever ready to further any philanthropic object with his purse and personal attention, and took a fatherly interest in the welfare of the inmates of the Quatt Industrial Schools whom Mr. and Mrs. Pritchard were often in the habit of entertaining at Stanmore. Up to the time of his decease Mr. Pritchard was a valued member of the Board of Management of the South East Shropshire School District. Mr. Pritchard was also on the Commission of the Peace for the county, and a magistrate for the Borough of Wenlock (although not acting as such of recent years), and forty years ago represented Bridgnorth in Parliament jointly with Mr. Henry Whitmore from 1853 to 1866 [recte 1868]. The deceased leaves a widow, but no family.

Coda

William Pritchard Gordon inherited considerable wealth on the death of his childless aunt Jane Pritchard in 1892. He inherited Stanmore Hall, an impressive art collection of works by or acquired on the advice of Ruskin, and extensive lands with a rental income of over £1,900 p.a.[32] Since he already owned and lived in a large residence at Danesford, near Bridgnorth, he let Stanmore Hall to Frederick St. Barbe Sladen. In Kelly's *Directory* of 1900, W. P. Gordon is described as one of the principal landowners of the parish of Worfield and of Chetton. Like his uncle, he was a respected Justice of the Peace and actively involved in the life of the community. In a sale catalogue printed for the auction of Stanmore Hall to take place at the Star & Garter, Wolverhampton on 20 October 1920, the Hall was described as "decorated in the Italian style".[33] W. P. Gordon's eldest son, Herbert Pritchard-Gordon (by now the name is hyphenated), disposed of the fine art collection at a sale at Sotheby's on 10 May 1933. Homage was paid to John Ruskin in the catalogue in the preface to the list of sixty-five sale items:

> The Property of H. Pritchard-Gordon, Esq. Berrington Hall, Shropshire.
> This Collection was formed by Mr. Gordon's Great-great Uncle, J. Pritchard, Esq. of Stanmore Hall, Bridgnorth, Shropshire, and was bought under the guidance of John Ruskin, who was a close personal friend.

Considerable changes took place to Stanmore Hall over the next few decades. Almost a century after Pritchard's former Venetian Gothic residence had been so splendidly described in *The Builder* in 1870, it was almost unrecognisable. A sale catalogue, on the instructions of Mr and Mrs J. Hickman, advertised the Hall as a "period Gentleman's Country Residence [...] fully centrally heated and completely renovated regardless of expense

[and] one of the most attractive Georgian style individual properties in the area".[34] No vestiges of Gothic are apparent in the
photograph of the house. Stanmore Hall was partly demolished
in the late twentieth century in order to construct a motor
museum.

John Pritchard MP.
By permission of Shropshire Archives, Shrewsbury.

Osborne Gordon.
From a photograph; by permission of Mr Roger Pope.

Chapter House, Wenlock Priory by Whymper.
Courtesy of Suzanne Boulos.

Lavabo at Wenlock Priory.
Photograph by Cynthia Gamble, 2004.

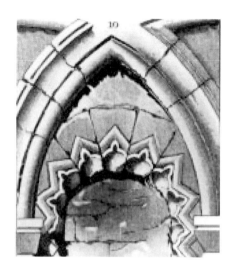

Edge Decoration at Wenlock Priory sketched by John Ruskin, engraved by J. C. Armytage, showing "zigzag effect", an example of "the simple decoration of the recesses" in which each "is worked into a small trefoiled arch round it to mark its outline, and another slight incision above, expressing the angle of the first cutting" (Plate IX, figure 10, *The Stones of Venice*, volume 1).

Blind arcade on the south wall of the Chapter House, Wenlock Priory, showing Ruskin's "zigzag effect".
Photograph by Cynthia Gamble, 2006

St Giles' Church, Badger.
Photograph by Cynthia Gamble, 2007.

Badger, trees in the park, pen and ink drawing by Robert Henry and/or Edward Cheney, dated 1847. Private Collection.

Buildwas Abbey looking East.
Courtesy of Tom Foxall.

Buildwas Abbey.
Courtesy of Tom Foxall.

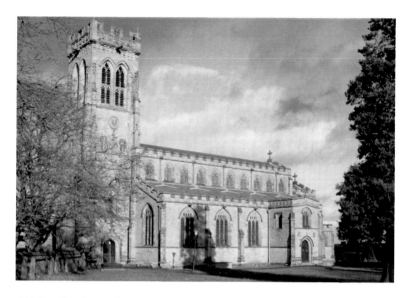

All Saints Church, Broseley.
Photograph by Tom Foxall, 2007.

The Gatehouse and Well, Stokesay Castle.
Courtesy of Julia Couchman.

The Hall, Stokesay Castle.
Courtesy of Julia Couchman.

Ludlow Castle.

Font at St Leonard's Church, Bridgnorth.
Photograph by Cynthia Gamble, 2004.

Tomb of the Rev. Osborne Gordon, in the churchyard of the
church of St Michael and St Mary Magdalene, Easthampstead.
Photograph by Cynthia Gamble, 2007.

Church of St Michael and St Mary Magdalene, Easthampstead.
Photograph by Cynthia Gamble, 2007.

RECTORS OF EASTHAMPSTEAD

DATE		DATE	
1298	Richard de Budham		John Clifton
1305	William de Marcheria	1583	Christopher Newman
		1594	Humphrey Goodinge
1392	John Russell	1620	William Paine
1400	John Pakenham	1656	John Brice B.D.
	John Guerdon	1662	Robert Stubbs M.A.
1417	Thomas Attebrouche	1698	John Power M.A.
	John Phillip	1746	Erasmus Dryden B.D.
1424	Laurence Horewode	1759	William Sharp D.D.
1425	Thomas Barry		Principal of Hertford College Oxford
1432	William Derby		Regius Professor of Greek
1433	Elias Martyn	1783	Thomas Pettingal B.D.
	John Swancote	1826	Abraham Boyle Townsend M.A.
1448	Richard Stacy	1860	Osborne Gordon B.D.
1449	John Roby	1883	Herbert Salwey M.A.
1458	Thomas Bland		Hon. Canon of Southwark
1477	John Dewe	1921	Arthur Groom Parham H.C. M.A.
			Bishop of Reading 1942
1542	George Horneby	1926	Wilfrid Thomas Stubbs M.A.
1545	James Hanncocke	1938	Alfred Clarkson M Maynard M.A.
1551	John Mabley	1950	Frederick William Cornell M.A.
1553	Richard Chandler	1957	Michael Charles Clarke M.A.
	Anthony Perke	1964	Colin Arnold Hill
1571	Nicholas Abbs	1973	Leonard George Tyler M.A.
		1985	Alan Frederick Christmas B.D.
			Hon. Canon of Oxford

1988	Oliver Simon M.A., M.Min.
2001	Guy Spenser Cole M.A. B.A.Hons.

Rectors of Easthampstead.
Photograph by Cynthia Gamble, 2007.

PART TWO

Chapter 12

A "sensuous education"
and the desire for England

Instead of joining the Gold Rush to California in the far West of America, young Henry James (1843-1916) was taken in an easterly direction from his home in New England to the Old World, to the cultural capitals of Europe – London, Paris and Geneva, and also Bonn. Henry James Sr., his wife Mary, their five children (William, Henry, Garth Wilkinson, Robertson and Alice) and French nanny, Annettte Godefroi, embarked on the *S. S. Atlantic* at New York docks on 27 June 1855. The trans-Atlantic crossing was not without considerable risks: on one occasion the non-arrival of that same steamer had caused such extreme anxiety among the public that its safe arrival was announced to a "huge and pronounced roar of relief" at the curtain fall in the theatre.[1] The *Arctic* and the *Pacific* both went down on that route. The crossing lasted eleven days and the family finally disembarked on the west coast of Lancashire, at Liverpool, then the second largest seaport in Great Britain after London, on 8 July.

Henry James Sr. wanted his children (particularly his sons) to experience a "sensuous education". He had already formulated his plan to Ralph Waldo Emerson as early as August 1849 when he wrote that he was gravely pondering "whether if would not be better to go abroad for a few years with them, allowing them to absorb French and German and get a better education than they are likely to get here".[2] So Henry James's first great European adventure had begun at the age of twelve and, apart from a short interlude back in America, he was not to return until late September 1860. Of all the places he visited, Paris and London were the great settings for James's boyhood education, the "formative forces"[3] in his "aesthetic evolution".[4] Both were exciting and fascinating and so full of history. Queen Victoria was firmly on the throne, and France was ruled by the self-styled Emperor Napoleon III and Spanish-born Empress Eugénie.

But his "sensuous education" commenced in England, where, after a lengthy journey by coach and horses from Liverpool to London, he recalled a hotel room with a "great fusty curtained [...] medieval four-poster"[5] bed and his first intense act of seizing the experience of the atmosphere both inside and outside. Young James was ill and feverish – he thought he had malaria – and the sensations he was experiencing were heightened, most probably, by his sickness.

When he first arrived in Paris in July 1855, an ambitious slum clearance and urban development programme was underway under the guidance of the Paris *préfet* Georges Eugène Haussmann (1809-1891). The whole city was an education for James. He spent hours in the great rooms of the Louvre – they were "educative, formative, fertilising"[6] – and acquired a sense of "reconstituted" history through such modern paintings as Delaroche's *The Execution of Lady Jane Grey* and *Edward V and the Duke of York in the Tower*. He discovered the paintings of Thomas Couture (1815-1879), in particular *The Romans of Decadence*, a work that had earned him the accolade of "the new Veronese" when, at the Paris Salon of 1847, it was likened to Veronese's huge canvas *The Marriage at Cana*. The young boy was awestruck by Géricault's *Raft of the Medusa* depicting dying and terrified men abandoned on a raft after a shipwreck in a storm on the West coast of Africa: it was "*the* sensation, for splendour and terror of interest".[7]

For a short time James attended, mornings only, a small experimental school, the Institution – or Pension – Fezandié (named after the owners) in the rue Balzac, in the 8th *arrondissement* in central Paris. It was, he recalled, "the oddest and most indescribable" of establishments, "a recreational, or at least a social, rather than a tuitional house". It was chosen by James's father, whom he described as one of "many free spirits of that time",[8] on account of its promotion of the utopian ideas of Charles Fourier (1772-1837): it must have been based on one of his experimental "phalanxes" or self-sufficient units, a kind of co-operative style of living. But young James coped with its eccentricities and indeed relished the place that he recalled as "positively gay – bristling [...] and resonant".[9] His French improved rapidly and he adapted easily to a cultured European life style.

Paris theatres, like those of London, provided James with a permanent source of enjoyment and delight. Rachel "alive, but dying", Mademoiselle Georges, Mademoiselle Mars, all famous actresses of the time, performed to wild acclaim.[10] He haunted the Café Foyot of the old Paris, and walked the streets "across the Champs-Élysées to the river, [...] over the nearest bridge and the quays of the left bank to the Rue de Seine",[11] browsing in second-hand bookshops and print-shops.

This was the city that was to become the second home to fellow American painter and dandy James McNeill Whistler. Twenty-two-year-old Whistler had arrived for the first time in Paris on 2 November 1855, after spending the previous month in London. The great Paris show, the *Exposition Universelle* – Burne-Jones and Morris had been there in July and admired English paintings by Hunt, Millais and Charles Allston Collins –[12] was a magnet for both James and Whistler. However, these two great Europeanised Americans did not meet each other until much later, according to Edel for the first time at a dinner *chez* the society hostess Christina Stewart Rogerson, in 1878/9.[13] First impressions were not very favourable for the novelist described his fellow-countryman as "a queer but entertaining creature".[14] But one wonders how Whistler reacted to James.

James's most memorable experiences of London around 1855-1856 were in the world of the theatre and art. He had at that early age eclectic tastes and was not subjected to parental censorship of any kind. That was in keeping with his parents' broadminded views and desire for their son to have a wide education. He experienced almost every kind of entertainment, from popular shows to Shakespeare. Albert Smith's dioramas, at the Egyptian Hall in Piccadilly, of his ascent of Mont Blanc attracted huge crowds who enjoyed being terrorised as they re-lived the dangers he experienced on his climb. James was there, having his senses charmed by the "big, bearded, rattling, chattering, mimicking Albert Smith"[15] whose presence in Chamonix in August 1851 had so offended Ruskin. James's thirst for the spectacular was assuaged by Charles Kean's production of Shakespeare's *Henry VIII*, a "momentous date" in his life. Memories of that prodigious, lavish revival, of such "historical and archaeological accuracy,"[16] with colours akin to stained-glass windows, remained with him for a long time.

He delighted in the National Gallery and Royal Academy displays, particularly Millais's *Autumn Leaves* and his prodigious *Blind Girl* and the awesomeness of Holman Hunt's *Scapegoat*. The very word Pre-Raphaelite had a particular resonance for him and "that intensity of meaning, not less than of mystery, that thrills us in its perfection".[17] Years later, James would enter more fully their world and become acquainted with some of these artists in person (Rossetti, Burne-Jones and Morris).

Returning to America, after the excitement of this European experience, seemed dull. Desultory law studies at Harvard in 1862-1864 did not provide James with inner satisfaction. The "muse of prose fiction"[18] had a stronger appeal and James began to publish literary reviews and short stories.

* * *

Henry James was twenty-six years old when he renewed contact with Victorian England in 1869. This was the first of several visits leading to his decision to take up more permanent residence and eventually become a British citizen in 1915. After disembarking at Liverpool docks from the *S. S. China* on a cold, windy day Saturday 27 February after a ten-day transatlantic voyage, the unaccompanied bachelor spent the night at the Adelphi Hotel before heading straight for London where, after staying a few days at Morley's Hotel in Trafalgar Square, he took lodgings at 7 Half-Moon Street, off Piccadilly.

His detailed letters to his family in America recount the extremely busy social life into which he plunged. He engaged intensely with London life, absorbing, observing, getting as close as possible to the metropolis. Many may have considered him to be a dilettante – the same charge that was to be erroneously levelled at Marcel Proust (1871-1922) – but his thirst for continuous social intercourse, in which he revelled, was also the essential foundation, the gathering of material for his becoming a great novelist. James was a relatively wealthy man who could have travelled by brougham or taken a victoria, but instead, he deliberately chose to walk "for exercise, for amusement, for acquisition".[19] Most effective and productive were his nocturnal London walks: "above all I always walked home at the evening's end", he wrote in his preface to *The Princess Casamassima*, "when the evening had been spent elsewhere, as happened more often than not".[20] This 1869 sojourn, in which James really discovered himself and his vocation, was of defining importance. His imagination reacted swiftly to the many impressions that "sought an issue" in the birth of a book. The habit of walking with "one's eyes greatly open" that he acquired resulted in an almost symbiotic relationship with people and places: "a mystic solicitation, the urgent appeal, on the part of everything, to be interpreted and, so far as may be, reproduced."[21] Ideas for his novels might come from a stray suggestion, a word, even a vague echo could start a train of thought in his imagination as though it had been pricked by a sharp pin: "one's subject is in the merest grain, [...] the seed [...] transplanted to richer soil."[22] He jotted down these echoes in his notebooks where they matured.

One may wonder how James was able to enjoy such a fruitful social life so quickly. He had an engaging personality, certainly, but he also had the right contacts. Of these, the most important was the American writer, scholar, art historian and art collector Charles Eliot Norton, who became Professor of Fine Art at Harvard in 1875, a post he held until 1898. Norton was a sensitive, sophisticated man, profoundly Europeanised – he regularly stayed in Switzerland, Italy, France and England – and was regarded by his lifelong friend and confidant John Ruskin as having a "genius for friendship".[23] He became an ardent enthusiast of Ruskin, Edward Burne-Jones and their circle and did much to promote their work in America. So great was his advocacy of Ruskin and the Pre-Raphaelites that at times it appeared to be counterproductive and caused some of his students to rebel.[24] James had been greatly indebted to Norton for his support for his early literary endeavours. As joint editor (with James Russell Lowell) of *The North American Review*, Norton had accepted for publication in October 1864 James's "first fond attempt at literary criticism":[25] this was a review of *Essays on Fiction*, a collection of reviews by the English political economist Nassau William Senior (1790-1864). Norton subsequently invited James to become a regular contributor. James remained immensely grateful to the "invaluable" Norton,[26] personal friend of so many eminent literary and scientific figures of the day – the Brownings, Thomas Carlyle, Charles Darwin, Charles Dickens, Ralph Waldo Emerson, Henry Wadsworth Longfellow, Leslie Stephen. James received many invitations to meals at the Nortons, then (in 1869) residing for a while in an old rectory at Keston, in Kent (England). He was also warmly welcomed by other members of the Norton family, by Charles's two sisters Grace (1834-1926) and Jane (1824-1877), his wife Susan, *née* Sedgwick (1838-1872), brother-in-law Arthur Sedgwick (1844-1915), and sister-in-law

Sara Sedgwick (1839-1902) who married Darwin's son, William. The entire family devoted a great deal of time to James, ensuring that he was embedded in an important artistic and literary network that extended far beyond anything he could have imagined.

Barely ten days after arriving in England James was taken by the Nortons (after dining with them) to University College, London, to hear, for the very first time, John Ruskin. The subject of his lecture, on the evening of Tuesday 9 March 1869, was the "Greek Myths of Storm", particularly the legends of Athena and Bellerophon. James's immediate reaction was brief but positive: "I enjoyed it much in spite of fatigue", he wrote to his sister Alice, adding, "but as I am to meet him someday thro' the N's, I will reserve comments".[27]

The next day, James was plunged into the world of the Pre-Raphaelites and the burgeoning Arts and Crafts movement, and more Greek myths in poetry. "My crowning day"[28] was how he resumed Wednesday 10 March – his first encounter with William Morris. At 4.30pm, he was taken by Norton and "ladies" to Morris's home, showroom, *fabrique* and company office at 26 Queen Square, Bloomsbury. His first impression of Queen Square was unfavourable: "an antiquated ex-fashionable region, smelling strong of the last century, with a hoary effigy of Queen Anne in the middle".[29] For James, Morris had been first and foremost an imaginative poet whose lengthy works, *The Life and Death of Jason* and *The Earthly Paradise* he had favourably reviewed in American journals in 1868. Now it was a revelation to discover that Morris was principally "a manufacturer of stained glass windows, tiles, ecclesiastical and mediaeval tapestry altar-cloths, and in fine everything quaint, archaic, pre-Raphaelite – and I may add exquisite".[30] James was impressed not only by the quality and design of Morris's work – "so handsome, rich and expensive (besides being articles of the very last luxury) [...] superb and beautiful" – but also by his method of working: "He designs with his own head and hands all the figures and patterns used in his glass and tapestry and [...] works the latter, stitch by stitch with his own fingers – aided by those of his wife and little girls."[31]

James fell under the spell of Morris's thirty-year-old wife, Jane. He was ecstatic: "Ah, *ma chère*," he wrote to his sister Alice, "such a wife! *Je n'en reviens pas* – she haunts me still".[32] So often in moments of heightened emotion, James interjects fragments of French expressing his own linguistic duality and the strength of his feeling for French culture. Jane, complex, magnificent and hard to define, was the embodiment of the Pre-Raphaelite ideal:

> A figure cut out of a missal – out of one of Rossetti's or Hunt's pictures – to say this gives but a faint idea of her, because when such an image puts on flesh and blood, it is an apparition of fearful and wonderful intensity. It's hard to say [whether] she's a grand synthesis of all the pre-Raphaelite pictures ever made – or they a 'keen analysis' of her – whether she's an original or a copy. In either case she is a wonder.[33]

In his penetrating description focusing on her dress, face and hair, he captures, in that same letter, some of the mystery of her sexuality: her remote, detached, immobile exterior conceals her hidden desires and charged sensuality. She is both medieval ("a figure cut out of a missal") and modern. Yet her identity and sexuality are blurred: her eyes are likened to those of Algernon Charles Swinburne (1837-1909), and her mouth resembles William Holman Hunt's engraving of Oriana for Alfred Tennyson's (1809-1892) *The Ballad of Oriana*. Her striking resemblance to Swinburne is apparent in Dante Gabriel Rossetti's watercolour of the redheaded, flamboyant young poet in 1861.[34] The predominant Pre-Raphaelite colours of purple and black frame and accentuate her sexless exterior, her pallor, sadness and longing for her lover, Dante Gabriel. She seems sickly, unhealthy, "lean" rather than slim, wearing a dress of some "dead" material:

Imagine a tall lean woman in a long dress of some dead purple stuff, guiltless of hoops (or of anything else, I should say,) with a mass of crisp black hair heaped into great wavy projections on each of her temples, a thin pale face, a pair of strange, sad, deep, dark Swinburnish eyes, with great thick black oblique brows, joined in the middle and tucking themselves away under her hair, a mouth like the 'Oriana' in our illustrated Tennyson, a long neck, without any collar, and in lieu thereof some dozen strings of outlandish beads – in fine Complete.[35]

Hanging on the wall was Rossetti's "large nearly full-length portrait of her", possibly *The Blue Silk Dress*.[36] It was "so strange and unreal" wrote James, "that if you hadn't seen her, you'd pronounce it a distempered vision, but in fact an extremely good likeness".[37]

The unhealthy, anorexic picture of Jane – an appearance that belied her strength for she outlived her husband by nearly twenty years and died in 1914 – is reinforced by her retreat, after dinner, into a corner of the apartment, where she lounged unsociably on a sofa, passive, silent and supposedly suffering: a "medieval woman with her medieval toothache". The couple's incompatibility becomes more apparent: Morris was, James observed, "extremely pleasant and quite different from his wife". He related the incongruous and almost unreal scene to his sister, contrasting Morris's demonstrative reading aloud of his mythological poetry (an appropriate link with Ruskin's lecture of the previous evening) with the stillness and remoteness of Jane:

There was something very quaint and remote from our actual life, it seemed to me, in the whole scene: Morris reading in his flowing antique numbers a legend of prodigies and terrors (the story of Bellerophon, it was), around us all the picturesque bric-a-brac of the apartment (every article of furniture literally a 'specimen' of something or other,) and in the corner this dark silent medieval woman with her medieval toothache.[38]

He described Morris as "short, burly and corpulent, very careless and unfinished in his dress" with "a very loud voice and a nervous restless manner and a perfectly unaffected and business-like address". James continued: "His talk indeed is wonderfully to the point and remarkable for clear good sense. He said no one thing that I remember, but I was struck with the very good judgment shewn in everything he uttered. He's an extraordinary example, in short, of a delicate sensitive genius and taste, served by a perfectly healthy body and temper. All his designs are quite as good (or rather nearly so) as his poetry."[39]

James was soon to meet Rossetti in person, introduced by Norton who took him to his Cheyne Walk studio "in the most delicious melancholy old house at Chelsea on the river".[40] It was packed with curios, cabinets, ornaments, mirrors, furniture, strange pets, and exotic, lush, erotic paintings and drawings inspired by his relationships with Fanny Cornforth (his model), Elizabeth Siddal (his wife from 1860 who died of an overdose of laudenum two years later), Jane Burden Morris and Swinburne. But James was disappointed, for the promise of such a "home and haunt" did not match the reality of the occupant. The forty-one-year-old Rossetti struck him as "unattractive" and "horribly bored": this may have been due to one of his bouts of depression (he would attempt suicide in 1872). As regards his portraits, "they were all large, fanciful portraits of women, of the type *que vous savez*, narrow, special, monotonous, but with lots of beauty and power".[41]

Norton arranged for James to be invited (along with some members of the Norton family) to dine with Ruskin at his home at 163 Denmark Hill, in what was then a small leafy town, known as the "Belgravia of the South",[42] to the south of London. We do not know the date of the visit other than it took place after the lecture on Greek Myths and before 26 April 1869 when Ruskin left for the continent. James had the opportunity to experience the life of a well-off, comfortable, middle-class household consisting of Ruskin's frail and increasingly deaf and partially blind eighty-seven-year-old widowed mother Margaret, her nurse and companions, servants, housekeeper and gardeners. The large, detached, three-storey-house, with a lodge and a keeper who turned away unwelcome callers, was set in seven acres of land, part of it, to the rear, being meadow, flower and vegetable gardens. By 1869, many of the rooms in the house were more like art galleries, crammed with dozens of works by Turner (including the now celebrated canvas *Slavers throwing overboard the Dead and Dying – Typhon coming on*), by Samuel Prout, David Roberts, Copley Fielding and others that Ruskin and his father (until his death in 1864) had collected avidly for many years. So huge was the collection that Ruskin decided to sell forty-one of his Turners and other works at a Christie's sale that took place on 15 April, leaving their destiny and value to the vagaries of an auction.

"R[uskin] was very amiable" James wrote to his American friend, the painter John La Farge, "and shewed his Turners. The latter is assuredly great".[43] But the painting in the Ruskin collection that James most enjoyed was a portrait by Titian – "an old Doge, a work of transcendent beauty and elegance such as to give one a new sense of the meaning of art".[44] This was the *Portrait of the Doge, Andrea Gritti* (now in The National Gallery, London), an oil on canvas then attributed to Titian but since 1931 considered to be the work of Vincenzo Catena. At the Whistler-Ruskin trial in 1878, it was taken into court as evidence of what a properly finished work should be: "a most perfect specimen [...] an arrangement in flesh and blood"[45] was how Burne-Jones, one of the witnesses for the defendant (i.e. Ruskin), described it.

But much more revealing was James's letter to his mother in which he records his impressions of Ruskin:

Ruskin himself is a very simple matter. In fact, in manner, in talk, in mind, he is weakness, pure and simple. I use the word, not invidiously, but scientifically. He has the beauties of his defects;

but to see him only confirms the impression given by his writing, that he has been scared back by the grim face of reality into the world of unreason and illusion, and that he wanders there without a compass or guide – or any light save the fitful flashes of his beautiful genius. The dinner was very nice and easy, owing in a great manner to Ruskin's two charming young nieces who live with him – one a lovely young Irish girl with a rich virginal brogue – a creature of a truly British maidenly simplicity – and the other a nice Scotch lass who keeps house for him.[46]

Ruskin had seemingly given the impression, perhaps by the abundance of familiar expressions he used to address them, that the two young women were his nieces. The girl with the Irish accent was Lily Armstrong (a former pupil at Winnington School, near Northwich, in Cheshire, with which Ruskin developed close links): she was the daughter of Serjeant Armstrong, MP for Sligo, and was a guest at the house.[47] The "nice Scotch lass" would have been Joan Agnew (later Severn), then aged twenty-three. She was a very distant cousin of Ruskin and had come from Wigtown, in Scotland, to Denmark Hill in 1864 to be a companion to the widowed Margaret Ruskin. Joan called Mrs Ruskin "Auntie".

Lunch with the former cleric, writer, critic and mountaineer Leslie Stephen (1832-1904) marked the beginning of a fruitful and life-long relationship. As influential editor of the *Cornhill Magazine* 1871-1882, Stephen accepted James's short story *Daisy Miller* "with effusion" (it was published in two numbers of the *Cornhill Magazine* in 1878). This controversial story (of Daisy, an unconventional and independent young American in Europe, whose defiance of certain mores coupled with a degree of naïvety contribute to her untimely death in Rome) was hugely popular and established James's fame on both sides of the Atlantic. A long-time admirer and reviewer of George Eliot's works, he finally met the revered writer one Sunday in April (1869), escorted there, as he recalled in *The Middle Years*, "by one of the kind door-opening Norton ladies".[48]

James's activities, however, were not solely London based. He toured many English counties, and spent several weeks, for health reasons, in Great Malvern, the attractive market and spa town with the ruins of a fine Abbey, nestling in the Malvern Hills in Worcestershire. It was the presence of the English countryside, recalling in a not un-Proustian way memories of childhood reading, that he carried back with him to America as he sailed on the *Scotia* on 30 April 1870:

> elm-scattered meadows and sheep-cropped commons and the ivy-smothered dwellings of small gentility, and high-gabled, heavy-timbered, broken-plastered farmhouses, and stiles leading to delicious meadow footpaths and lodge-gates leading to far off manors – with all these things suggestive of the opening chapters of half-remembered novels, devoured in infancy [...].[49]

The "pleasure of cathedral-hunting"[50] occupied much of his time in the spring of 1872, when he haunted and explored the old cathedral cities of Chester and its Roman ruins, Lichfield, Exeter, Wells, Salisbury and savoured what he called, in a way redolent of Ruskin, the "tone of things".[51]

* * *

Back in Paris of the Third Republic in 1876, James encountered many literary figures – Gustave Flaubert, Alphonse Daudet and the Russian writer Ivan Turgenev. He went on numerous excursions to Normandy, Picardy, the Marne, and published travel sketches about the ancient cathedral towns of Rheims, Laon, Soissons and Rouen. Other essays were devoted to Chartres and Étretat, and a longer sketch entitled "From Normandy to the Pyrenees". He returned to London in late 1876, decided to settle, and took accommodation at 3 Bolton Street, off Piccadilly, two streets away from his previous lodgings in Half-Moon Street.

Charles Eliot Norton had been instrumental in opening doors for James in 1869: now that role was taken over, to some extent, by another Europeanised and much travelled compatriot, the historian Henry Brooks Adams (1838-1918), son of the American diplomat and author Charles Francis Adams and grandson of John Quincy Adams, 6th President of the USA. James was immensely grateful to Adams and expressed his thanks to his long-standing friend in a letter of 5 May 1877: "Your introductions rendered me excellent service and brought about some of the pleasantest episodes of my winter."[52]

With astuteness and rapidity, the engaging, increasingly cosmopolitan budding writer, on the verge of being an expatriate, cultivated an ever-widening circle of interesting and influential people – leading literary figures, politicians, scientists, aristocrats – often through contacts made at prestigious London clubs. Massachusetts-born historian and diplomat, John Lothrop Motley (1814-1877), put James on the honorary list of the Athenaeum,[53] a club he was to "frequent and prize".[54] How greatly James delighted in the history of that prestigious club in Pall Mall. To his father he proudly declared: "I am writing this in the beautiful great library of the Athenaeum Club." Occupying seats around him were "Herbert Spencer, asleep in a chair [...] and a little way off is the portly Archbishop of York with his nose in a little book".[55]

James needed the stimulation of intellectual company in order to work. He had expressed this need to his parents a few years earlier: "What I desire now more than anything else, and what would do me more good, is a *régal* of intelligent and suggestive society, especially male. But I don't know how or where to find it. [...] I chiefly desire it because it would, I am sure, increase my powers of work."[56] He was now revelling in such company. In a detailed letter of 10 July 1877 to his elder brother William, then a lecturer in comparative anatomy at Harvard where he had graduated in medicine, he painted a lively, frank and often amusing picture of many of his social activities. On Sunday 8 July 1877, he dined *en famille* with Darwin's "bulldog", the biologist Thomas Henry Huxley (1825-1895). He dined, uncomfortably on one occasion, at the home of Mme Van de Weyer (the wealthy English woman *née* Bates, wife of Silvain Van de Meyer, Belgian Minister in London) at "a big luscious and ponderous banquet, where [he] sat between the fat Mme V. de W. and the fatter Miss *ditto*".[57]

One of James's most influential and stimulating acquaintances at this time was Richard Monckton Milnes (Lord Houghton), with whom Ruskin had breakfasted in 1844. Monckton Milnes had the reputation of knowing everybody in society. He was a flamboyant, temperamental character who enjoyed the domineering and controlling role of patron of budding writers – provided they accepted his conditions. He befriended Swinburne and secured the poet laureateship for Tennyson, his friend and contemporary at Trinity College, Cambridge. Milnes was renowned for his trenchant wit, malicious gossip and sexual excesses. His library of erotica at Fryston was reputed to be unrivalled. He was a close friend of Captain (later Sir) Richard Burton (1821-1890) – also an acquaintance of Ruskin –[58] traveller, poet (perhaps *manqué*) and an accomplished translator of erotic, oriental literature including *The Kama Sutra*, *The Perfumed Garden* and the *Arabian Nights*. Not only was "the bird of paradox"[59] a collector of books, but a collector of people. James was invited to his literary breakfasts, lunches and dinners, and even became a guest at Fryston Hall, his country house in his constituency.

At the same time, James was busy writing and publishing articles about his first-hand experiences of London life: the crowds at events in the social calendar – the Oxford and Cambridge boat race, Derby Day on the Epsom Downs,[60] and people in parks.[61] He reported on the Grosvenor Gallery exhibition in his article "The Picture Season in London, 1877". Among the exhibits were works by Burne-Jones – his six panels depicting *The Days of Creation* and his oil painting *The Beguiling of Merlin*: the latter James admired as "a brilliant piece of *rendering* [that] could not have been produced without a vast deal of 'looking' on the artist's part",[62] thereby helping to establish Burne-Jones's reputation. The Grosvenor would soon be known as the gallery in which Whistler's controversial painting, *Nocturne in Black and Gold: The Falling Rocket,* had first been exhibited and which became the subject of a *cause célèbre* following Ruskin's libellous comments.

It was almost mid-July 1877 and the London season was drawing to a close. Henry James felt exhausted after his usual hectic round of invitations. After seven months in London, he was longing to get away, to escape to France or Italy, to collect his thoughts and to "get into some quiet rural spot and at work". Life as an inveterate diner-out was beginning to take its toll: he needed to harness his experiences and devote time to sustained writing. His plans to go to Spain had been thwarted by news of the troubled political situation. Perhaps he would go to Dieppe or along the Normandy coast for a few weeks. But momentary doubts remained, nevertheless, about the direction of his work: "I don't even know whether to begin work upon a novel I have projected for next year."[63] In spite of his professed feelings of uncertainty, novels were germinating in his mind: *The Europeans* was published in 1878, followed by *Washington Square* in 1880 and *The Portrait of a Lady* in 1881.

But just before James finalised his decision to go abroad, he received a letter from America that would have an impact both on his immediate plans and the course of his life and writing.

Chapter 13

Life in a Shropshire Abbey

The letter James received was from Henry Brooks Adams, then a teacher of history at Harvard University. From his home in America, Adams wrote a most insistent letter to the effect that if James received an invitation to stay at Much Wenlock Abbey and Priory, the Shropshire residence of the wealthy barrister and landowner Charles Milnes Gaskell (1842-1919) and his wife Lady Catherine, he must accept.

Why was Adams so insistent? Who was Charles Milnes Gaskell?

* * *

Henry Adams's friendship with Charles George Milnes Gaskell, then a Cambridge undergraduate at Trinity College, began at nine o'clock on the morning of 27 April 1863, when both were invited to breakfast, in Brook Street, Mayfair, with Sir Henry Holland, the Court physician.[1] Adams was then (between 1861-1868) Private Secretary to his father, Charles Francis Adams, US minister to Britain.

Charles G. Milnes Gaskell was the eldest son of James Milnes Gaskell (1810-1873), Conservative MP for the Borough of Wenlock between 1832-1868, and a distant cousin of Richard Monckton Milnes. James Milnes Gaskell entered the House of

Commons at the age of twenty-two. His political career had been enhanced and promoted by his marriage in 1832 (the year he entered Parliament) to Mary Williams Wynn (d. 1869), second daughter of fellow MP, the Rt. Hon. Charles Williams Wynn (1775-1850) who represented Montgomeryshire in central Wales from 1799 until his death. The wealthy and powerful Williams Wynn family had owned large estates in Wales and Shropshire for generations: their main residence was Wynnstay Hall, near Ruabon (Rhiwabon in Welsh), a small town half-way between Wrexham and Llangollen, but geographically and psychologically close to the Shropshire border. Both Members of Parliament (father-in-law and young son-in-law) are depicted in the huge and historic painting by Sir George Hayter entitled *The House of Commons 1833* commemorating the passing of the first Reform Bill of 1832 and the first session of the new House of Commons on 5 February 1833.[2]

The Gaskell parents showed Adams immense kindness, considered him a member of their family and an excellent friend for their son, "perhaps a less dangerous friend than some Englishman might be".[3] As the friendship developed – Gaskell was addressed familiarly as "Gask" or "Carlo", "*Caro amico mio*", "My dear Karl", "My dear Carlo" – Adams was invited to their Yorkshire residence, Thornes House, near Wakefield and also became a frequent guest at their Shropshire residence, customarily known as Wenlock Abbey, although it comprises a Priory and an Abbey. The property had belonged to the Williams Wynn family from whom James Milnes Gaskell purchased it in 1858.[4] The new owners set about restoring first of all the decaying fifteenth-century Prior's house – for their own living accommodation – that had been used as a farmhouse. In addition, they had a London home at 12 Stratford Place, in a quiet cul-de-sac of mainly eighteenth-century houses just off Oxford Street (on the north side).

Adams was invited to Wenlock Abbey in the early autumn of 1864 as one of the first guests of Mary Milnes Gaskell whom he regarded as "one of the most intelligent and sympathetic women in England".[5] In his *Autobiography*, he recalls the impact of his first taste of Shropshire when he "drove about Wenlock Edge and the Wrekin with her [Mary Milnes Gaskell], learning the loveliness of this exquisite country, and its stores of curious antiquity". "It was", he continued, "a new and charming existence; an experience greatly to be envied – ideal repose and rural Shakespearean peace".[6] The immediacy of that experience was shared in letters to his older brother, Charles Francis Adams Jr. (1835-1915), then a Colonel in the American Civil War (1861-1865). Adams was a prolific and engaging letter writer and almost immediately after returning from Wenlock on 6 October 1864, wrote enthusiastically to his brother about his "very enjoyable" visit.[7] The twenty-six-year-old American provides a valuable insight into life at the old Abbey, that Henry James was to complement thirteen years later. Here are his first impressions of parts of the interior – the Great Hall and Adams's bedroom with a spiral staircase:

> God only knows how old the Abbot's House is, in which they are as it were picnic-ing before going to their Yorkshire place for the winter. Such a curious edifice I never saw, and the winds of Heaven permeated freely the roof, not to speak of the leaden windows. We three, Mrs Gaskell, Gask and I, dined in a room where the Abbot or the Prior used to feast his guests; a hall on whose timber roof, and great oak rafters, the wood fire threw a red shadow forty feet above our heads. I slept in a room whose walls were all stone, three feet thick, with barred, square Gothic windows and diamond panes; and at my head a small oak door opened upon a winding staircase in the wall, long since closed up at the bottom, and whose purpose is lost.[8]

Adams was a most congenial guest whose lively conversation almost competed with that of the jackdaws who had taken up permanent residence in the ruins:

The daws in the early morning, woke me up by their infernal chattering around the ruins, and in the evening we sat in the dusk in the Abbot's own room of state, and there I held forth in grand after-dinner eloquence, all my social, religious and philosophical theories, even in the very holy-of-holies of what was once the heart of a religious community.[9]

He was also a practical guest who assisted with the ongoing excavation of the ruins and participated in the discovery of some ancient tiles:

Wherever we stepped out of the house, we were at once among the ruins of the Abbey. We dug in the cloisters and we hammered in the cellars. We excavated tiles bearing coats of arms five hundred years old, and we laid bare the passages and floors that had been three centuries under ground.[10]

With Gaskell, he explored the Shropshire countryside and got to know some of the local farmers and their rustic dwellings, probably some of Milnes Gaskell's tenants: "Then we rambled over the Shropshire hills, looking in on farmers in their old kitchens, with flitches of bacon hanging from the roof, and seats in the chimney corners, and clean brick floors, and an ancient blunderbuss by the fire-place."[11] They visited some of the large estates in the vicinity (perhaps Attingham Park renowned for its deer and pheasants, or Willey Park) and "drove through the most fascinating parks and long ancient avenues, with the sun shining on the deer and the pheasants, and the 'rabbit fondling his own harmless face'".[12] Near Attingham Park and Hall, the Roman settlement of Uriconium (Wroxeter) provided the picturesque setting for their gastronomic picnic "in the ruins of what was once the baths" where they ate "partridge and drank Château Léoville, where once a great city flourished, of which not one line of record remains, but with which a civilisation perished in this country".[13] But they were also sipping their top-of-the-range Bordeaux wine on ground that had once been a great Roman vineyard.

In 1864, the two Members of Parliament for the Borough of Wenlock were James Milnes Gaskell and George Cecil Weld Forester (1807-1886),[14] for whose father's cousin John Pritchard Senior had been agent. Forester's country house was Willey Hall – about three miles east of Much Wenlock – an impressive early nineteenth-century mansion designed in the neo-classical style by the English architect Lewis Wyatt, with landscaped parkland, lakes and pools. The relationship between the two MPs was close – they had known each other for many years – and it is not inconceivable that Gaskell and Adams were invited to Willey Hall. Perhaps that was what Adams had in mind when he wrote to his brother: "Then we dined with a neighboring MP whose wife was eccentric in her aspirates and asked me if I didn't like that style."[15]

Adams was delighted with his Shropshire stay and had enjoyed the Gaskells' "rather sensual and intellectual style". The visit was, he told his brother, "a species of quiet success, so curiously different from the usual stiffness of English society, that I shall always feel a regard for the old barn, though it was as cold a place as one wants to be near".[16]

In the summer of 1870, that same Abbey provided an oasis of calm and stability away from from Paris and the beginning of the Franco-Prussian war. Adams took refuge in its profound peace and found comfort in the timelessness of the surroundings: "Only the few remaining monks, undisturbed by the brutalities of Henry VIII – three or four young Englishmen – survived there, with Milnes Gaskell acting as Prior."[17] It was much older than the medieval period: its roots went back millions of years to the age of the pteraspis, the primitive fish that inhabited the area and whose fossils remain in the stone that built the Abbey. In a passage that seems to draw on James's impressions, Adams recalled in his autobiography:

The August sun was warm; the calm of the Abbey was ten times secular; not a discordant sound – hardly a sound of any sort except the cawing of the ancient rookery at sunset – broke the stillness; and, after the excitement of the last month, one felt a palpable haze of peace brooding over the Edge and the Welsh Marches. Since the reign of *Pteraspis*, nothing had greatly changed; nothing except the monks. Lying on the turf, the ground littered with newspapers, the monks studied the war correspondence.[18]

A photograph taken in July 1873 depicts a group of guests – Lady Pollington, Lady Cunliffe, Marian (Clover) Adams and her husband Henry Adams, Sir Robert Cunliffe, Lord Pollington – with Charles Milnes Gaskell and his faithful hound in the centre, in a romantic, picturesque setting before the ruined chapter house of Wenlock Abbey. Clover Adams wrote engagingly to her father about the house party and her enjoyment at being there: "Lady Cunliffe and I sketch in the ruins and gossip and wind up the day with 5 o'clock tea in my room, which is the pleasantest in the house, I think – stone walls with a fireplace eight feet wide cut out of it, furniture and floor black oak, white roses flattening their cheeks against the mullion windows."[19]

This setting is the subject of Whymper's sketch in which he depicts a farmer, smoking a pipe and resting against one of the arches, as he guards his flock of sheep grazing and resting among the ruins. This sketch, signed in the bottom right-hand corner by Whymper (the initial is indistinct), was one of the illustrations in Mandell Creighton's *The Story of Some English Shires* published in 1897.

* * *

Adams was well aware of James's desire for rest and for the continent. But, an astute judge of character, he also sensed that Gaskell and James would be compatible companions with interests in common and that the relationship would be beneficial: and so it proved, for they were to become lifelong friends.

Adams also knew of James's fascination for inhabited medieval castles and abbeys and his overriding concern was for him to experience such things at first hand: Wenlock Abbey was the ideal place and presented an exceptional, indeed unique, opportunity. James was in a quandary, for he barely knew Gaskell. He "had seen next to nothing of Gaskell & his wife in town", had had "but 10 minutes' talk" with him, and "had but admiringly looked upon" Lady Catherine, for he had "been unable to accept their invitation to dinner", James explained in a letter to Adams.[20] James had first met Gaskell and his wife – "a very old-English beauty"[21] – in late May or early June 1877 at the home of Francis Turner Palgrave (1824-1897), the English poet and critic best known today as the editor of the *Golden Treasury of the Best Songs and Lyrical Poems in the English Language* (1861). F. T. Palgrave was Gaskell's brother-in-law, having married his sister Cecil Grenville Milnes in 1862.

Gaskell had followed this up with an abortive visit to James who was not at home when he called, as James explained to Adams in his letter of June 5th 1877: "Gaskell called on me 2 days since (I didn't see him), & shall return his visit to day & hope to see something of him."[22]

Adams had prepared the ground for the invitation by writing to Charles Milnes Gaskell on 22 June 1877:

Harry James writes me that you called on him of which I am glad, for I like him though I don't read his books. Some people admire them. If you ask him to Wenlock, you will I doubt not, find him much after your own taste. He would appreciate Wenlock, which is quite after his theory of life and imagination, so I hope you will try him.[23]

James explained to his brother William the somewhat unusual circumstances of the invitation, "to go down for three days to Wenlock Abbey". He was on the point of declining, "when, by an odd chance, came a letter from H. Adams saying – 'If Gaskell asks you to Wenlock don't for the world fail to go';

and adding other remarks, of a most attractive kind: the upshot of which has been that I have accepted the invitation, and go on the 12th, to stay to the 16th".[24]

*   *   *

James prepared for the visit by consulting Murray's *Handbook for Shropshire, Cheshire and Lancashire*, published in 1870: the entry relating to Much Wenlock concentrated on the Abbey. "It is", James wrote to his brother William, "according to Murray's *Shropshire*, a very exquisite place: a medieval Abbey, half ruined, half preserved and restored".[25] The reputation, authority and reliability of all the series of *Handbooks* were based on the name of Murray, the well-established family firm in Albemarle Street, London. It was generally assumed that the author was John Murray: however, research in the Murray archives has since shed light on the identity of many of the contributors. That first *Handbook for Shropshire, Cheshire and Lancashire* was compiled by the Welsh-born industrialist George Phillips Bevan (1830-1889) and the history writer William Edward Flaherty (1807-1878).[26] Bevan and Flaherty relied to some extent on existing accounts by "Mr Parker" – a reference to the Oxford historian and friend of Ruskin, John Henry Parker (1808-1884), author of *Some Account of Domestic Architecture in England: from Richard II to Henry VIII* (1859) – and by "Mr Blore" – almost certainly Edward Blore (1787-1879) the English architect and draughtsman who sketched Wenlock Abbey –, as well as *Archaeologia Cambrensis*, the Journal of the Cambrian Archaeological Association.

Clearly this was no ordinary abbey. In an exceptional setting of thirty acres were the monastic ruins of St Milburga's Abbey and a Cluniac Priory, deep in the heart of the Shropshire countryside. The chapter house, a "beautiful specimen of Norman architecture", featured chevron mouldings and rows of intersecting arches (sketched by Ruskin). The 100ft.-long two-storey

secular building, the late fifteenth-century Prior's Lodge or
Lodging, with a very high, sloping, oak roof, "light and elegant
open cloister extending the whole length and communicating
with the rooms on either floor", abutted at an angle the twelve-
century infirmary. The guidebook revealed parts of the private
residence of the then owner James Milnes Gaskell. Glimpses
were afforded of the kitchen and bakehouse, and unusual or
even unique features such as the *garde-robe* (privy), the private
oratory with an altar "open underneath for the reception of
relics" and stone reading-desk "rudely carved with Norman
foliage" (the lectern now in the Victoria and Albert Museum,
London), the abbot's Hall "a fine room of 3 bays, lighted by 4
windows of 2 lights each, on the 1st floor, over which is now the
kitchen" and abbot's parlour.

A well-crafted invitation in the form of "a gracious note from
Lady Catherine Gaskell",[27] Henry Adams's persuasion and influence, and an evocative Murray's *Handbook* sufficed to attract
James to the little market town of Much Wenlock with a population of around 1500, to experience life in an unusual country
house inaccessible to the general public, as were most British
country houses at the time. So for five days James turned his
back on London and headed, for the first time, to Shropshire,
the rich agricultural county on the border with Wales. It was to
provide material for one of his travel sketches, "Abbeys and
Castles", first published in *Lippincott's Magazine* in October 1877
and later in *Portraits of Places* in 1883.

* * *

Chapter 14

Medieval immersion in Much Wenlock

However late in the evening I may arrive at a place, I never go to bed without my impression.[1]
Henry James

James arrived by steam locomotive, on the "noiseless little railway running through the valley",[2] at Much Wenlock station on Thursday, 12 July 1877. The Welsh slate, gabled, stationmaster's house, designed by the local railway engineer Joseph Fogerty and built in 1864 when the passenger station opened, was already partly covered with ivy and climbing plants. Beneath the finial of the central gable was the insignia of the private Wenlock and Severn Junction Railway company, a "Wen and Lock". The platform was decorated with pots of shrubs and summer flowers in bloom. In front of a white fence, a board with the name, Much Wenlock, blazoned in large letters, welcomed the traveller. The porter unloaded James's trunk from the luggage-van and placed it in the great square two-horse barouche, an old-fashioned, high-hung vehicle, with a green body and a faded hammer-cloth,[3] waiting for him in front of the station. How different this was from young James's first coach journey from Liverpool to London in 1855.

He cut a dashing figure with his long, silky, black beard, receding hairline, smooth forehead and penetrating eyes, not unlike an Elizabethan sea captain.[4] He was certainly most attractive. This was confirmed by the famous actress Fanny Kemble who described her guest that Christmas, at Alveston Manor House, near Stratford-upon-Avon, as "our dark-bearded, handsome American friend".[5] Crawley, Gaskell's Yorkshire coachman,[6] proudly drove the foreign guest down Station Road, turned left into Sheinton Street, past the Almshouses, Holy Trinity Church with its lofty steeple, the black and white timber-framed Elizabethan Guildhall, along Barrow Street before veering left at No. 16, known as Sir Thomas Butler's house. Thomas Butler was vicar of Much Wenlock from 1538 until his death in 1562: he kept a detailed record of that turbulent period of English history spanning four sovereigns, Henry VIII, Edward VI, Queen Mary and Queen Elizabeth. They rumbled past what is purported to be St Milburga's mystical well, noted for its healing properties – it was reputed to cure eye problems –, before taking a sharp turn left into the drive leading to the Abbey guesthouse.[7] A footman dressed in livery greeted James and took charge of his belongings. Lady Catherine had placed a nosegay of flowers from her garden on his dressing table, along with notepaper, envelopes and a supply of pens and ink, a delicate touch that she called "the welcome of mute courtesies".[8] In *The Europeans*, published a year after James's Shropshire visit, there is an echo of this act when the "beneficent invalid" Mrs Acton showers her European visitor Baroness Münster with "a great many nosegays from her garden, and baskets of beautiful fruit".[9]

* * *

James was always at home in the world of the landed gentry and aristocracy. His host's pedigree and coat of arms were in Burke's *Landed Gentry*, while his hostess's could be found in Burke's *Peerage*.

Charles Milnes Gaskell had inherited two large estates,

Thornes House, Wakefield, Yorkshire, and Wenlock Abbey, on the death of his father on 5 February 1873. He was now landowner of much of the town and parish of Much Wenlock. The large, brick vicarage, in which the Rev. Frederick Robert Ellis had resided since 1875 when he was first appointed to Holy Trinity Church, belonged to Gaskell who also provided him with a generous living of about £235 a year. After studies at Eton and Trinity College, Cambridge, Gaskell was called to the bar in 1866. But politics was in his blood and in spite of contesting several seats (Pontefract in 1868, Wenlock in 1874 and Knaresborough in 1881), it was not until 1885 that he achieved his ambition and was elected Liberal MP for Morley, in Yorkshire, until 1892.

James enjoyed the generous hospitality of the Gaskells. "I certainly like them" he wrote, adding that he found his host "an excellent fellow, an entertaining companion & the pearl of hosts".[10] The feeling was mutual.[11] The mid-summer bad weather contributed to the bonding, enabled them to get to know each other for they "talked together as people talk in an English country-house when, during the three days of a visit, two, alas, turn out too brutally pluvial. This is a rather big thorn on the Wenlock rose, which, however, on my first day, bloomed irreproachably".[12] How very grateful James was to receive the invitation: "It was therefore all the more meritorious in them to invite me hither, where they have come only for a week, to interrupt London & be alone."[13]

Gaskell's young bride, whom he had married on 7 December 1876, was Lady Catherine Henrietta Wallop: she was the daughter of the 5th Earl of Portsmouth, of Hurstborne Park, Whitchurch, Hampshire, a descendant of the great scientist Sir Isaac Newton. At the time of James's visit, Lady Catherine was only twenty years old and was six months' pregnant with her first child, a son Evelyn, to be born on 19 October 1877. A second child, her daughter Mary, was born in 1882. It was not until late February 1877 that Gaskell brought his bride to

Wenlock where she was warmly welcomed as the Lady of the Manor and celebrations took place in the town throughout the day.

Although Adams knew Gaskell well, he had never met Lady Catherine – they were not to meet until June 1879.[14] Aware of James's great literary skill in portraying female beauty, he requested a description of her. James was delighted to comply, for he was enchanted by her youth, charm and her Englishness, and, he dared to admit, a little in love with her. He sent Adams "not only a full-length, but a colossal, portrait" of the Wenlock "rose without a thorn", likening her to a character in a Shakespeare play or a Gainsborough painting. But he avoids a factual description of her and instead uses the power of suggestion through literary metaphors. We do not know what she is wearing other than being "expensively & picturesquely ill-dressed":

A rose without a thorn, moreover, is Lady Catherine G., of whom you asked for a description. I can't give you a trustworthy one, for I really think I am in love with her. She is a singularly charming creature – a perfect English beauty of the finest type. She is, as I suppose you know, very young, girlish, childish: she strikes me as having taken a long step straight from the governess-world into a particularly luxurious form of matrimony. She is very tall, rather awkward & not well made, wonderfully fresh & fair, expensively & picturesquely ill-dressed, charmingly mannered &, I should say, intensely in love with her husband. She would not in the least strike you at first as a beauty (save for complexion:) but presently you would agree with me that her face is a remarkable example of the classic English sweetness & tenderness – the thing that Shakespeare, Gainsborough &c, may have meant to indicate. And this not at all stupidly – on the contrary, with a great deal of vivacity, spontaneity & cleverness. She says very good things, smiles adorably & appeals to her husband with beautiful inveteracy & naturalness. There is something very charming in seeing a woman in her 'position' so perfectly fresh & girlish. She will doubtless, some day, become more of a British matron or of a fine lady; but I suspect she will never lose (not after 20 London seasons) a certain bloom of shyness & softness.– But I am drawing not only a full-length, but a colossal, portrait.[15]

James is a model of discretion about her pregnancy: the reference to her as "a woman in her 'position'" being a veiled allusion to her physical state.

Lady Catherine was a sensitive, caring person with a keen interest in gardening, history, literature and the arts. She kept records of conversations and made copious notes, many of which are incorporated into *Spring in a Shropshire Abbey* (1905) chronicling a cycle of her life between January and July at Wenlock Abbey with her daughter Bess (Mary), her staff (gardener, gamekeeper, butler, cook, housekeeper), friends and local characters. She enjoyed some fame as a writer, especially about Shropshire life. Over the years she welcomed to her home the novelist Thomas Hardy (1840-1928), the Arts and Crafts architect and designer Philip Webb (1831-1915), the explorer Henry Morton Stanley and other eminent people. She was skilled with a bodkin and, with a team of helpers, including her friend Constance who lived nearby in the Red House, produced a colourful embroidery, a "huge text worked in wool", depicting four angels praising God: it was based on Burne-Jones's *Angeli Laudantes*, a design that was used for stained-glass windows and tapestries. Sometimes she worked alone on the embroidery and on one occasion she referred to her work on a particular motif, a blue dragon:

> Ten minutes later, and I was seated before my embroidery. Today I had a blue dragon to work. I tried to see and to reproduce in my mind's eye Burne Jones' wonderful tints of blue with brown shades and silver lights, and so the hours passed.[16]

Lady Catherine described more fully the embroidery:

The background is of yellow linen and is thickly covered with fourteenth and fifteenth century birds, beasts, and flowers, and in the centre of each there is an angel.

Each curtain is three yards four inches, by two yards four inches. The birds, beasts, and flowers are all finely shaded and are worked in crewels, tapestry wools divided, in darning and fine Berlin wools, and all these various sorts seem to harmonize and mingle wonderfully well together.

The picture, for it really is a picture, was drawn for me by a very skilful draughtsman. The birds, beasts, and angels have been taken from old Italian work, from mediæval stained-glass windows, and from old missals, and then drawn out to scale. There are Tudor roses, Italian carnations, sprays of shadowy love-in-the-mist, dusky wallflowers, and delightful half-heraldic birds and beasts, running up and hanging down the stems. It is a great work.[17]

Her work was created for the oratory in her Abbey. It was eventually placed in Holy Trinity Church, where it still hangs.[18]

James would have nurtured her interest in the Arts and Crafts with first-hand accounts of his meetings with Morris and his circle, and descriptions of Burne-Jones's paintings. He may also have shared his impressions of the Turners he had seen at the Ruskin family home at Denmark Hill on his visit in 1869. Perhaps memories of these were revived by the sight of "two Turners" hanging on the panelled wall of the chapel hall in Wenlock Abbey?[19] One of Turner's wealthy patrons was Sir Watkin Williams Wynn II (1749-1789): Lady Catherine's husband was a descendant of the Williams Wynn family and would most likely have inherited the two Turner paintings.

Lady Catherine died in 1935 and is buried in the churchyard of Holy Trinity Church, Much Wenlock, in the shadow of her beloved Abbey and Priory.

* * *

James lived for five days at Wenlock Abbey – he was the sole guest of Charles Milnes Gaskell and Lady Catherine, not part of a large house party – in a state of heightened awareness and creativity, conscious of every detail and nuance, observing, recording and accumulating a wealth of impressions. He was a sophisticated, sensitive guest and in his writings about his stay – and James felt compelled to write – he mingled "discretion with enthusiasm",[20] not wishing to violate the hospitality, the "act of private courtesy"[21] afforded him by his host. This was his very first experience of living in an inhabited, authentic medieval abbey, far removed from William Morris's "medieval *mise-en-scène* of Queen Square".[22] It was the essence of what was lacking in America and exactly what James craved. Nathaniel Hawthorne, in his preface to his novel *Transformation*, had recognised the "difficulty of writing a romance about a country where there is no shadow, no antiquity, no mystery, no picturesque".[23] James listed at length and with greater emphasis things that were "absent from the texture of American life" and, to a degree, obstacles to his creativity:

> No sovereign, no court, no personal loyalty, no aristocracy, no church, no clergy, no army, no diplomatic service, no country gentlemen, no palaces, no castles, nor manors, nor old country-houses, nor parsonages, nor thatched cottages nor ivied ruins; no cathedrals, nor abbeys, nor little Norman churches; no great Universities nor public schools – no Oxford, nor Eton, nor Harrow; no literature, no novels, no museums, no pictures, no political society, no sporting class – no Epsom nor Ascot![24]

Gaskell epitomised so much that James admired and sought: educated at Eton and Trinity College, Cambridge, of a prestigious and ancient lineage, inhabiting a medieval abbey.

James steeped himself in the atmosphere and recreated the working abbey, priory and church of the Middle Ages: life before the vandalism and dissolution of the monasteries in the 16th century, an iconoclastic act that art critic Waldemar Januszczak has described as "a cultural tsunami that eradicated a millenni-um's worth of British artistic achievement".[25] How ironic that Gaskell's *alma mater* (Trinity) was founded by the same powerful man (King Henry VIII) who expelled the monks from Wenlock Abbey. James's abbey is soon peopled with ghosts of the monks, friars and abbots, carrying on with their centuries-old rituals in silence and in obedience to the rules of their order. Some came from Burgundy in 1080, from the priory at La Charité-sur-Loire, a daughter house of the great Cluny Abbey.

Among the ruined Priory church and other remains, James attempts to recreate the vast edifice and restore it to its original grandeur:

> Adjoining the house is a beautiful ruin, part of the walls and windows and bases of the piers of the magnificent church administered by the predecessor of your host, the abbot. These relics are very desultory, but they are still abundant, and they testify to the great scale and the stately beauty of the abbey.[26]

As James lies on the grass near the stumps of the four central pillars that supported the tower, he is well placed to grasp the huge girth – approximately twelve yards – of these diamond-shaped columns, some four yards in diameter:

> You may lie upon the grass at the base of an ivied fragment, measure the girth of the great stumps of the central columns, half smothered in soft creepers, and think how strange it is that in this quiet hollow, in the midst of lonely hills, so exquisite and elaborate a work of art should have arisen.[27]

Those ruins that were visible were overgrown and in a state of considerable decay. They were the Romantic subject matter of picturesque paintings by artists such as Paul Sandby Munn (1773-1845), Paul Sandby (1730/31-1809), the Rev. Edward Pryce Owen (1788-1863) and John Sell Cotman (1782-1842). Cotman and Munn travelled together in the summer of 1802,

leaving London in early July, reaching Bridgnorth on 8 July and
then Wenlock where both drew the Priory: they continued to
Broseley, Ironbridge, Coalbrookdale and Buildwas.[28] Horses,
cattle and sheep were often depicted grazing among the ruins.
As the roofs collapsed and the walls fell down and crumbled,
local people collected the rubble in barrow loads for building
cottages, sheds, outhouses and roads. In *Spring in a Shropshire
Abbey*, Lady Catherine Milnes Gaskell documents the vivid
memories of local people who used the Priory and Abbey ruins
as a quarry and took whatever stone they needed. One of the
worst offenders appears to have been "'King Collins', as the old
people used to call Sir Watkin's agent, who lived in the red-brick
house which is now the vicarage, [who] carted away whatever he
had a mind to".[29] The vandalism of Sir Watkin Williams Wynn's
trusted employee – W. W. Wynn was then the owner of the
Priory and Abbey estate – seems to have been widely known and
this shocking state of affairs is confirmed in Murray's *Handbook*:
"A large portion of the abbey was pulled down many years ago
by a Vandal in the shape of a house agent, but further ruin was
stopped by the then Sir W. W. Wynn."[30]

At the time of James's visit, many of the ruins were hidden
deep beneath long grass and briar. He did not know that he was
sitting near a grassy mound that concealed part of a rare feature
– the great free-standing lavabo or *lavatorium*. It was strategically situated in the south west corner of the cloister, near the
entrance to the refectory, for the monks' cursory ablutions after
their heavy and dirty manual work in the fields, forests and
gardens, before they ate in the communal room or went into the
church. The existence of the lavabo may have been unknown to
Gaskell and his family: it is not mentioned in Murray's first
Handbook for Shropshire of 1870. In its heyday in the twelfth
century, the covered octagonal open arcaded building, three
storeys high, supported by columns, could accommodate
sixteen monks simultaneously washing their hands. Water from
a nearby well was piped into a large, round basin in the centre of

the lavabo, and like an elaborate fountain gushed through the mouths of sixteen carved heads into the circular trough below. The gargoyles or spout heads were embedded in the lower part of highly decorative sculpted designs. The base of this trough was faced with carved slabs, cut to the curve, approximately two and a half feet high. The entire construction was of local limestone, the famous Wenlock marble known locally as bellstone on account of its sonority. It must have been a magnificent and awe-inspiring monument until much of it was destroyed after the dissolution of the Priory in 1540. However, the inner part partially survived, protected through the centuries by the covering of mother earth, and was not unearthed until after James's first visit.

In keeping with the aesthetics of the construction, the panels around the base were probably all carved with religious scenes, although only two of these survive. On 16 October 1882, Gaskell sent Henry Adams photographs of some saints he had discovered. Adams replied, on 3 December 1882:

> My dear Carlo,
> Your letter of Oct. 16 has been lying some weeks on my table, and the photographs of your discovered saints have adorned my library. They are interesting, and if you find out when they were done, I would like to know.[31]

This may be a reference to the two existing panels. One of the sculptured stone panels around the base represents two contemplative saints, standing in coupled arches. The beardless saint on the left is supporting his chin and cheek with his left hand whereas the stocky, bushy-bearded figure on the right – possibly St John the Evangelist or St Paul whose usual attributes are a book – is pressing a heavy tome, the Word of God, to his chest. Another panel depicts two rowing boats, one above each other, framed beneath a trefoiled arch. There is an oarsman and a male passenger in each. In the upper boat, the passenger appears to be sleepy: his head is drooping and his raised hand gesture implies a rejection of some kind. The lower boat is clearly half immersed in turbulent water, and the right hand of the bearded passenger (possibly one of the disciples) is gripped tightly by a Christ-like figure standing on water. The symbolism of water would have been most appropriate for the lavabo.

As soon as James crosses the threshold of his host's abode, "through an old Norman portal, massively arched and quaintly sculptured, [...] the ghosts of monks and the shadows of abbots pass noiselessly to and fro". "This aperture admits you to a beautiful ambulatory of the thirteenth century – a long stone gallery or cloister, repeated in two stories, with the interstices of its traceries now glazed, but with its long low, narrow, charming vista still perfect and picturesque – with its flags worn away by monkish sandals, and with huge round-arched doorways opening from its inner side into great rooms roofed like cathedrals."[32]

These "great rooms" are "furnished with narrow windows, of almost defensive aspect, set in embrasures three feet deep, and ornamented with little grotesque mediæval faces".[33] They are omnipresent and belong there: "to see one of the small monkish masks grinning at you while you dress and undress, or while you look up in the intervals of inspiration from your letter writing, is a mere detail in the entertainment of living in a *ci-devant* priory."[34] In this ancient house, the remote past is all around and inescapable: so intense is the experience that "you feast upon the pictorial, you inhale the historic".[35] On arrival at Medley Park, Hyacinth Robinson (hero of *The Princess Casamassima*) experiences a not dissimilar reaction: "Round the admirable house he revolved repeatedly; catching every point and tone, feasting on its expression."[36] James's senses are heightened: his vision becomes acute, his sense of smell is laden with layers of the past, his historic consciousness flows.

The ancient building is imbued with mystery and life. Like an infusion, six hundred years of living history are transmitted, effortlessly yet with such force, so that even after only twenty-four hours he feels that he has lived in the place for six centuries. Here is "an accumulation of history and custom" that forms "a fund of suggestion for a novelist"[37] that is indispensable. He is part of the process of time and contributes to the wearing away of the fabric: "You seem yourself to have hollowed the flags with your tread," he reflects, "and to have polished the oak with your touch".[38] This Jamesian motif is echoed, nearly forty years later, in Marcel Proust's great novel *In Search of Lost Time*. In the little church of Combray, the worshippers' actions of gentle touching contribute, slowly and almost imperceptibly, to the "destructive force" of time:

> The old porch by which we entered, black, pocked like a skimming ladle, was uneven and deeply hollowed at the edges […], as if the gentle brushing of the countrywomen's cloaks as they entered the church and of their timid fingers taking holy water could, repeated over centuries, acquire a destructive force, bend the stone and carve it with furrows like those traced by the wheel of a cart in a boundary-stone which it knocks against every day. Its tombstones, under which the noble dust of the abbots of Combray, who were buried there, formed for the choir a sort of spiritual pavement, were themselves no longer inert and hard matter, for time had softened them and made them flow like honey beyond the bounds of their own square shapes […].[39]

As James strolls along the stone ambulatory on his way to the drawing-room, he is particularly aware of the passage of time, manifest in the crooked step and in the cracked lintels "worn by the myriad-fingered years". So acutely does he sense the perpetuation and continuity of life, that he dons, metaphorically, the mantle of a monk, and repeats their age-old rhythms, motions and gestures, even to the extent of casting a glance back down the cloister just before going through the round-arched doorway at the end:

You walk along the little stone gallery where the monks used to pace, looking out of the gothic window-places at their beautiful church, and you pause at the big round, rugged doorway that admits you to what is now the drawing-room. The massive step by which you ascend to the threshold is a trifle crooked, as it should be; the lintels are cracked and worn by the myriad-fingered years. This strikes your casual glance. You look up and down the miniature cloister before you pass in; it seems wonderfully old and queer.[40]

Past and present happily co-exist and even fuse. As he turns into "what is now the drawing-room", where he will find "modern conversation and late publications and the prospect of dinner", he is fully aware that the "new life and the old have melted together; there is no dividing-line".[41]

In the "drawing-room wall" an unusual detail attracts his attention: "a queer funnel-shaped hole, with a broad end inward, like a small casemate."[42] James asked what it was, "but people have forgotten". His enquiries did not elicit satisfactory answers: "It is something of the monks; it is a mere detail" was the response. It was indeed "something of the monks" who had cut the funnel-shaped hole so that herbs and medicines could be dropped down through it to be picked up by the highly infectious and often severely disfigured lepers and untouchables, who were confined to a lazaret a few minutes' walk away in the woods at a place known as the Spittle. They were obliged to carry a bell to announce their arrival.

Occupying "a distinguished position in the drawing room" was a three-panelled, six-foot-high screen. Each was decorated with floral motifs: a large white lily with leaves on the left-hand panel, and smaller white flowers (different types of lilies) on the other two panels. This "handsomest appurtenance" was a wedding present from Henry and Clover Adams and James reports that the screen had been a particular subject of conversation:

[Gaskell] furthermore calls my attention to the screen you sent him on his marriage & which occupies a distinguished position in the drawing room, & bids me say that he & his wife consider it their handsomest appurtenance. It is indeed very handsome & 'reflects great credit' as the newspapers say, on American workmanship. I pretend, patriotically, to Gaskell, that in America *nous n'en voyons pas d'autres*; but, in fact, I seem to myself to recognise in it the exceptional inspiration of your wife.[43]

James's evening would not be complete without a ghost appearing in the haunted Abbey:

> After dinner you are told that there is of course a ghost – a gray friar who is seen in the dusky hours at the end of passages. Sometimes the servants see him; they afterwards go surreptitiously to sleep in the village. Then, when you take your chamber-candle and go wandering bedward by a short cut through empty rooms, you are conscious of a peculiar sentiment toward the gray friar which you hardly know whether to interpret as a hope or a reluctance.[44]

At Medley Park, Hyacinth Robinson is shown a "haunted chamber [...] where a dreadful individual at certain times made his appearance – a dwarfish ghost, with an enormous head, a dispossessed brother, of long ago".[45] Ralph Touchett's Winchester Square abode, in *The Portrait of a Lady*, has a "hint of the supernatural" in the "ghostly presence as of dinners long since digested".[46] Isobel Archer, recently arrived from America, yearns to see a ghost in the old country house of Gardencourt and asks: "Please tell me – isn't there a ghost?"[47] The question is answered at the end of *The Portrait of a Lady* when the ghost of kind Ralph, who has just died after a long illness, appears to Isabel as a sign of comfort, not terror.[48] *The Turn of the Screw*, James's most masterly and spooky of stories, set in a rambling country house, has a plot in which two of the characters are ghosts – the servant Peter Quint and the previous governess Miss Jessel, both most likely murdered. Like the ghost of the gray friar whom

James accommodated so seemlessly and gently at Wenlock Abbey, Quint and Jesssel are alive and an integral part of Bly, a fictional country house in Essex. James's interest in the supernatural coincided with the rise of spiritualism that gained credence in the nineteenth century with the developing telecommunications systems. The tapping or knocking of the telegraph transmitting messages across continents was thought by some to be spirits communicating. In November 1863, he had heard the spiritualist, Cora L.V. Hatch, lecture in New York. As we have seen, Ruskin too was not immune to spiritualism in the hope of speaking to Rose La Touche.

* * *

The small, rural market town in which James found himself in 1877 was still in many ways a medieval settlement. Farms with livestock were attached to dwellings (Brook House Farm in Queen Street, in the town centre, was still a working farm in the twenty-first century). There were regular stock markets for the sale and purchase of horses, sheep and cattle, as well as general markets for fruit, vegetables, flowers, homemade cakes, pies, jams, pickles and other produce. Animals roamed around the streets: bull-baiting, by dogs, was a popular form of entertainment. Waggoners and farmers with their carts and horses drove noisily up and down the cobbles.

Alongside the many timber-framed dwellings of all shapes and sizes – weavers' cottages, smithy, Raynald's Mansion, Ashfield Hall – fine red brick town houses for the local gentry had been built. One of these solid red brick houses was No. 4 Wilmore Street, the two-storey home of Dr William Penny Brookes (1809-1895), medical practitioner and surgeon. Penny Brookes was, like Ruskin, a polymath and philanthropist. He was a botanist who not only collected and recorded specimens that he kept in his many herbaria, in special cabinets with shelves, but aimed to enhance the environment by planting trees and shrubs. He took a keen and active interest in Much Wenlock. He founded the Agricultural Reading Society, mainly for local farmers, in 1841 and organised educational classes in Drawing (copying anatomical specimens), Music and Botany. For him, Physical Education was a priority, in and out of school, especially competitive sport – running, bicycle races, athletics and traditional country games. His organised games flourished and were described as "Olympian", as in "Olympian Class" and "Wenlock Olympian Society". From these local initiatives Brookes and a small committee (John Murray, the publisher was a member) founded a National Olympian Association in November 1865. In France, the great apostle of sport was a wealthy, intelligent, energetic Parisian Baron Pierre de Coubertin (1863-1937). The work and zeal of Brookes came to his attention and he visited his mentor in Much Wenlock in 1890. Coubertin, inspired by Brookes, set up a large sports federation and founded in 1896, shortly after Brookes's death, the modern Olympic movement. It is true to say that the Olympic Games were revived thanks to Anglo-French cooperation and enthusiasm. Brookes also campaigned vigorously and successfully for a railway to come to Wenlock. He is buried in Wenlock churchyard, near the tombs of the Gaskell family.

While physical health was being championed by Brookes, public health was threatened by poor sanitation. It was still basic: an open sewer (euphemistically called a brook) ran through the middle of the town, from the high ground on the Stretton Road in the west, down the High Street, past the Fox Hotel, along Back Lane, by Brook House Farm (hence the name) and across the road into the precincts of the remains of the monastery. People crossed over Rea Brook on the many wooden bridges. Even as late as 1890, Charles Milnes Gaskell complained of "the present offensive state of the brook that passed through the town".[49] Flooding was also a common occurrence.

It was a town with many old alehouses ("publics"), hostelries and important coaching inns such as the Wynnstay Arms (now the Gaskell Arms) and the Fox. There were malthouses for the drying of hops and the preparation of ale, a safer beverage than water drawn from one of the wells with a high risk of being infected with cholera. At least two wells were dedicated to saints – to St Owen and to St Milburga. As well as honouring their piety, this was no doubt also an attempt to invoke their protection of the purity of the water and the health of the townsfolk. St Owen was an early Christian missionary who was reputed to have come to Much Wenlock, from Brittany, in the 6th century. St Milburga was the second Abbess of the early Wenlock monastery for both monks and nuns founded around 680 by her father King Merewalh of Mercia.

However, this seemingly sleepy town was part of an important borough that, up until 1868, had been represented by two MPs in the Westminster parliament: that privilege was gradually reduced under the Reform Acts. When James stayed in Much Wenlock, the only MP (a Conservative) was The Hon. Cecil Theodore Weld Forester of nearby Willey Hall: he was the last MP for the borough, from 1874 until he retired in 1885, at which date the "Redistribution of Seats Act" removed Wenlock's independent representation. Cecil Forester's contender for the one remaining Wenlock seat in 1874 had been the unsuccessful Liberal candidate, Charles Milnes Gaskell!

James resumed Much Wenlock as "an ancient little town at the abbey-gates – a town, indeed, with no great din of vehicles, but with goodly brick houses, with a dozen 'publics', with tidy, whitewashed cottages, and with little girls [...] bobbing curtsies in the street".[50]

* * *

Chapter 15

Possessing Stokesay and Ludlow

On Friday 13th July, Gaskell accompanied James to the historic border towns of Ludlow in south Shropshire, and Shrewsbury, the Salopian capital, both famed for their timber-framed buildings, cobbled streets, alley ways, historic churches and castles. They also stopped at the village of Stokesay, nestling in the Onny valley, with its impressive castle, one of the earliest fortified mansions of the thirteenth century, and large timber-framed Tudor gatehouse, surrounded by a deep, wide moat. We do not know the order of their itinerary, nor the kind of transport used, but all of these places were easily accessible at that time by rail from Much Wenlock, thanks to the efforts of Penny Brookes and other prominent local people. A straightforward round trip of approximately sixty-five miles would have been the following: Much Wenlock to Shrewsbury via Buildwas (change); Shrewsbury to Craven Arms (for Stokesay); Craven Arms to Ludlow; returning from Ludlow to Craven Arms (change) where they could take a direct train to Much Wenlock. James summarised the day in his letter to Adams: "The morning after my arrival, luckily, Gaskell & I started off & made an heroic day of it – a day I shall always remember most tenderly. We went to Ludlow, to Stokesay & to Shrewsbury & we saw them all in perfection."[1] James's only other comment about Shrewsbury, the birthplace of Charles Darwin, was that it was "most capital".

* * *

Henry Adams had given James lots of information about Shropshire and had told him "not to fail [...] to go to Stokesay and two or three other places [in the neighbourhood where] Edward IV and Elizabeth are still hanging about".[2] Adams would have been pleased to receive James's report of his immense enjoyment:

> You spoke of Stokesay, & I found it of course a gem. We lay there on the grass in the delicious little *préau*, beside the wall, with every feature of the old place still solid & vivid around us, & I don't think that, as a sensation, I ever dropped back, for an hour, more effectually into the past. Ludlow, too, is quite incomparable & Shrewsbury most capital. The whole thing made a delightful day.[3]

Adams would have been even more delighted to identify himself as "a friend of mine, an American" and to read of James's intense response to Stokesay (and other places) in his essay "Abbeys and Castles" published later that year.

After alighting at the railway junction of Craven Arms, James and Gaskell walked about a mile along the road in the direction of Stokesay. Near the church, they turned into a narrow path in the churchyard with holly trees and ancient yews. There they were among monuments made of sandstone, granite, limestone, polished black marble, and a variety of memorials – chest tombs, altar tombs, standing gravestones. The little church of St John the Baptist, with its castellated square tower, was founded in the twelfth century and rebuilt in the seventeenth century owing to extensive damage in the Civil War. At the time of James's visit, the vicar was the Rev. James Digues La Touche (1824-1899), an enthusiastic amateur naturalist, geologist and historian. He belonged to the powerful Irish family one of whose members, Rose La Touche, had been romantically involved with John Ruskin.

On approaching the castle grounds, adjoining the churchyard, they crossed a little bridge over "a good deep moat, now
filled with wild verdure", went through the large oak, nail-
studded gatehouse door, then entered the inner courtyard.
There they lay, stretched out on a warm summer's day on that
"grassy, æsthetic spot":[4] "a couple of gentlemen in search of
impressions [...] one of whom has taken a wine-flask out of his
pocket and has coloured the clear water drawn for them out of
the well in a couple of tumblers by a decent, rosy, smiling,
talking old woman, who has come bustling out of the gatehouse,
and who has a large, dropsical, innocent husband standing
about on crutches in the sun."[5] The two well-dressed city gents,
enjoying their claret diluted with water from the medieval well,
speaking with accents that set them apart as foreigners from
America and London, attracted the curiosity of the incongruous
couple – the talkative, bustling housekeeper and her uncommu-
nicative, sickly husband. James's attempt to converse with him
and enquire about his health met with silence and a stony stare.
   Since 1992, Stokesay Castle has been under the guardianship
of English Heritage and has been open to the public. But at the
time of James's visit, it was in private hands and had been purchased in 1869 by John Derby Allcroft (1822-1893). Allcroft
owed his fortune to the success of his London business making
and selling ladies' leather gloves, essential articles of clothing in
a Victorian lady's wardrobe. Allcroft was a philanthropist and
gave large sums of money to charities. He also gave freely of his
time as Treasurer of Christ's Hospital, a boys' school in Newgate
Street, London: Ruskin was a governor of the school. When
Ruskin gave an address, "A Lecture on Stones", to the boys in
April 1876, Allcroft proposed a vote of thanks.[6] From 1873 and
for the next twenty years until his death he devoted himself to
the repair and restoration of Stokesay, "at very considerable
expense and with much skill and judgment",[7] a task continued
by the Allcroft family who opened the castle to the public in
1908. Allcroft also built for himself a splendid country mansion

called Stokesay Court (approximately two miles south of Stokesay Castle in the village of Onibury), designed by architect Thomas Harris (1829/30-1900) and completed in 1889.

Unlike Ruskin, who avoids any mention of the human presence in his depiction of cathedrals and churches (*The Seven Lamps of Architecture* and *The Stones of Venice* are literally about stones), James needs, even craves, a picturesque scene. On his little tour of France in 1882, he wrote: "I stopped at Beaune in pursuit of the picturesque."[8] He found that at Stokesay. Although the rooms in the uninhabited castle – no one had lived in it since Queen Anne's time – were "in a state of extreme decay",[9] a male artist was "reproducing its mouldering repose".[10] Outside, a young, female artist was also at work: "From one of the windows I see a young lady sitting under a tree, across a meadow, with her knees up, dipping something into her mouth. It is a camel's hair paint-brush; [...]. These are the only besiegers to which the place is exposed now, and they can do no great harm, as I doubt whether the young lady's aim is very good."[11]

They gazed at the gables of the great Banqueting Hall with mullion windows flanked by massive buttresses against the solid, thick stonewalls of this "small *gentilhommière* of the thirteenth century". James became totally absorbed in the past, crossing the centuries: "I have rarely had, for a couple of hours, the sensation of dropping back personally into the past in a higher degree than while I lay on the grass beside the well in the little sunny court of this small castle, and lazily appreciated the still definite details of mediæval life."[12]

He was particularly struck by the incongruity of the "curious gatehouse of a much later period"[13] and the "fortress" (castle): "This gate-house, which is not in the least in the style of the habitation, but gabled and heavily timbered, with quaint cross-beams protruding from surfaces of coarse white plaster, is a very effective anomaly in regard to the little gray fortress on the other side of the court."[14]

It is through the observation of an architectural detail – the castle's unusually large windows, instead of the more secure, narrow protective slits associated with defences – that James constructs the genteel life of its former inhabitants. The fortress, he observes, "must have assumed its present shape at a time when people had ceased to peer through narrow slits at possible besiegers. There are slits in the outer walls for such peering, but they are noticeably broad and not particularly oblique, and might easily have been applied to the uses of a peaceful parley".[15] This contributes to the "charm of the place; [when] human life there must have lost an earlier grimness [and] was lived in by people who were beginning to believe in good intentions".[16]

James and Gaskell "wandered about the empty interior, thinking it a pity such things should fall to pieces". They went in the "beautiful great hall [...] with tall, ecclesiastical-looking windows, and a long staircase at one end, climbing against the wall into a spacious bedroom".[17] The room at the top of the stair-case, with its "irregular shape, its low-browed ceiling, its cup-boards in the walls, and its deep bay windows formed of a series of small lattices"[18] was particularly evocative of the past. It stim-ulated James's imagination and from it he recreated what he called "the historic vision":[19] "You can", he continued, "fancy people stepping out from it upon the platform of the staircase, whose rugged wooden logs, by way of steps, and solid, deeply-guttered hand-rail, still remain". From that vantage point, "they looked down into the hall, where [...] there was always a con-gregation of retainers, much lounging and waiting and passing to and fro, with a door open into the court".[20] It was the ideal place from which the lord and lady of the house could view fes-tivities in the court below – "groups on the floor [...], the calling up and down, the oaken tables spread, and the brazier in the middle"[21] – and if necessary issue orders. But the courtyard in the middle ages was a rough terrain, not grassy and soft: "there were beasts tethered in it, and hustling men-at-arms, and the earth was trampled into puddles."[22] James's "historic vision" became more complete as he pursued it through the rest of the building, "through the portion which connected the great hall with the tower […] through the dusky, roughly circular rooms of the tower itself, and up the corkscrew staircase of the same to that most charming part of every old castle, where visions must leap away off the battlements to elude you – the bright, dizzy platform at the tower-top, the place where the castle-standard hung and the vigilant inmates surveyed the approaches".[23] The past becomes present again. In a final flourish of the pen, Stokesay Castle is anthropomorphised – it becomes a trapped animal of the chase – thereby enabling James to grasp, possess and appropriate it more easily: "Here, always, you really overtake the impression of the place – here, in the sunny stillness, it seems to pause, panting a little, and give itself up."[24] He has at last totally absorbed what he calls "the aesthetic presence of the past".[25] His feelings were an extension of those exuberant words he uttered in his letter of 1 November 1875, to his family, shortly after arriving in London from America: "I take possession of the old world – I inhale it – I appropriate it! I have been in it now these twenty-four hours […] and feel as if I had been here for ten years."[26]

In 1882, James visited Aigues-Mortes ("Dead Waters"), the curiously named walled town on the edge of the marshy Camargue on the delta of the river Rhône in the south of France. Although his impressions are much less personal and less dramatic that those of Shropshire, when concluding his visit, he climbed the thirty-metre-high fortress *Tour de Constance* and experienced similar feelings of possession-taking:

> From the battlements at the top, […] you see the little compact rectangular town, which looks hardly bigger than a garden-patch, mapped out beneath you, and follow the plain configuration of its defences. You take possession of it, and you feel that you will remember it always.[27]

* * *

Ludlow is situated about six miles south east of Stokesay. Its fortress castle was strategically built on the highest point of the town, originally to fend off the then hostile Welsh. Its other important landmark is the pink sandstone church of St Laurence, the largest parish church in Shropshire and known as the "cathedral of Shropshire". In the wooded valley the gentle river Teme partly encircles Ludlow before continuing on its seventy-five-mile journey from the hills on the Welsh border to Powick in Worcestershire where it joins the river Severn.

Ludlow railway station opened in 1852, due in large measure to the engineering skills of Thomas Brassey (1805-1870), complete with a gabled stationmaster's house, passengers' waiting-rooms and other facilities. On arrival, Gaskell and James walked up some steps and as they crossed the footbridge over the railway line, they saw in the distance St Laurence's Church. Its pinnacled, lofty square tower, one hundred and thirty-five feet high, rebuilt in the fifteenth century in the perpendicular style, dominated the town. The visitors would have many opportunities to hear the famous eight bells in the tower chime with their different melodies. They walked along Station Drive, then turned left into Corve Street, a mainly residential area with stately, solid, Georgian brick houses and inviting doorways enhanced with elegant pediments and traceries. Gaskell and James became increasingly aware that they were in a hilltown for as they approached the Bull Ring the gradient was noticeably steeper. On their left, in Corve Street, they admired the richly decorated, timber-framed Feathers Hotel of 1603, and facing it, the Bull Hotel. They turned right into King Street, past St Laurence's, and continued up a gentle slope, along the historic High Street that opened into Castle Square, a bustling market place in the shadow of the castle.

They then made their way to the castle, whose solidity was painted by Turner on several occasions as a picturesque scene. It was here in the great council chamber that John Milton's *Masque of Comus* was first performed in 1634. This was a revelry starring Comus a pagan god of Milton's invention, written specially for the Earl of Bridgewater to celebrate his appointment as Lord President of the Council of the Marches, the governing body for the border counties (known as Marches), with the seat of power at Ludlow Castle. The tradition of a performance of *Comus* in the castle, usually in the open air, has continued for centuries. Ludlow Castle had many royal connections. Young Prince Edward (the uncrowned King Edward V) spent much of his childhood there, before his imprisonment and subsequent death in the Tower of London in 1483. This was a story that James had learnt about from Delaroche's painting when he first visited the Louvre in 1855. The seventeen-year-old Catherine of Aragon once lived in the castle for five months with her fifteen-year-old husband Prince Arthur (son of King Henry VII) until his death from consumption in 1502. She later married her husband's brother, King Henry VIII. Another royal visitor was Queen Mary Tudor who spent three winters at Ludlow between 1525 and 1528. In the late seventeenth century the castle was abandoned and fell into decay. It was not until 1811 that it was rescued and purchased by the 2nd Earl of Powis: it remains in the ownership of that same family in the twenty-first century.

Gaskell, a man of exquisite courtesy, would almost certainly have contacted the Earl of Powis prior to the visit, but James does not mention meeting the owner or members of his family or indeed anyone else. They entered via the principal gateway in the outside curtain wall, crossed the castle yard or outer bailey and made their way to the little two-arched stone bridge over the dry, deep moat. Once through the massive studded oak door at Sir Henry Sidney's gateway, they stepped into the heart of the fortress, the inner bailey, also protected by a thick curtain wall. There they walked among the ruined remains of the little round chapel of St Mary Magdalene, the Great Hall or council chamber some sixty feet long and thirty feet wide, private apartments, kitchens, towers and other buildings. But it was the oldest part of the castle, the massive Norman keep, seventy-feet high, that

James wished to experience most of all. They entered through a low doorway immediately to the left of the entrance to the inner bailey, and climbed the steep, winding eight-hundred-year-old steps, peering at times through the slits hewed through the four-foot-thick wall. They paused on the platforms marking the storeys, until eventually reaching the summit crowned with battlements and all open to the sky. The magnificent countryside of Shropshire with the Wrekin to the north stretched far into the horizon: the Clee Hills stood out in the east, and nearer was wooded Whitcliffe Common and Dinham Bridge over the Teme in the west. The church of St Laurence and the medieval grid town of Ludlow nestled in the south east corner.

James was again in search of impressions, sensations and pulsations, and from that lofty vantage point he lingered in order "to enjoy the complete impression so overtaken".[28] Similarly, at Stokesay, he had positioned himself on a "platform at the tower-top" in order to "really overtake the impression of the place" (not forgetting the vantage point of Wenlock Edge). James was experiencing at first hand what he would develop as a recurring theme in his fiction, that of the protagonist observing from a privileged viewpoint such as a balcony or other height.[29] In *The Turn of the Screw*, little Flora takes her new governess on a tour of Bly "through empty chambers and dull corridors, on crooked staircases", but it is on reaching "the summit of an old machicolated square tower" that the governess feels dizzy.[30] This is a premonition of its significance later in the story, for the first terrifying apparition of the ghostly figure of the dead servant Peter Quint takes place high up at the very top of a square, crenellated tower among the battlements. As the governess observer-narrator confronts the past, the experience intensifies as the man stares at her, then moves to another crenellation, continues to pierce her with his eyes until he eventually turns away and disappears. The observer-writer experiences some of her/his most powerful emotions, "the whole feeling of the moment returns" intensified by the silence of the cawing rooks and the realisation that the scene was "stricken with death".[31] The medieval border castles of Ludlow and Stokesay provided James with possible models for Bly.

But away from the fortress castle, it was the elegant Georgian centre of Ludlow, so rich in literary, artistic and musical activities, that suited James. The carefully planned town was the exemplar of the setting for the novels of those quintessential English writers, Frances (Fanny) Burney – whose father Charles Burney was born in Shrewsbury and studied music there – and Jane Austen. It was a place where their heroines "might perfectly well have had their first love-affair", and to which a journey "would certainly have been a great event to Fanny Price or Emma Woodhouse, or even to those more exalted young ladies, Evelina and Cecilia".[32] It is "a place on which a provincial 'gentry' has left a sensible stamp". Seldom had Henry James seen "so good a collection of houses of the period between the elder picturesqueness and the modern baldness". The sight of these dwellings transports him to a pre-Victorian age, to a more insular English society with its traditions and its "narrowness of custom". In short, a non-cosmopolitan society that James, "a stranger", would, he recognises, have had difficulty in penetrating, not only in London but also in the provinces and in "a genteel little city like the one I am speaking of".[33]

James delights in being transported to this "most impressive and magnificent of ruins" that has remained intact and untouched by industrialisation and retains "a remarkable air of civic dignity". "Ludlow is", he writes, "an excellent example of a small English provincial town that has not been soiled and disfigured by industry: it exhibits no tall chimneys and smoke-streamers, with their attendant purlieus and slums."[34] The effects of good town planning, as well as the care people take in maintaining standards, are noticeable: "its streets are wide and clean, empty and a little grass-grown, and bordered with spacious, mildly-ornamental brick houses, which look as if there had been more going on in them in the first decade of the century than there is in the present, but which can still, nevertheless, hold up their heads and keep their window-panes clear, their knockers brilliant and their door steps whitened." Everything suggests to James that this was a very good "centre of a large provincial society".[35]

In a pre-railway age, James imagines society arriving for the season "in rumbling coaches and heavy curricles" to enjoy the abundance of cultural and social activities such as "balls at the assembly rooms". Assembly Rooms, mainly places for fashionable gatherings, were immensely popular in the eighteenth and nineteenth centuries: those to which James alludes date from 1840 and occupy a site on the corner of Mill Street and Castle Street in the town centre.

Celebrities left behind the London stage and flocked to perform in Ludlow: "Mrs Siddons to play" and her friend the renowned Italian soprano Angelica Catalani "to sing". The reference to the great English actress Sarah Siddons had a particular resonance for James for he knew her niece, Fanny Kemble, whom he described in *A Small Boy and Others* as "my fine old friend".[36] He also knew Adelaide Sartoris (Sarah Siddons's sister) and her daughter.[37] James adored the theatre from a very early age, and at one time even considered becoming a playwright but his theatrical novel, *The Tragic Muse,* was the closest he came to achieving that thwarted ambition. He was fascinated with Georgian England and admired the strong role and success of Mrs Siddons, immortalised in portraits by Gainsborough and Reynolds. In his short story *The Aspern Papers,* astonishment that the elderly English lady Miss Juliana Bordereau, the former lover of the great American poet Jeffrey Aspern and keeper of his valuable manuscripts, is alive in Venice is equal to that of learning that Mrs Siddons (or Queen Caroline or Lady Hamilton) still existed.[38] Sarah Siddons and her actor husband William were on stage for three consecutive nights, 15-17 August 1803, at Ludlow Theatre. She played the role of Desdemona, and her husband that of Iago in the first Ludlow performance of Shakespeare's tragedy *Othello* on Monday 15 August 1803. On Tuesday 16 August, sandwiched between *Othello* and *Hamlet*, they starred in *The Mountaineers* by George Colman 'the Younger' (1762-1836) and in *Deuce is in him*, a two-act farce by his father, George Colman 'the Elder' (1732-1794). In the grand finale in their honour on Wednesday 17 August, Mrs Siddons played Ophelia, and Mr Siddons was cast as Hamlet. A poster advertising these performances is preserved in Ludlow Museum and it is not inconceivable that James, seventy-four years later, visited the museum and obtained this information from that source.

Angelica Catalani (1780-1849), known as "Mme Cat" or "Mme Catalani", was the convent-educated daughter of a tradesman from Sinigaglia on Italy's Adriatic coast who became one of the most famous prima donnas of her day. One of her memorable operatic performances in London was on 3 July 1813 when news was announced of Wellington's victory at the battle of Vittoria. Madame de Staël, who was present on that occasion, reported that Catalani's rendering of "God save the King" caused all the ladies to rise to their feet and pray for their country.[810]

* * *

Chapter 16

A rainy English weekend:
Wenlock Edge and Buildwas Abbey

Plans for another excursion on Saturday 14 July had to be shelved owing to continuing heavy rain and bad weather, and necessitated staying indoors, at least for part of the day:

> Gaskell had proposed another for the morrow, but I am sorry to say that the heavens *dis*posed, otherwise. There is, however, a very handsome entertainment in simply loafing – lounging about such an interesting old house as this. I imagine, from what G. tells me, that it is better now than when you saw it – has more of its ancient detail uncovered & disentangled.[1]

James and Gaskell both enjoyed the Shropshire countryside and walking. Clover Adams noted in 1873 how vigorous Gaskell and his male friends were, how they "behave like young colts in a pasture" and "scour the hills on foot."[2] Their "afternoon's walk"[3] on Wenlock Edge ("the Edge" as it is known locally) took place, most likely, on Saturday 14 July, the only time not accounted for with precision in the reconstruction of the timetable of James's stay. Wenlock Edge is a steep, coppiced escarpment – a rich geological limestone seam with fossils and rare wild flowers – that stretches in unbroken line for approximately eighteen miles from the Ironbridge Gorge, via Much Wenlock, Presthope,

Wilderhope, Church Stretton to Craven Arms. This is the ridge beloved of A. E. Housman in his poem *A Shropshire Lad* of 1896 when he wrote:

> On Wenlock Edge the wood's in trouble,
> His forest fleece the Wrekin heaves;
> The gale, it plies the saplings double,
> And thick on Severn snow the leaves.

To reach the crest of the Edge, James and Gaskell walked along the High Street, reaching the Gaskell Arms, past the vicarage on the left and on the right an eighteenth-century house with bow windows named "Pinefield": in the late nineteenth-century this was the home of the Rev. D. H. S. Cranage, vicar of Holy Trinity Church and learned local historian who became Dean of Norwich Cathedral. They went under the Wenlock to Craven Arms railway bridge, turned into the Church Stretton road and took the old packhorse road (leading to Shrewsbury) up Blakeway Hollow. Dense woods covered the steep slope on the right of the track: on the left (to the east), well beyond the fields of sheep, was the county of Staffordshire with the Black Country and Cannock. They looked down a cutting, which was in fact a vestige of the old road going towards Shrewsbury. As they climbed higher, among the wild orchids, wild garlic, spindle trees, maples, hawthorn, oak, beech, silver birch and ash, the Clee Hills unfolded to the south: they continued to follow the long ridge up to the Major's Leap, a cliff over which a local Royalist, Major Thomas Smallman, was reputed to have leapt, on horseback, to make a deft escape from his pursuers during the English Civil War. James had an impression of danger and awe. "The 'edge' plunged down suddenly", he wrote, "as if the corresponding slope on the other side had been excavated".[4] The two friends chatted and with great pride and affection Gaskell proclaimed: "I do believe it is the loveliest corner of the world!"[5] James concurred. When they reached the highest point, Ippikin's

Rock – so named after a legendary highwayman who inhabited a cave beneath the rock – the vast panoramic view encompassed Wales and the line of blue Welsh hills, Caer Caradoc and the Wrekin (both ancient Iron Age hill forts), the Lawley and the Long Mynd (5000 acres of heather-clad grouse moor), North Shropshire and the Cheshire Plains. From here, James looked across at the "hills and blue undulations" – the range of shades of pale to dark and threatening blue, purple and green is truly breathtaking – at this "exquisite modulation, something suggesting that outline and colouring have been retouched and refined by the hand of time". Such a landscape, with "the definite relics of the ages, [...] seems historic".[6]

From his "vantage-point", the seemingly small and compact county expands before his eyes, as the rich patchwork of colours and tones delineates the estates of the landed gentry. He associates the gradations of colour with wealth: thus "a darker patch across the lighter green [represents] the great estate of one of their lordships".[7] "Beyond these", he continues, "are blue undulations of varying tone, and then another bosky-looking spot, which constitutes [...] the residential umbrage of another peer. And to right and left of these, in wooded expanses, lie other domains of equal consequence".[8] In "this delightful region", he is enchanted by the "old red farmhouses lighting up the dark-green bottoms" of the hillsides, "gables and chimneytops of great houses peeping above miles of woodland" and "in the vague places of the horizon, [...] far away towns and sites that one had always heard of".[9] The half-timbered, late fifteenth-century Larden Hall, and the great Elizabethan country houses of Lutwyche Hall, Shipton Hall and Wilderhope Manor were all in the vicinity of the Edge.

The landscape oozes history: the "hand of time"[10] is present just as acutely as in ancient buildings. The view is characteristic of English scenery with its "density of feature", in which "there are no waste details [in which] everything in the landscape is something particular – has a history, has played a part, has a value to the

imagination".[11] The patchwork effect of the hedgerows is the result
of history, of the eighteenth and nineteenth-century Enclosure
Acts which divided land into parcels, a development from the
system of open farming. And well before that, even in the Middle
Ages, attempts were made to define much of England's farm and
grazing lands by simple wooden gates and fences.

The Edge was, and still is, dotted with limestone quarries and
limekilns. The high quality Wenlock limestone, known as
Wenlock marble because it can be polished so finely, is packed
with fossil corals and shells. James was treading the very earth
that created Wenlock Abbey – the solid lectern from which the
monks read their religious books, although hewed and carved in
the twelfth century, was made of local stone that was millions of
years old. The steep-gradient railway that opened in 1867 was
built mainly to facilitate the transportation of this important
mineral. Lower down, James was also treading the earth of the
ancient Spittle where lepers were confined in the Middle Ages
and who were given medical help at Wenlock Abbey, through
that mysterious hole that was "something of the monks".

Seen through his American eyes, the Shropshire landscape
seemed "almost suburban in its smoothness and finish",[12] in such
contrast to the wildness perceived by local people. Chapter
twenty-five of *The Princess Casamassima* opens with a description of the countryside where Hyacinth Robinson, while a guest
of the Princess at her country home, went walking. This is the
Shropshire scenery that James knew and loved (with echoes of
the "little girls bobbing curtsies in the street" that he had seen in
Much Wenlock) compressed in one long sentence:

> Hyacinth took several long walks by himself, beyond the gates of
> the park and through the neighbouring country – walks during
> which [...] he had still a delighted attention to spare for the
> green dimness of leafy lanes, the attraction of meadow-paths
> that led from stile to stile and seemed a clue to some pastoral
> happiness, some secret of the fields; the hedges thick with
> flowers, bewilderingly common, for which he knew no names,

the picture-making quality of thatched cottages, the mystery and sweetness of blue distances, the bloom of rural complexions, the quaintness of little girls bobbing curtsies by waysides (a sort of homage he had never prefigured); the soft sense of the turf under feet that had never ached but from paving-stones.[13]

* * *

Henry James was not a practising Christian. He had observed not without a certain cynicism the power of custom in the "universal church-going"[14] so closely linked to the State in England. Church-going was, for him, a performance or sublime spectacle, a ritual that was repeated throughout the land. When he visited "the picturesque little town of Abergavenny" in Monmouthshire in late April 1879, he deliberately stayed away from going to church on the Sunday because "the sacred edifice had a mediæval chill"[15] and he was fearful of catching a chill, or lumbago or rheumatism. It was an aesthetic experience that he preferred to watch, observe and enjoy from a distance: "The outside of an old English country-church in service-time is a very pleasant place; and this is as near as I often care to approach to the celebration of the Anglican mysteries."[16] In a deeply moving letter to his grieving friend Grace Norton in 1883, James proffered stoicism rather than a belief in God: "I am determined not to speak to you except with the voice of stoicism. I don't know *why* we live – the gift of life comes to us from I don't know what source or for what purpose; but I believe we can go on living for the reason that [...] life is the most valuable thing we know anything about."[17]

James refused to be institutionalised and by keeping a safe distance ensured his independence. Although he may well have appreciated the aesthetics of the ceremony and ceremonial for their feeling, he could not make any compromise and be seen to be part of the establishment. He had had a very broad, even anarchical religious and secular education and his tastes were largely ecumenical. So as with so many aspects of his stay, he remained the outside observer of society.

He did not attend morning service with the Gaskells to hear their *protégé*, the Rev. Frederick Ellis, deliver his sermon at Holy Trinity Church. Instead he stayed indoors, on that cold Sunday morning, "with a great raw rain-storm howling outside", an "unpleasantness" that had "lasted 48 hrs.",[18] and penned a long letter to Henry Adams, then at home in Beverly Farms, Massachusetts. He commenced: "This is my last day, & I can't let it pass without thanking you for your share in bringing about so agreeable an episode."[19]

The letter – and that Sunday morning – concludes with the portrait of beautiful Lady Catherine in a medieval setting emerging from her private chapel with its recessed oratory and altar with seven blind panels before a three-light window. She announces not something spiritual but what James desires most of all:

> But Lady Catherine comes in from the 'chapel' – you remember the chapel – to inform me with her own rosy lips that lunch is being served. Commend me humbly to your wife, the memory of whose merits even the presence of those of Lady Catherine does not obscure.[20]

*   *   *

Sunday in much of Victorian England was a traditional day of rest: shops were closed and, in the strictest households, no work or entertainment of any kind was permitted. Church worship was *de rigueur*, sometimes several times a day. The Lord's Day Observance Society, established in 1831, exerted a powerful force and disapproved strongly of the consumption of alcohol, theatrical and musical entertainments, gambling and trading on a Sunday. Ruskin's evangelical parents restricted their young son's reading to certain kinds of books, such as *Pilgrim's Progress*,[21] and the family did not travel on a Sunday. For many people, it epitomised boredom and dullness and was something to be endured or even dreaded rather than enjoyed. James had been accustomed to the bustle of a continental Sunday with markets and cafés, and he disliked intensely the English Sunday: it "is so difficult" he wrote in *The Princess Casamassima*.[22] In *The Aspern Papers*, Miss Bordereau's *palazzo* is in a corner of Venice that is "as negative […] as a Protestant Sunday".[23] One of his most painful experiences was around Christmas-time in 1876 when he "encountered three British Sundays in a row – a spectacle to strike terror into the stoutest heart. A Sunday and a 'bank-holiday' […] had joined hands with a Christmas-day".[24] And when staying at Eggesford Manor, in North Devon, the country residence of Lord and Lady Portsmouth, so great was James's boredom and need to return to the city that he wrote home: "I don't think I could stick out a Sunday here."[25]

To relieve the monotony of the lengthy interval between lunch and tea on that "long, wet Sunday", his host took him on a walk, of about an hour, to a place that Gaskell described as "the paradise of a small English country-gentleman".[26] The destination was Buildwas, with its ruined twelfth-century Cistercian Abbey, dedicated to Our Lady and St Chad, standing in meadows by the fast-flowing river Severn: once it was teeming with monks from the Normandy village of Savigny, south of Mortain. In 1536, it fell victim to King Henry VIII who suppressed the monastery and appropriated its valuable possessions, including a fine collection of books, many of which had been produced by the monks themselves. The two men, both in their mid-thirties, set off, hesitating between two paths: the scenic route via Wyke with a grange originally belonging to Wenlock Abbey or the road through romantic Farley Dingle with its steam and water-powered corn mill. They walked down the steep, winding road through the woods into the valley, near the little railway that James had taken the previous Thursday. In the distance was the Wrekin, part shrouded in mist. James was spellbound by the magnificent Buildwas Park and its setting that reminded him of Northern Italy:

It was indeed a modern Eden, and the trees might have been trees of knowledge. They were of high antiquity and magnificent girth and stature; they were strewn over the grassy levels in extraordinary profusion, and scattered upon and down the slopes in a fashion than which I have seen nothing more charming since I last looked at the chestnuts on the Lake of Como. It appears that the place was not very large, but I was unable to perceive its limits.[27]

In 1873, on the drive from Bellinzona to Como, James had been enthralled by the beauty of the Swiss and Italian lakes and hills and "the lawn-like inclinations, where the great grouped chestnuts make so cool a shadow in so warm a light".[28]

James wrote sparingly about Buildwas Abbey, "another great ruin, which has held together more completely. There the central tower stands erect to half its altitude, and the round arches and massive pillars of the nave make a perfect vista on the unencumbered turf".[29] He did not record such interesting architectural features as the waterleaf motifs on the capitals or any technical details. The stones of Buildwas were dead without a human presence. Painters of the picturesque had depicted Buildwas Abbey as a welcoming place among whose ruins people could have picnics, rest and chat with their friends, let their animals roam freely and even store their hay. These were not religious scenes and were far removed from the monastic piety of medieval times. Michael 'Angelo' Rooker (1746-1801) included a large family group, possibly gypsies, around a campfire waiting for the pot to boil (the cooking-pot is suspended from a tripod of sticks) and the food to cook, next to one of the round pillars in the north aisle of the church. In that same watercolour, there is a group of goats, and a wagon is parked beneath the crossing and hay piled high in what used to be the holy presbytery. In John Sell Cotman's Romantic watercolour of Buildwas Abbey seen from the south-west, a cow (or is it a goat?) is positioned in the foreground. Philippe de Loutherbourg sketched *The Ruins of Buildwas Abbey* depicting the central ruined tower, Buildwas Bridge over the river Severn, a boat with two oarsmen, a lady with a basket and a man pointing the way, an artist sketching, two washerwomen and the Wrekin in the background. Paul Sandby and Turner also painted the ruins.

However, particularly on such a cold, wet day, and in order to yield to the seduction of the place, James needed living history: that he found in the private residence, formerly the Abbey House or Abbot's House, situated in the north-east corner of the grounds of Buildwas Abbey. Viewed from the outside, it was "most agreeable" and "stood", wrote James, "on a kind of terrace, in the middle of a lawn and garden, and the terrace overlooked one of the most copious rivers in England [...]. On the terrace also was a piece of ornamental water, and there was a small iron paling to divide the lawn from the park".[30]

Gaskell left his visiting card with the butler, but due to their "bespattered", muddy condition, walked away. Much to James's relief and expectation, they were recalled by the butler and invited into the house. He had rightly gauged that the occupants would welcome company in such a quiet place, on a rainy Sunday afternoon! Although "the house was charming, the terrace delightful, the oaks magnificent, the view most interesting [...] the whole thing was quiet".[31] This was an opportunity not to be missed, to gather more material for his writing, to penetrate the mysteries of another inhabited Abbey House, and establish, if possible, the existence of "a curious series of underground passages, said by tradition to communicate with Wenlock". Perhaps the blocked doorway with early carving on it concealed a secret passageway? Once again, James's curiosity had been whetted by the enticing, albeit brief, account of Buildwas Abbey House in Murray's *Handbook*:

> The abbot's house (recently restored) contains the ambulatory, the chapel, and a large hall of the 13th century, with some interesting doorways and carved stones. There is also a curious series of under-

ground passages, said by tradition to communicate with Wenlock. The ceiling of the hall is of oak and Spanish chestnut. It is entered by a good Norman doorway, and lighted by beautifully moulded Norman windows, one being on either side of the door.[32]

So, James writes, "we went back, and I carried my muddy boots into the drawing-room – just the drawing-room I had imagined – where I found – I will not say just the lady I had imagined, but a lady even more charming. Indeed, there were two ladies, one of whom was staying in the house".[33] The lady of the house whom James met was Miss Moseley, whose family had owned Buildwas Abbey, Park and estate since the seventeenth century.

Learning that one of the ladies is "staying" leads James, also "guilty of 'staying'", to conclude that this is a custom that typifies English life:

In whatever company you find yourself in England, you may always be sure that someone present is 'staying'. I seldom hear this participle nowadays without remembering an observation made to me in France by a lady who had seen much of English manners. 'Ah, that dreadful word *staying*! I think we are so happy in France not to be able to translate it – not to have any word that answers to it'.[34]

The theme of "staying" in country houses is a leitmotiv in some of James's novels: Hyacinth Robinson at Medley Park in *The Princess Casamassima* and Isabel Archer at Gardencourt in *The Portrait of a Lady*.

James and Gaskell approached the house by a lodge entrance over a gravelled, sweep drive. The butler escorted them through a side hall, up a staircase, through round, early Norman arches with simple *bâtons rompus/bâtons brisés* mouldings, and opened a heavy oak door leading to the drawing-room on the first floor. Did James really carry his muddy boots into the drawing-room? From the magnificent, oak-floored drawing-room, measuring approximately 44′ by 15′, warmed by an open stone fireplace, there are stunning views. Looking south, through the five Gothic windows, beyond the lawn with its fountain and ornamental terraced gardens, are the wooded slopes on both sides of the steep, winding road between Buildwas and Wenlock, and also some of Buildwas Abbey ruins. Through the four, deeply recessed, tall, Gothic windows at the east end of the drawing-room, can be seen the powerful river Severn – this is one of its most dangerous stretches – rushing among woods and hills on its way towards Ironbridge and Coalbrookdale, the cradle of the Industrial Revolution, before eventually disgorging into the Bristol Channel, having commenced its journey on the Welsh peak of Plynlimmon. James described the view (now partly obscured by tall trees): "The large windows of the drawing-room [...] looked away over the river to the blurred and blotted hills, where the rain was drizzling and drifting."[35] This strong river had provided power and energy for the monastery mills, as well as being a conduit for sewage disposal.

James harboured doubts about the apparently idyllic country life. He recalled the vast literature "of manners" – Jane Austen for example – that had exposed its dullness and the "recorded occupations and conversations [that] occasionally strike one as lacking a certain indispensable salt".[36] His doubts were confirmed, for, in spite of the beauty of the place, an impression of languor and boredom prevailed. The conversation unveiled the ladies' longing for a more interesting life in the town:

> It was very quiet [...]; there was an air of large leisure. If one wanted to do something here, there was evidently plenty of time – and indeed of every other appliance – to do it. The two ladies talked about 'town': that is what people talk about in the country. If I were disposed I might represent them as talking about it with a certain air of yearning. At all events, I asked myself how it was possible that one should live in this charming place and trouble one's head about what was going on in London in July.[37]

Likewise, in *The Portrait of a Lady*, Henrietta Stackpole is bored with country life and longs for the stimulation of London: "I've described all the scenery in this vicinity […] scenery doesn't make a vital letter. I must go back to London and get some impressions of real life."[38] The boredom and tedium of the reclusive lives of aunt and niece, Miss Juliana and Miss Tina Bordereau, in a crumbling Venetian *palazzo*, with their "mystic rites of ennui", is the setting of *The Aspern Papers*.[39]

"Then we had excellent tea", wrote James.[40] Did the tea table offer "an anomalous and picturesque repast"[41] such as that served to Baroness Münster at the great house of Mr Wentworth in *The Europeans*? The ritual of afternoon tea or "tea time" was well established in the nineteenth century and James valued highly that pleasant, relaxing period. China or Indian tea was prepared in a silver (or china) teapot and served in the best china cups. This was accompanied by delicately cut sandwiches filled with sliced cucumber or gentleman's relish, home-made scones with fresh butter, strawberry jam and clotted cream, and a selection of sponge and fruit cakes. Echoes of this Sunday afternoon at Buildwas can be found in the opening scene of *The Portrait of a Lady*, a tea ceremony on the lawn in the English country house of Gardencourt. Pure tea was then an expensive, heavily taxed commodity and the drink of the gentry – the poor drank adulterated tea or gin.

It is to be hoped that James was shown more of this historic Abbey House, with its chapel, ambulatory, library, winding staircases and passageways. One of the finest rooms is the great dining hall on the ground floor with a garden entrance, stone fireplace, serving hatch, old tiled floor, half panelled walls and moulded ceiling. The motifs on the plasterwork ceiling include portcullis, rose, *fleur-de-lys*, designs also found in Wilderhope Manor.[42]

It was not until 1925 that the Abbey ruins, in a perilous condition, were placed in the care of the state (HM Office of Works, later English Heritage) by Major H. R. Moseley. The Abbey House, however, remained in private hands until it was sold in the early 1960s. It was then owned by Ironbridge Power Station and used as a private club.

* * *

At Wenlock, Stokesay, Buildwas and Ludlow, James achieved what he had failed to experience on his first visit to Venice in September 1869. Whereas Ruskin had engaged mainly in a technical way with the stones of Venice and often moralistically towards its artistic treasures, James was unable to respond at all. He explained to his brother William how he tried in vain to follow some of Ruskin's recommendations "to frequent and linger in a certain glorious room at the Ducal Palace where Paolo Veronese revels on the ceilings and Tintoret rages on the walls".[43] He was unable to respond to the "Italian tone of things" that lay "as a cold and foreign mass – never to be absorbed and appropriated".[44] Perhaps too much under the didactic influence of Ruskin and with memories of the evening at his Denmark Hill home only a few months before, James remained a Venetian outsider who could not shed what he called his "inexorable yankeehood".[45] That feeling of "yankeehood" would be well and truly shed as he became absorbed into British life and culture. It was in Shropshire in particular that he responded fully to the "tone of things". The metaphor of the images of "the pierced aperture, either broad or balconied or slit-like and low-browed" representing James's "literary form", his "house of fiction", was inspired by these country houses.[46] This Shropshire idyll contributed to making 1877 the "happiest and most 'lived' year yet".[47]

* * *

In a letter to his brother William, written from the Reform Club on 23rd July 1878, James states his intention to remain in London all summer, where he has a busy work schedule and as usual, plenty of invitations. However, the attraction of staying again at Wenlock Abbey was strong: "I have received several invitations to pay short visits, but have declined them all, save one for a week at Wenlock Abbey (Charles Gaskell's) on August 10th."[48]

* * *

Chapter 17

A taste of Yorkshire

James consolidated his friendship with Charles Milnes Gaskell and was invited to experience an English Christmas in 1878 with the family at Thornes House, Wakefield, in "the well-appointed, well-administered, well-filled country-house".[1] Thornes House provided a complete architectural contrast to Wenlock Abbey. It was – Thornes House was destroyed by fire in 1951 – a fine building constructed between 1779 and 1782 for the Milnes family. The architect was the Yorkshire-born John Carr (1723-1807): he came from Horbury, a small town a few miles west of Wakefield. In the Palladian style, Thornes appeared larger than it was owing to a two-hundred-foot-wide façade integrating the main part of the house in the centre – a three-storey block with seven bays and a three-bay pediment supported on four fluted Ionic pilasters – flanked at a lower level by one-storey matching service blocks, housing the stables on one side and the kitchen, laundry and wash-house on the other. At the lower level, doors crowned with classical urns were substituted for windows. A particular feature inside the house was an oval drawing-room with a semi-circular bay at one end overlooking the gardens, and, at the opposite end, also semi-circular, two niches, one on either side of the door, to house classical statues or vases. Carr created a feeling of space and of classical ruins, by placing, in the inner hall, a pair of free-standing columns supporting the landing above through which one had to pass to reach the staircase on the side of the house. Although James described Thornes as a country-house, it was in fact a grand town house, a classical villa, and of such importance that it was included in the 1802 edition of *Vitruvius Britannicus* and chosen as one of only twenty-seven buildings in Britain worthy of being illustrated.

The House was situated in Westgate, as the name implies slightly to the west of the centre of the industrial town of Wakefield, with its woollen mills and factories with tall chimneys belching out smoke, coal mines and row upon row of 'back-to-backs', the 'two-up, two-down' brick houses, usually rented, accommodating workers and their families. An outdoor lavatory, with a wooden seat with a hole, in a shed at the bottom of the garden or in a yard, would be shared by several house-holds. A chamber pot (known as a 'guzunder') was placed under the bed for urgent urinal needs during the night. There was no running water, no bathrooms: the weekly ritual of filling a small tin bath with water fetched from a pump or well, then boiled over a coal fire, formed part of a miner's life (the practice was well described by D. H. Lawrence and Émile Zola).

Thornes was part of a one hundred and twelve-acre estate, allowing James ample space to enjoy country walking. But above all he had been so engrossed in Gaskell's private library that he had neglected his letter writing, as he explained to his sister Alice: "But what more particularly, I found to go against epis-tolizing at Thornes was Gaskell's beautiful and interesting library; for whenever I was not talking or walking, or lunching or dining, I was turning over the charming collection of books, in that charming great room."[2]

One particular event left its mark on James – a visit to a grim Victorian workhouse. It was on that very cold, dusky Christmas Eve in 1878 that James was driven, with the lady of the house, in a "lamp-lit brougham" that pulled up in "the snowy quadrangle of a grim-looking charitable institution". He was suddenly plunged into the world of Dickens and transported "to the early pages of *Oliver Twist*".[3] He was invited by a "lady [who] had made a present of a Christmas-tree to the children of a work-house [...] to go with her and assist at the distribution of the toys". This act of charity by a wealthy lady was part of the ritual of life among the English gentry. The "beautiful Lady Bountiful" in question was probably his hostess, the twenty-one-year-old Lady Catherine Milnes Gaskell, then mother of a one-year-old son. He witnessed the Dickensian scene in a "large frigid refectory" where "some hundred and fifty little children of charity" dressed in pinafores lined up to receive "little offerings" distributed by "their benefactress" to whom they "directed a melancholy hymn".[4] The juxtaposition of these two very different worlds geographically close but so far apart left a strong and lasting impression on James: "The scene was a picture I shall not forget, with its curious mixture of poetry and sordid prose – the dying wintry light in the big, bare, stale room; the beautiful Lady Bountiful, standing in the twinkling glory of the Christmas-tree; the little multitude of staring and wondering, yet perfectly expressionless, faces."[5] James had been sheltered from poverty all his life and here for the first time he came face to face with the reality of life in the workhouse.

The Yorkshire countryside, in the north of England, was harsher than that of Shropshire, and its industrial landscape, particularly to the south, was dotted with coalmines. Returning to London and from the comfort of an armchair in the Reform Club, James wrote to Grace Norton revealing his true feelings: "that Yorkshire smoke-country is very ugly and depressing, both as regards the smirched and blackened landscape and the dense and dusky population."[6] In his essay "An English New Year" he was more circumspect and described it as "a populous manu-facturing region, full of tall chimneys and of an air that is gray and gritty".[7]

That year the weather was bitterly cold with heavy snowfalls and severe frost and James suffered from a recurrence of chill-blains. So deep was the snow that Gaskell and James went by sledge to nearby Bretton Hall (built in the early eighteenth century) to call on Lady Margaret Beaumont to whom James took an instant dislike! She was, he wrote, "a drawling, lisping fine lady [...] enclosed in her great wintry park and her immense dusky, pictured luxurious house – with her tea table at one elbow and a table-full of novels at the other".[8]

From Thornes House, it was only a short distance – approximately twelve miles in a north-easterly direction – to Lord Houghton's "hospitable house", Fryston Hall, about one mile north of Ferrybridge, to which James was invited for New Year. James was to experience life in yet another English country-house, in the vicinity of the pit village of Fryston (its colliery has since closed).

This was the Hall (demolished in 1934) to which Thomas Carlyle (friend of Henry James, Sr., and Emerson) had been invited in April 1841 and had been accommodated in an apartment "furnished as for Prince Albert and Queen Victoria; the most absurd place I ever lived in".[9] Richard Monckton Milnes was a great admirer of Carlyle and his writings, in particular his monumental work *The French Revolution*. Both men shared a common interest in books and had worked together on the (library) committee of the London Library. But there were considerable drawbacks in being a country-house guest. In exchange for lavish hospitality, the guest – and particularly a prestigious writer – was expected to entertain and be entertaining from breakfast until very late at night. James suffered from being deprived of his personal independence and remarked to American diplomat William Jones Hoppin that "to be obliged to be agreeable morning, noon and night for several days is a great task upon one's spirits – if not one's intellect".[10] Carlyle found the experience so disruptive of his routine that he could not sleep. He described Fryston Hall as "a large, irregular pile, of various ages, rising up among ragged old wood, in a rough large park ... chiefly beautiful because it does not set up for beauty".[11]

When Henry Adams stayed there in December 1862,

Laurence Oliphant and Swinburne were also guests.[12] It was an all-male party and no doubt a jolly affair for, as John Batchelor observed, "there was never anything serious about Monckton Milnes, who […] introduce[d] Swinburne to the dubious joys of flagellant pornography".[13] Oliphant's cutting observations were incorporated into his satirical novel *Piccadilly* (1870) in which Fryston Hall is depicted as Dickiefield and where R. Monckton Milnes figures as Lord Dickiefield.

A library was an essential feature of these country-houses. As at Thornes, it was Lord Houghton's fine collection of books that appealed to James. It must have been a devastating experience for the bibliophile when a terrible fire in November 1876 swept through Fryston's eighteenth-century front, containing the drawing-room and long library and destroyed much of the fabric and many of the rare books. Repairs had not been completed at the time of James's stay. He wrote to his sister Alice that "poor Lord Houghton's immense library was thrown into hopeless confusion at the time of the partial burning of his house, two years ago, and is now scattered all over the place".[14]

For the New Year there was a small party of guests including the witty Mrs Anne Procter (widow of writer Barry Cornwall), the dowager Lady Galway (Lord Houghton's sister), "a pretty Miss Bland", the great Macaulay and others. On one occasion, Lord Houghton took James to visit the elderly Duchess of Somerset.

James was a compulsive writer – it was his trade – and sitting by "a luxurious fireside"[15] or in the privacy of his bedroom he had been constantly recording his impressions of those two country-houses. Some of his experiences as a house guest *chez* Milnes Gaskell at Christmas and *chez* Lord Houghton at New Year provided the inspiration for his article "The New Year in England" – the title is slightly misleading for the essay also discusses Christmas – published in the New York-based magazine *Nation* on 23 January 1879, remarkably soon after his Yorkshire stay. As always, James is totally discreet – therefore socially acceptable – and no names or places are mentioned. But the essay is unusual in that it begins and ends with a commentary on social conditions in England at the time. He was enjoying assuming the role of transatlantic correspondent in England and presenting to Americans a certain image of the Old World: a forerunner of Alistair Cooke's "Letter from America" in reverse. Both were outsiders presenting a fresh perspective on life in their adopted country.

In private, James penned a fair, but perhaps cutting portrait of R. Monckton Milnes to Grace Norton soon after his New Year visit. He was:

a battered and world-wrinkled old mortal, with a restless and fidgety vanity, but with an immense fund of real kindness and humane feeling. He is not personally fascinating, though as a general thing he talks very well, but I like his social, democratic, sympathetic, inquisitive old temperament.[16]

James seemed to thrive on such an exhausting schedule that required huge stamina, resilience and an ability to adapt. His social life continued to increase – he was the ideal guest – and he became so popular that during the winter of 1878-1879 he confessed to dining out "107 times":[17] Leon Edel counted 140 engagements.[18] His cosmopolitan entourage, with a vast number of French, British and American acquaintances, provided the subject matter for his novels.

James had witnessed the heyday of the country squire, a powerful force in Parliament, in local justice, in the Church and in the countryside. He could enjoy a romanticised and picturesque vision of their life. But only a few years later, in 1882, Charles Milnes Gaskell published an article in *The Nineteenth Century* on the plight of the country squire in which he bemoaned, with some degree of exaggeration, the financial difficulties:

He has given up his deer, has dismissed his servants; he is advertising his house for a Grammar School or a Lunatic Asylum; he is making arrangements with little Premium for the sale of his ancestors, and with the nearest timber-merchant for that of his trees [...]. He has made permanent reductions in three or four of his principal farms, and he has 800 acres on his hands.[18]

Although the role of the country squire may have diminished, C. M. Gaskell was to some extent unnecessarily pessimistic. His family home, Wenlock Abbey and Priory, is, at the beginning of the twenty-first century, well-preserved and maintained partly as a family residence: the ruins are protected and cared for by English Heritage. Stokesay Castle and Ludlow Castle are both beautifully preserved: the former in the care of English Heritage, the latter the property of the Earl of Powis and Trustees. Vast tracts of land upon which Henry James trod and which he admired are also protected for generations to come through bodies such as The National Trust, one of whose founders was John Ruskin.

Notes

Part One

Chapter 1

1. Joan Evans and John Howard Whitehouse (eds.), *The Diaries of John Ruskin*, The Clarendon Press, Oxford, three volumes, 1956-1959, vol. I, p. 1. Henceforth, *Diaries*, followed by the volume and page number(s).

2. E. T. Cook and Alexander Wedderburn (eds.), *The Works of John Ruskin*, George Allen, London, in thirty-nine volumes, 1903-1912, vol. 35, p. 622. Henceforth, CW followed by the number of the volume and page(s).

3. CW35: 95.

4. CW16: 445.

5. CW1: 191.

6. Van Akin Burd (ed.), *The Ruskin Family Letters. The Correspondence of John James Ruskin, His Wife, and Their Son, John, 1801-1843*, in two volumes, Cornell University Press, Ithaca and London, 1973, vol. I, p. 267. Henceforth, Burd, *The Ruskin Family Letters*, followed by the volume and page number(s).

7. CW35: 95-96.

8. George Borrow, *Wild Wales, its People, Language and Scenery*, Fontana/Collins, Glasgow, 1977 [1862]. Borrow describes a tour in 1854.

9. He mentions the town in a letter to his son, written from Liverpool on 24 February 1832, as the place where he will be, and where he can be contacted, after 28 February (Burd, *The Ruskin Family Letters*, I, p. 266, and see also p. 260).

10. Listed in *Pigot and Co.'s Directory of Shrewsbury* (1839). In the Salop Directory, published by Tibham & Co., Shrewsbury, 1828, both businesses are in Claremont Street.

11. Burd, *The Ruskin Family Letters*, II, p. 671.

12. See *Crockford's Clerical Directory*, 1860 and subsequent years. In 1860, he is listed as The Venerable Edward Bickersteth, Prebendal House, Aylesbury, Bucks.

13. *Henry IV, part I*, 5.4. 141-142.

14. *Henry IV, part I*, 5.4. 138-146.

15. Burd, *The Ruskin Family Letters*, II, pp. 705-706.

16. CW35: 139.
17. Burd, *The Ruskin Family Letters,* I, p. 252, n. 1.
18. Burd, *The Ruskin Family Letters,* I, p. 260, n. 3.
19. John Newman and Nikolaus Pevsner, *Shropshire,* Yale University Press, New Haven and London, 2006, p. 538. Henceforth, Newman and Pevsner, *Shropshire* (2006).
20. See Burd, The Ruskin Family Letters, I, p. 261, n. 11.
21. Burd, *The Ruskin Family Letters,* I, p. 261, n. 13.
22. Burd, *The Ruskin Family Letters,* I, p. 326, n. 1.
23. CW35: 138-139.
24. Letter of John Ruskin to Henry Acland, undated, The Ruskin Foundation (Ruskin Library, Lancaster University), B 13. Henceforth, Lancaster RF followed by the reference.
25. See CW2: 429-438.
26. CW2: 433.
27. CW35: 441, n. 2.
28. CW2: 434.
29. CW3: 415-416.
30. CW2: 470-473.
31. Quoted in Tim Hilton, *John Ruskin: The Early Years 1819-1859,* Yale University Press, New Haven and London, 2000 [1985], p. 29. Henceforth, Hilton, *John Ruskin: The Early Years.*
32. John Batchelor, *John Ruskin: No Wealth but Life,* Pimlico, London, 2001 [Chatto & Windus, 2000], p. 40. Henceforth, Batchelor, *John Ruskin.*
33. CW35: 299.
34. On 18 January 1843 (*Diaries,* I, p. 239); 22 February 1843 (*Diaries,* I, p. 244); 21 February 1844 (*Diaries,* I, p. 266).
35. CW35: 440.
36. CW35: 441.
37. CW35: 441.
38. CW35: 441.
39. CW35: 441, n. 2.
40. Burd, *The Ruskin Family Letters,* I, p. 260, n.3.

Chapter 2

1. Information about their births, baptisms and deaths can be found in Box 13, Broseley Parish Register, Shropshire Archives (S.A.), Shrewsbury, and

on microfiche. The initials are not clearly legible in the register.

2. *VCH Shropshire*, x, p. 257.

3. See page 71 of Broseley baptisms, 1813-1916, microfiche, S.A., Shrewsbury.

4. *Dictionary of National Biography*, edited by Leslie Stephen and Sidney Lee, Smith, Elder & Co., London, 1890. Henceforth, *DNB*.

5. *Oxford Dictionary of National Biography*, in 60 volumes, edited first by H. C. G. Matthew, then by Brian Harrison and from 2004 by Lawrence Goldman, Oxford University Press, Oxford, 2004. Henceforth, *Oxford DNB*.

6. *VCH Shropshire*, x, pp. 287-288.

7. See tablet of cast iron on south transept wall of Broseley Parish Church.

8. Jane Onions died on 30 May 1825: Mary died on 30 November 1825: Martha died on 25 April 1860. See tablet of cast iron on south transept wall of Broseley Parish Church.

9. *VCH Shropshire*, x, p. 276.

10. H. E. Forrest, *The Old Houses of Wenlock and Wenlock Edge, their History and Associations*, Wilding & Son, Shrewsbury, 1922, third edition, [1914], p. 87. Hereafter, Forrest, *The Old Houses of Wenlock* followed by the page number(s).

11. Oil on canvas, 68 x 106.7 cm: in the Science Museum, London.

12. Listed in CW13: 255 and 633.

13. CW13: 255.

14. Evelyn Joll, Martin Butlin and Luke Herrmann, *The Oxford Companion to J. M. W. Turner*, Oxford University Press, Oxford, New York and other places, 2001, p. 280. Henceforth, Joll, Butlin, Herrmann, *The Oxford Companion to J.M.W.Turner.*

15. Joll, Butlin, Herrmann, *The Oxford Companion to J. M. W. Turner*, p. 280.

16. Caption in exhibition *A Picture of Britain*, at Tate Britain, London, 15 June-4 September 2005.

17. An exhibit at the exhibition *A Picture of Britain*, Tate Britain, 15 June-4 September 2005.

18. In the Ironbridge Gorge Museum, Ironbridge. Exhibited at *A Portrait of Britain*, Tate Britain, 15 June-4 September 2005.

19. *VCH Shropshire*, x, p. 261.

20. In 1849, the population of Bridgnorth was 6198 according to the Law List of that year.

21. Murray, *A Handbook for Shropshire, Cheshire and Lancashire*, 1870, p. 24.

22. This painting was sold at Christie's, London, on 21 November 2002: it was dated as c. 1798 (see *Turner Society News*, no. 93, March 2003, p. 17).

23. J. F. A. Mason, "Thomas Rowley: Energy and Pre-eminence 1821-1850",

in Maureen Jones (ed.), *Bridgnorth Grammar & Endowed Schools. Five Hundred Years of Change 1503-2003,* 2003, pp. 14-15. Henceforth, Jones, *Bridgnorth Grammar & Endowed Schools.*

24. George Marshall (ed.), *Osborne Gordon. A Memoir: With a Selection of his Writings,* Parker & Co., Oxford & London, 1885, p. 3. Henceforth, Marshall, *OG.*

25. Marshall, *OG*, pp. 2-3.

26. In the National Portrait Gallery, London.

27. Reproduced in E.G. W. Bill and J. F. A. Mason, *Christ Church and Reform 1850-1867,* The Clarendon Press, Oxford, 1970, facing p. 66, by permission of Mr Roger Pope. Hereafter, Bill and Mason, *Christ Church and Reform.*

28. Joseph Foster, *Alumni Oxonienses* 1715-1886.

29. Henry Maas (ed.), *The Letters of A. E. Housman,* Rupert-Hart-Davis, London, 1971, pp. 11-12.

30. Ruskin matriculated as a gentleman commoner on 20 October 1836: see Burd, *The Ruskin Family Letters,* II, p. 424, n. 1.

31. Hilton, *John Ruskin: The Early Years,* p. 42.

32. *DNB,* p. 221.

33. CW23: 229. A cast was in the Oxford University Galleries. See also a brief reference to Chantrey's sculpture at CW35: 348.

34. Marshall, *OG*, p. 3.

35. Marshall, *OG*, p. 3.

Chapter 3

1. Keith Grahame Feiling, *In Christ Church Hall,* Macmillan, London, 1960, p. 175.

2. Quoted in Hilton, *John Ruskin: The Early Years,* p. 48.

3. CW35: lxiii: from William Holman Hunt, *Pre-Raphaelitism and the Pre-Raphaelite Brotherhood,* vol. I, Macmillan, 1905, p. 323.

4. CW35: 192.

5. CW35: 198.

6. Burd, *The Ruskin Family Letters,* II, p. 490 (letter of Margaret Ruskin to her husband, 15 February 1838).

7. Burd, *The Ruskin Family Letters,* II, p. 500 (letter of Margaret Ruskin to her husband, 4 March 1838).

8. Burd, *The Ruskin Family Letters,* II, p. 550 (letter of Margaret Ruskin to her husband, 4 December 1838).

9. Burd, *The Ruskin Family Letters*, II, p. 565 (letter of Margaret Ruskin to her husband, 23 January 1839).

10. Marshall, *OG*, p. 3.

11. Burd, *The Ruskin Family Letters*, II, p. 592 (letter of Margaret Ruskin to her husband, 27 February 1839).

12. Burd, *The Ruskin Family Letters*, II, p. 624 (letter of Margaret Ruskin to her husband, 5 June 1839).

13. CW35: 249.

14. CW35: 255.

15. CW35: 249-250.

16. CW35: 250.

17. W. G. Collingwood, *Ruskin Relics*, Isbister & Co., London, 1903, pp. 18-21.

18. CW35: 254 (and see 252).

19. CW35: 251.

20. W. G. Collingwood, *The Life and Work of John Ruskin*, in two volumes, Methuen, London, 1893, vol. I, p. 82. Henceforth, Collingwood, *The Life and Work of John Ruskin*.

21. CW36: 21, from J. B. Atlay, *Sir Henry Wentworth Acland: A Memoir*, 1903.

22. CW35: 252.

23. CW35: 255.

24. Burd, *The Ruskin Family Letters*, II, p. 634 (letter of John James Ruskin to his wife, 24 January 1840).

25. Burd, *The Ruskin Family Letters*, II, p. 635.

26. Burd, *The Ruskin Family Letters*, II, p. 635.

27. Burd, *The Ruskin Family Letters*, II, p. 640 (letter of John James Ruskin to his wife, 13 February 1840).

28. Burd, *The Ruskin Family Letters*, II, p. 656, n.1.

29. Burd, *The Ruskin Family Letters*, II, p. 484, n.11.

30. Burd, *The Ruskin Family Letters*, II, pp. 655-656 (letter of John James Ruskin to his wife, 25/26 February 1840).

31. Burd, *The Ruskin Family Letters*, II, p. 661, n. 4.

32. Burd, *The Ruskin Family Letters*, II, p. 660 (letter of John James Ruskin to his wife, 5 March 1840).

33. CW35: 259.

34. Robert Hewison, *Ruskin and Oxford: The Art of Education*, The Clarendon Press, Oxford, 1996, p. 4.

35. CW35: 259.

36. CW35: 260.

37. See Diary of John Ruskin, 1871-1873, Lancaster RF Ms 18, [containing the Diary of John James Ruskin, 1840-1841]: reproduced in Jeanne Clegg and Paul Tucker, *Ruskin and Tuscany*, Ruskin Gallery, collection of The Guild of St George, Sheffield in association with Lund Humphries, London, 1992, p. 26, exhibit 10.

38. CW35: 299-300.

39. Burd, *The Ruskin Family Letters*, II, p. 691 (letter of John James Ruskin to John Ruskin, 7 October 1841).

40. Gordon had been ordained priest in June 1840.

41. *Diaries*, I, p. 214 (entry of 7 October 1841).

42. Possibly a reference to Charles, 2nd Earl (1764-1845), one time Whig Prime Minister, whose name is associated with a kind of China tea flavoured with bergamot.

43. *Diaries*, I, pp. 214-215. Most likely a reference to the Venerable Thomas Whitbread, a Catholic martyr executed at Tyburn in 1679. Peel had fought against Catholic rights in Ireland for two decades, but had been forced to support the Catholic Emancipation Act of 1829.

44. Burd, *The Ruskin Family Letters*, II, p. 691 (letter of John James Ruskin to John Ruskin, 7 October 1841).

45. Burd, *The Ruskin Family Letters*, II, pp. 694-695 (letter of Margaret Ruskin to John Ruskin, 7-8 October 1841).

46. Burd, *The Ruskin Family Letters*, II, p. 700 (letter of John James Ruskin to John Ruskin, 9 October 1841).

47. Collingwood, *The Life and Work of John Ruskin*, I, p. 96.

48. Collingwood, *The Life and Work of John Ruskin*, I, p. 96.

49. Burd, *The Ruskin Family Letters*, II, p. 732 (letter of John James Ruskin to John Ruskin, 19 April 1842).

50. *Hamlet*, I. 2. 149.

51. Burd, *The Ruskin Family Letters*, II, p. 727 (letter of John James Ruskin to John Ruskin, 12 April 1842).

52. CW36: 340 (letter of John Ruskin to Dr John Brown, 6 August 1860).

53. CW36: 340.

54. CW35: 315.

55. *Diaries*, I, p. 228.

56. *Diaries*, I, p. 231.

57. Reproduced in CW35 facing p. 328, Plate XX.

58. CW3: xxiv.

59. CW3: 666 (letter of John Ruskin to Osborne Gordon, 10 March 1844).

Chapter 4

1. James S. Dearden, *John Ruskin's Camberwell*, Brentham Press, St Albans, 1990, p. 16. The information was taken from the Account Book of John James Ruskin 1845-1863, Lancaster RF Ms 29.

2. Diary of John Ruskin 1840, 1843-1844, 1846, Lancaster RF Ms 3, folio 123 (cf. *Diaries*, I, p. 239).

3. Literally "sin strongly". Luther believed that since God's forgiveness had no effect on the soul, consisting merely of overlooking, or as it were cloaking sins, those who sinned more offered greater scope for divine mercy. This was in contradiction to the Roman Catholic doctrine on grace.

4. Contrary to Luther's doctrine of justification which held that faith alone was sufficient for salvation, the Catholic Church taught that good works were also needed.

5. Diary of John Ruskin 1840, 1843-1844, 1846, Lancaster RF Ms 3, folio 123 (cf. *Diaries*, I, pp. 239-240).

6. CW35: 386-387 for Ruskin's recollections of Melvill.

7. CW35: 386, n. 4.

8. *Oxford DNB*.

9. Diary of John Ruskin 1840, 1843-1844, 1846, Lancaster RF Ms 3, folio 123 (cf. *Diaries*, I, p. 240).

10. Diary of John Ruskin 1840, 1843-1844, 1846, Lancaster RF Ms 3, folio 123 (cf *Diaries*, I, p. 240).

11. CW35: 250.

12. CW35: 250.

13. Diary of John Ruskin 1840, 1843-1844, 1846, Lancaster RF Ms 3, folio 124 (cf. *Diaries*, I, p. 240).

14. Diary of John Ruskin 1840, 1843-1844, 1846, Lancaster RF Ms 3, folio 124 (cf. *Diaries*, I, p. 240).

15. Diary of John Ruskin 1840, 1843-1844, 1846, Lancaster RF Ms 3, folio 124 (cf. *Diaries*, I, p. 240).

16. CW3: 454-457.

17. Diary of John Ruskin 1840, 1843-1844, 1846, Lancaster RF Ms 3, folio 124 (cf. *Diaries*, I, p. 240).

18. Diary of John Ruskin 1840, 1843-1844, 1846, Lancaster RF Ms 3, folio 124 (cf. *Diaries*, I, pp. 240-241).

19. Diary of John Ruskin 1840, 1843-1844, 1846, Lancaster RF Ms 3, folio 124 (cf. *Diaries*, I, p. 240).

20. Burd, *The Ruskin Family Letters*, II, p. 740 (letter of Margaret Ruskin to John Ruskin, 12 June 1843).

21. *Diaries*, I, p. 260.

22. CW35: 254.

23. CW35: 253.

24. CW3: 235 note.

25. *Diaries*, I, 260 (18 January 1844).

26. Gordon's letter is so far untraced.

27. CW3: 665-667.

28. CW3: 666-667.

29. Diary of John Ruskin 1840, 1843-1844, 1846, Lancaster RF Ms 3, folio 189 (cf. *Diaries*, I, p. 272).

30. Diary of John Ruskin 1840, 1843-1844, 1846, Lancaster RF Ms 3, folio 189 (cf. *Diaries*, I, p. 272).

31. In early May 1843 and on 30 March 1844.

32. CW8: xxv, n. 3.

33. CW36: 37 (letter of John Ruskin to his father, 28 April 1844).

34. CW36: 37.

35. "Will you come and breakfast with me – Tuesday at 10?" Rogers asked Ruskin (CW36: 37). Ruskin accepted and arrived at 9.30 punctually but was told he had arrived an hour too soon: see *Diaries*, I, p. 274 (1 May 1844).

36. CW35: 252.

37. *The Valley of Chamouni* is reproduced as a photogravure as Plate 4, in CW3, facing page 240. It can be compared in relation to Turner's *The Valley of Chamouni* reproduced as a photogravure as Plate 3, facing page 238 in the same volume.

38. Flora of Chamouni 1844: An album of pressed flowers with notes on them by John Ruskin, Lancaster RF Ms 65, folio 13.

39. Ruskin's dog.

40. Diary of John Ruskin 1844, Lancaster RF Ms 4 (cf. *Diaries*, I, p. 298).

41. My rough calculations are: Chamonix to Martigny 30 km; Martigny to Sion 25 km; Sion to Sierre 20 km; Sierre to Visp 30km; Visp to Zermatt 35 km.

42. Mary Lutyens (ed.), *Effie in Venice*, John Murray, London, 1965, p. 49: henceforth, Lutyens, *Effie in Venice*. Effie wrote, from Chamonix, to her mother on Wednesday 17 October 1849 about getting from Chamonix to Martigny: "We leave tomorrow crossing the Tête Noir[e] and getting to Martigny next day. We ought to go in one day but eight hours on mule-back is too much for us and we are going to do half one day and do the next four hours next day".

43. Lutyens, *Effie in Venice*, p. 50.

44. Effie and John Ruskin posted between Martigny and Sion in October 1849: see letter of Effie to her brother, 21 October 1849, in Lutyens, *Effie in Venice*, p. 50.

45. James D. Forbes, *Travels through the Alps*, revised and annotated by W. A. B. Coolidge, Adam and Charles Black, London, 1900, p. 309.

46. CW35: 333.

47. CW35: 333-334.

48. CW35: 334.

49. Quoted by Ruskin in CW35: 334-335. The French text quoted is from Saussure's *Voyages dans les Alpes*, an influential book that Ruskin had received on his fifteenth birthday.

50. *Diaries*, I, 304.

51. CW4: xxv, n. 1.

52. The itinerary is given in CW4: xxiv.

53. CW4: xxxv.

54. CW35: 414.

55. CW35: 414.

56. CW35: 414.

57. CW4: 334.

58. Batchelor, *John Ruskin*, p. 70.

59. CW35: 269.

60. CW 4: xxxii (letter of John Ruskin to his father, 4 June 1845).

61. CW4: xxxii.

62. CW4: xxxiii.

63. Harold I. Shapiro, *Ruskin in Italy, Letters to his Parents, 1845*, The Clarendon Press, Oxford, 1972, p. 137 (letter of John Ruskin to his father, 3 July 1845). Henceforth, Shapiro, *Ruskin in Italy*.

64. CW5, Plate XIII, facing p. 396.

65. CW3: 180 (letter of John Ruskin to his father, 2 June 1845).

66. CW36: 47.

67. CW4: 202.

68. CW4: 320-321.

69. CW4: 280.

70. CW35: 413.

71. Ruskin wrote "in the Gallery" (CW36: 50) which I assume to be the Uffizi.

72. *Diaries*, I, p. 240 (entry of 26 January 1843).

73. CW36: 50 (letter of John Ruskin to his father, commenced on 17 June 1845).

Chapter 5

1. At least from 1678 when Sir John Weld and William Forester were the two MPs for Wenlock. See Forrest, *The Old Houses of Wenlock*, p. 127 *seq.*

2. John Randall, *Old Sports and Sportsmen*, 1873, p. 181.

3. See Browne's Law List of 1788.

4. John Randall, *Old Sports and Sportsmen*, pp. 182-183 for letter to Pritchard Senior.

5. Broseley Parish Register, Box 13, S. A., Shrewsbury.

6. Broseley Parish Register, Box 13, S. A., Shrewsbury.

7. Kelly's *Directory* 1900, p. 48.

8. See Law Lists of 1839 and 1841.

9. Ernest H. H. Shorting, "John Pritchard, a Shropshire Solicitor, 1759-1837", in *Notes and Queries*, 23 January 1915, p. 62.

10. *Records of the Honourable Society of Lincoln's Inn, The Black Books*, vol. IV, Lincoln's Inn, 1902, p. 258. Pritchard did not have a university degree.

11. Marshall, *OG*, p. 18.

12. In the census return of 1841, listed at Linley were Elizabeth Gordon, aged 55; Jane Gordon, aged 20; Alexander John Gordon, farmer, aged 25. The ages given do not accord with the dates of birth obtained elsewhere and must be treated with caution and circumspection. The census was certified by Alexander John Gordon, Enumerator, on 14 June 1841: see Fiche H0107/0928/11 in S.A., Shrewsbury.

13. Shapiro, *Ruskin in Italy*, pp. 109-110 (letters of John Ruskin to his mother, 9 and 10 June 1845).

14. Shapiro, *Ruskin in Italy*, p. 113.

15. CW36: 50 (letter of John Ruskin to his father, 17 and 18 June 1845).

16. Shapiro, *Ruskin in Italy*, p. 137.

17. Shapiro, *Ruskin in Italy*, p. 165 (letter of John Ruskin to his father, 29 July 1845).

18. Shapiro, *Ruskin in Italy*, pp. 178-179 (letter of John Ruskin to his father, 19 August 1845).

19. Shapiro, *Ruskin in Italy*, pp. 182-183 (letter of John Ruskin to his father, 23 August 1845).

20. Shapiro, *Ruskin in Italy*, p. 220 (letter of John Ruskin to his father, 7 October 1845).

21. Marshall, *OG*, p. 18.

22. Marshall, *OG*, pp. 18-19.

23. Marshall, *OG*, p. 19.

24. Marshall, *OG*, p. 19.

25. Marshall, *OG*, p. 19.

26. Marshall, *OG*, p. 19.

27. Shapiro, *Ruskin in Italy*, p. 199 (letter of John Ruskin to his father, 11 September 1845).

28. Marshall, *OG*, pp. 19-20, note e.

29. Diary of John James Ruskin, 1845-1864, Lancaster RF Ms 33.

30. Diary of John James Ruskin, 1845-1864, Lancaster RF Ms 33.

31. Register of Burials in the Parish of Broseley, S.A., Shrewsbury.

32. Diary of John James Ruskin 1845-1864, Lancaster RF Ms 33.

33. Lutyens, *The Ruskins and the Grays*, p. 81 (letter of John Ruskin to Effie, 24 January 1848).

34. Oxford, Bodleian Library, MS. Eng. c. 7054, fols. 1-94.

35. Lutyens, *The Ruskins and the Grays*, p. 82, note.

36. Published in Oxford by John Henry Parker.

37. Quoted in Batchelor, *John Ruskin*, p. 38.

38, Lutyens, *The Ruskins and the Grays*, p. 82 (letter of John Ruskin to Effie, 24 January 1848).

39. Lutyens, *The Ruskins and the Grays*, p. 82.

40. Lutyens, *The Ruskins and the Grays*, p. 92 (letter of John Ruskin to Effie, late February 1848).

41. Lutyens, *Effie in Venice*, p. 23.

42. William James (ed.), *The Order of Release*, John Murray, London, 1947, p. 115 (letter of Effie to her parents, 4 July 1848). Henceforth, James, *The Order of Release*.

43. James, *The Order of Release*, pp. 115-116 (letter of Effie to her parents, 4 July 1848).

44. James, *The Order of Release*, p. 115 (letter of Effie to her parents, 1 July 1848).

45. James, *The Order of Release*, p. 116 (letter of Effie to her parents, 4 July 1848).

46. Feiling, *In Christ Church Hall*, p. 185.

47. James, *The Order of Release*, p. 115 (letter of Effie to her parents, 4 July 1848).

48. CW8: 6.

49. Links, *The Ruskins in Normandy*, pp. 26-27.

50. Links, *The Ruskins in Normandy*, p. 27.

51. Lutyens, *The Ruskins and the Grays*, p. 157.

52. James, *The Order of Release*, p. 135.

53. Diary of John James Ruskin 1845-1864, Lancaster RF Ms 33.

54. Murray, *A Handbook for Travellers in Switzerland*, part I, 1891, p. 40.

55. CW5: xxviii (letter of John Ruskin to his father, August 1849).

56. CW5: xxvi.

57. See Ray Haslam, "Ruskin, Drawing and the Argument of the Lens", *The Ruskin Review and Bulletin*, Michaelmas Term, vol. 2, no. 1, 2005, p. 23.

58. Collingwood, *The Life of John Ruskin*, in one volume, 1905 [1900], fifth and cheaper edition, p. 116. Henceforth, Collingwood, *The Life of John Ruskin*.

59. Lutyens, *Effie in Venice*, p. 89 (letter of Effie to her mother, 15 December 1849).

60. Hilton, *John Ruskin: The Early Years*, p. 146.

Chapter 6

1. Diary of John James Ruskin 1845-1864, Lancaster RF Ms 33: quoted in Hilton, *John Ruskin: The Early Years*, p. 286, n. 4.

2. CW9: facing p. 318.

3. CW9: xvi.

4. CW9: figure 8 (g) and (h), p. 97.

5. Lutyens, *Effie in Venice*, p. 108 (letter of Effie to her father, Sunday 6 January 1850).

6. *Diaries*, I, p. 274.

7. See Rebecca Jenkins, *Fanny Kemble: A Reluctant Celebrity*, Simon & Schuster, London, New York, Sydney, Toronto and Dublin, 2005, pp. 305-306.

8. R. Monckton Milnes, Baron Houghton, "Edward Cheney. *In Memoriam*" in *Miscellanies of the Philobiblon Society*, vol. xv, London, 1877-1884. Henceforth, Milnes, "Edward Cheney. *In Memoriam*".

9. Milnes, "Edward Cheney. *In Memoriam*".

10. Lutyens, *Effie in Venice*, p. 170.

11. *VCH Shropshire*, x, 216. The service buildings of the old Hall were refurbished as a private house in the early 1980s after the demolition of most of Badger Hall in c. 1953.

12. Collingwood, *The Life of John Ruskin*, p. 350.

13. Newman and Pevsner, *Shropshire* (2006), p. 131.

14. In April 1851, Effie and John Ruskin made a very brief visit to Badger Hall where all three Cheney brothers were in residence: see Lutyens, *Effie in Venice*, p. 173.

15. Diary of John Ruskin, 1850, Lancaster RF Ms T7A. At the beginning of

Ms T7A Ruskin has written "some notes of Wenlock, p. 188": however, I have been unable to find these notes.

16. Diary of John Ruskin, 1850, Lancaster RF Ms T7A.
17. Lutyens, *Effie in Venice*, p. 171 (letter from Effie to Rawdon Brown, undated).
18. *Diaries*, II, p. 467 (Sunday 3 October 1850).
19. Hilton, *John Ruskin: The Early Years*, p. 150.

Chapter 7

1. *Diaries*, II, p. 469.
2. Hilton, *John Ruskin: The Early Years*, p. 157.
3. *Diaries*, II, p. 469.
4. Lutyens, *Effie in Venice*, pp. 179-180 (letter from Effie to her mother, 15 August 1851).
5. *Diaries*, II, p. 469 (Wednesday 12 August 1851).
6. CW35: 447. See Ruskin's sketch of bridge, Plate XXXIII, facing p. 447 (date uncertain).
7. CW35: 433.
8. CW33: xxxii.
9. Lutyens, *Effie in Venice*, p. 180.
10. CW2: facing 224. The impressive glacier had been the inspiration for some of Ruskin's poetry in 1842 (CW2: 224).
11. CW36: 454.
12. Lutyens, *Effie in Venice*, p. 181 (letter of Effie to her mother, 15 August 1851).
13. Lutyens, *Effie in Venice*, p. 181.
14. Yves Ballu, *À la conquête du Mont-Blanc*, Gallimard, Paris, 1993, p. 73.
15. Letter of John James Ruskin to Elizabeth Fall, written from the Hotel Liverpool, no. 11 Rue Castiglione, Paris, Lancaster RF Ms L 3/3/3.
16. CW35: 436.
17. CW6: 456.
18. CW6: 456, n. 1.
19. CW36: 117.
20. Raymund Fitzsimons, *The Baron of Piccadilly: The Travels and Entertainments of Albert Smith 1816-1860*, Geoffrey Bles, London, 1967, p. 111. Hereafter, Fitzsimons.
21. Fitzsimons, p. 115.

22. Fitzsimons, p. 121

23. CW36: 117.

24. Letter of John James Ruskin to Elizabeth Fall, 16 September 1856, Lancaster RF Ms L 3/3/3. The "e" in Forman has been struck through, possibly a correction made by John James on realising his mistake.

25. Diary of John Ruskin 1856, 1857, 1858, 1859, Lancaster RF Ms 11, folio 26.

26. CW35: 166.

27. CW36: 117 (letter of John Ruskin to his father, 16 August 1851).

28. John Lewis Bradley, *Ruskin's Letters from Venice 1851-1852*, Yale University Press, New Haven, 1955, p. 15 (letter of John Ruskin to his father, 18 September 1851). Henceforth, Bradley, *Ruskin's Letters from Venice 1851-1852*.

29. Bradley, *Ruskin's Letters from Venice 1851-1852*, p. 66.

30. Lutyens, *Effie in Venice*, p. 189.

31. Bradley, *Ruskin's Letters from Venice 1851-1852*, p. 35 (letter of John Ruskin to his father, 11 October 1851).

32. Bradley, *Ruskin's Letters from Venice 1851-1852*, p. 35 (letter of John Ruskin to his father, 11 October 1851).

33. Lutyens, *Effie in Venice*, p. 192 (letter of Effie to her mother, postmarked 22 Sept. 1851).

34. Lutyens, *Effie in Venice*, p. 214.

35. Lutyens, *Effie in Venice*, p. 237 (letter of Effie to her parents, 28 December 1851).

36. Lutyens, *Effie in Venice*, p. 238.

37. Lutyens, *Effie in Venice*, p. 259 n. 1.

38. Lutyens, *Effie in Venice*, p. 264 (letter of Effie to her mother, 8 February 1852).

39. Bradley, *Ruskin's Letters from Venice 1851-1852*, p. 195 (letter of John Ruskin to his father, 24 February 1852).

40. Bradley, *Ruskin's Letters from Venice 1851-1852*, p. 195, n. 4.

41. CW35: 392-393.

42. Bradley, *Ruskin's Letters from Venice 1851-1852*, p. 171 (letter of John Ruskin to his father, 8 February 1852).

43. James noted the "rapidly increasing decay" of the Tintorettos: see Henry James, *Italian Hours*, edited with an introduction and notes by John Auchard, Penguin Books, Harmondsworth, 1995, p. 57. Henceforth, *Italian Hours* (1995).

44. CW12: lx.

45. CW11: 366.

46. CW11: 366-367; 429-431.

47. Bradley, *Ruskin's Letters from Venice 1851-1852*, pp. 281-282 (letter of John Ruskin to his father, 17 May 1852).

48. Quoted in Lutyens, *Effie in Venice*, p. 225, from an unpublished letter from Venice, August 1851.

49. Lutyens, *Effie in Venice*, p. 224.

50. CW24: 187.

51. CW24: xxxix-xl.

52. British Library Add. Ms 36304, folio 111.

53. CW35: 504.

54. Lutyens, *Effie in Venice*, p. 304.

55. Lutyens, *Effie in Venice*, p. 316 (letter of Effie to her parents, 23 May 1852).

56. CW12: lxi.

57. Lutyens, *Effie in Venice*, p. 297 (letter of Effie to her parents, 17 April 1852).

58. Lutyens, *Effie in Venice*, p. 301 (letter of Effie to her parents, 26 April 1852).

59. Lutyens, *Effie in Venice*, p. 313 (letter of Effie to her parents, postmarked 17 Maggio 1852).

60. Lutyens, *Effie in Venice*, p. 313 (ibid.).

61. Lutyens, *Effie in Venice*, p. 318 (letter of Effie to her parents, 29 May 1852).

62. Inscription on her memorial stone carved by John Gibson in Badger Church.

63. Lutyens, *Effie in Venice*, p. 320 (letter of Effie to her parents, 12 June 1852).

64. Lutyens, *Effie in Venice*, p. 323 (letter of Effie to her parents, postmarked 16 Guigno 1852).

65. Lutyens, *Effie in Venice*, p. 326 (letter of Effie to her parents, 20 June 1852).

66. Bradley, *Ruskin's Letters from Venice 1851-1852*, p. 304 (letter of John Ruskin to his father, 18 June 1852).

67. Letter reproduced in Lutyens, *Effie in Venice*, pp. 331-332.

68. Lutyens, *Effie in Venice*, p. 339.

69. Lutyens, *Effie in Venice*, p. 327.

70. Bradley, *Ruskin's Letters from Venice 1851-1852*, p. 308 (letter of John Ruskin to his father, 24 June 1852).

71. Lutyens, *Effie in Venice*, p. 334 (letter of Effie to her parents, 4 July 1852).

72. Lutyens, *Effie in Venice*, p. 335 (letter of Effie to Rawdon Brown, 4 July 1852).

73. Lutyens, *Effie in Venice*, p. 341.

74. *The Times*, 6 February 1852.

75. Bradley, *Ruskin's Letters from Venice 1851-1852*, p. 273.

76. Bradley, *Ruskin's Letters from Venice 1851-1852*, p. 276.

77. Bradley, *Ruskin's Letters from Venice 1851-1852*, p. 299.

78. CW10: xxxiii (letter of John Ruskin to his father, 16 September 1851).

79. Lutyens, *Effie in Venice*, p. 189, n. 2.

80. Quoted in John Dixon Hunt, *The Wider Sea: A Life of John Ruskin*, Dent, London, Melbourne and Toronto, 1982, p. 223.

81. Lutyens, *Millais and the Ruskins*, p. 26 (letter of John Ruskin to Mr Gray, 10 November 1852).

82. Marshall, *OG*, p.32.

Chapter 8

1. See full report in *The Times*, Wednesday 23 March 1853, p. 7, col. B.

2. *The Times*, Friday 20 May 1853, p. 8.

3. *The Times*, 23 March 1853.

4. *Who's Who of British Members of Parliament*, volume 1, 1832-1885, [compiled by] Michael Stenton, Harvester Press, Hassocks, 1976.

5. *Eddowes's Shrewsbury Journal*, 28 February 1866, p. 8 (letter to the editor from 'Turn-him-out', Bridgnorth). Information kindly supplied by George C. Baugh.

6. *Eddowes's Shrewsbury Journal*, 28 February 1866, p. 8.

7. [Dr R.H.Moore], *The Pritchard Family and Businesses*, Pitt & Cooksey 1190/3/1 – boxes 39-41 & 64-85, S.A., Shrewsbury. Information kindly supplied by George C. Baugh.

8. Eric Mercer, *English Architecture to 1900: The Shropshire Experience*, Logaston Press, Little Logaston, 2003, p. 227.

9. *The Builder*, 1 October 1870, p. 784.

10. Diary of John James Ruskin, 1845-1864, Lancaster RF Ms 33, folio 38.

11. John Batchelor, *Lady Trevelyan and the Pre-Raphaelite Brotherhood*, Chatto & Windus, London, 2006, p. 80 (excerpt from her diary of 27 April 1853). Hereafter, Batchelor, *Lady Trevelyan*.

12. Information in her unpublished diary kindly communicated to me by John Batchelor.

13. Batchelor, *Lady Trevelyan*, p. 80

14. Batchelor, *Lady Trevelyan*, p. 232.

15. Batchelor, *Lady Trevelyan*, p. 86.

16. Diary of John James Ruskin 1845-1864, Lancaster RF Ms 33.

17. CW35: 423-424.

18. Hilton, *John Ruskin: The Early Years*, p. 112.

19. Diary of John James Ruskin 1845-1864, Lancaster RF Ms 33.

20. Lutyens, *Millais and the Ruskins*, p. 113 (letter of Effie to Rawdon Brown, 30 November 1853).

21. Diary of John James Ruskin 1845-1864, Lancaster RF Ms 33.

22. Diary of John James Ruskin 1845-1864, Lancaster RF Ms 33.

23. Lutyens, *Millais and the Ruskins*, p. 145 (letter of Effie to her parents, 28 February 1854).

24. Diary of John James Ruskin 1845-1864, Lancaster RF Ms 33.

25. Lutyens, *Millais and the Ruskins*, p. 168 (letter of Effie to her mother, 6 April 1854).

26. Lutyens, *Millais and the Ruskins*, p. 174 (letter of Effie to Rawdon Brown, 10 April 1854). Brown was staying with the Cheneys at 4 Audley Square, London.

27. Lutyens, *Millais and the Ruskins*, p. 176 (letter of Effie to Rawdon Brown, 11 April 1854).

28. Lutyens, *Millais and the Ruskins*, p. 178 (letter of Millais to Mrs Gray, 18 April 1854).

29. James, *The Order of Release*, p. 227.

30. Gladstone was MP for Oxford University from 1847 to 1866.

31. British Library Add. Ms. 44379, folio 226 (letter of Osborne Gordon to Gladstone, 11 April 1854).

32. British Library Add. Ms. 44379, folio 288 (letter of Osborne Gordon to Gladstone, 17 April (Easter Monday) 1854).

33. Four girls were also born: Jane Gordon (died in 1912), Clara Gordon, Hilda Gordon and Agnes Isabel Baker.

34. Diary of John James Ruskin 1845-1864, Lancaster RF Ms 33.

35. CW5: xlix.

36. CW5: xlvii.

37. Quoted in Michael W. Brooks, *John Ruskin and Victorian Architecture*, Thames and Hudson, London, 1989, p. 101.

38. Diary of John James Ruskin 1845-1864, Lancaster RF Ms 33.

39. Edward Wakeling (ed.), *Lewis Carroll's Diaries: The Private Journals of Charles Lutwidge Dodgson*, vol. I, January to September 1855, The Lewis

Carroll Society, 1993, p. 101.

40. Burd, *The Ruskin Family Letters*, II, p. 450 (letter of John Ruskin to his father, 15 March 1837).

41. CW35: 192.

42. Burd, *The Ruskin Family Letters*, II, p. 734.

43. CW35: 251.

44. Wakeling (ed.), *Lewis Carroll's Diaries*, p. 100.

45. Marshall, *OG*, p. 41.

46. Reported in *The Times*, Friday 15 June 1855.

47. CW36: 256-257 (letter of John Ruskin to Mrs Simon, 1857).

48. Diary of John James Ruskin 1845-1864, Lancaster RF Ms 33.

49. Diary of John James Ruskin 1845-1864, Lancaster RF Ms 33.

50. Bill and Mason, *Christ Church and Reform*, p. 96.

Chapter 9

1. CW35: 251.

2. See photograph of the slab in Jones, B*ridgnorth Grammar & Endowed Schools*, p. 14.

3. CW20: 112-113.

4. Osborne Gordon, *A Sermon Preached in The Cathedral Church of Christ in Oxford on Easter Day 1861*, J.H. and Jas. Parker, Oxford & London, 1861.

5. Murray, *A Handbook for Travellers in Berks, Bucks, and Oxfordshire*, 1860, p. 25.

6. Diane Collins, *Easthampstead its Manor, Church and People*, Juniper Publications, Bracknell, 2000, p. 86. Henceforth, Collins, *Easthampstead*.

7. W. B. C. Lister, *A Bibliography of Murray's Handbooks for Travellers*, Dereham Books, 1993, p. 76.

8. Murray, *A Handbook for Travellers in Berks, Bucks, and Oxfordshire*, 1860, p. 25.

9. Murray, *A Handbook for Travellers in Berks, Bucks, and Oxfordshire*, 1860, p. 25.

10. Collins, *Easthampstead*, p. 24.

11. Collins, *Easthampstead*, p. 25.

12. Nikolaus Pevsner, *Berkshire*, Penguin books, 1998 [1966], p. 92. Henceforth, Pevsner, *Berkshire* (1998).

13. Letter of John Ruskin to Henry Acland, commenced in January 1859, in

Notes

Henry W. Acland and John Ruskin, *The Oxford Museum*, Smith, Elder and Co., London, pp. 84, 88-89. Henceforth, Acland and Ruskin, *The Oxford Museum*.

14. Acland and Ruskin, *The Oxford Museum*, p. 107.
15. Acland and Ruskin, *The Oxford Museum*, p. 106.
16. Acland and Ruskin, *The Oxford Museum*, p. 103.
17. Acland and Ruskin, *The Oxford Museum*, p. 104.
18. Murray, *A Handbook for Travellers in Berks, Bucks and Oxfordshire*, 1872, p. 32.
19. Collins, *Easthampstead*, pp. 31-32.
20. Letter of Osborne Gordon to John Ruskin, 11 June 1874, Lancaster RF Ms L7.
21. Letter of Osborne Gordon to John Ruskin, 11 June 1874, Lancaster RF Ms L7.
22. Oliver Simon, *The Stained Glass in the Parish Church of St Michael & St Mary Magdalene, Easthampstead, Berkshire*, 1994, p. 8.
23. Collins, *Easthampstead*, p. 86 (letter of Osborne Gordon to Christ Church Censors, 1 May 1863).
24. Marshall, *OG*, p. 43.
25. Collins, *Easthampstead*, pp. 86-87 (letter of Osborne Gordon to Christ Church Censors, 1 May 1863).
26. Marshall, *OG*, p. 43.
27. Collins, *Easthampstead*, p. 86 (letter of Osborne Gordon to Christ Church Censors, 1 May 1863).
28. Collins, *Easthampstead*, p. 15.
29. Reproduced in Collins, *Easthampstead*, p. 87 (letter of Osborne Gordon to unidentified recipient).
30. Account Book of John James Ruskin 1845-1863, Lancaster RF Ms 29.
31. Marshall, *OG*, p. 71.
32. G. W. Kitchin, *Ruskin in Oxford and Other Studies*, Murray, London, 1904, p. 25.
33. Wakeling, *Lewis Carroll's Diaries*, p. 135 (entry of 31 December 1855).
34. Bradley, *Ruskin's Letters from Venice, 1851-1852*, p. 284 (letter of John Ruskin to his father, 22 May 1852).
35. Account Book of John James Ruskin 1845-1863, Lancaster RF Ms 29.
36. Collins, *Easthampstead*, p. 86 (letter of Osborne Gordon to Christ Church Censors, 1 May 1863).
37. CW27: 39 (February 1871, *Fors Clavigera*).
38. See for example CW27: 60-64 (April 1871, *Fors Clavigera*).

39. CW34: 597.

40. CW29: 250.

41. Published in Oxford and London by James Parker and Co., 1870, price Sixpence. See also Marshall, *OG*, p. 44.

42. Collins, *Easthampstead*, p. 49 (Department of the Environment description).

43. 15 May-12 November 1862; 15 December 1862-1 June 1863; 8 September-14 November 1863.

44. James L. Spates, "Ruskin in Milan, 1862", *The Journal of Pre-Raphaelite Studies*, vol. 13 (New Series), Fall, 2004, p. 61, n. 62.

45. James L. Spates, *The Imperfect Round: Helen Gill Viljoen's Life of Ruskin*, 2005.

46. James L. Spates and Van Akin Burd, "Ruskin in Milan, 1862: A chapter from 'Dark Star', Helen Gill Viljoen's Unpublished Biography of John Ruskin", *The Journal of Pre-Raphaelite Studies*, volume 13, Fall 2004, p. 21.

47. CW36: 430 (letter of John Ruskin to his father from Mornex, 2 January 1863).

48. Listed in the Catalogue of Ruskin's Drawings compiled by Hugh Allen and E. T. Cook, published in 1912, CW38: 260, no. 917: it was then owned by William Pritchard Gordon.

49. Listed in the Catalogue of Ruskin's Drawings, CW38: 235, no. 283.

50. CW36: 432 (letter of John Ruskin to his father from Mornex, 18 January 1863).

51. CW17: Plate 4, facing p. lx. See also CW17: cxv. William Pritchard Gordon lent the painting for exhibition at the Ruskin Exhibition held in the Manchester City Art Gallery in the spring of 1904 (CW38: 235). It was purchased by John Howard Whitehouse after the H.[erbert] Pritchard Gordon sale at Sotheby's on 10 May 1933 (J. S. Dearden, *Ruskin, Bembridge and Brantwood*, pp. 123-124). It is now in the care of The Ruskin Foundation (The Ruskin Library, University of Lancaster), catalogued as RF 1174.

52. CW36: 436 (letter of John Ruskin to his father from Mornex, 26 February 1863).

53. Dearden, *Ruskin, Bembridge and Brantwood*, p. 124. *Paestum* is now in the care of The Ruskin Foundation, Lancaster RF 755.

54. CW35: 316, and reproduced as Plate XVII.

55. Dearden, *Ruskin, Bembridge and Brantwood*, pp. 123-124.

56. Also spelt Breson or Brison: for its situation, see W. G. Collingwood, *The Limestone Alps of Savoy*, George Allen, Orpington, 1884, pp. 10 and 76 ff.

57. CW36: 444-445 (letter of John Ruskin to his father, 14 May 1863).

58. CW36: 444 (letter of John Ruskin to his father, 14 May 1863).

59. CW36: 445 (letter of John Ruskin to his father, 26 May 1863).

60. CW17: lxxiv-lxxv.

61. Van Akin Burd (ed.), *The Winnington Letters: John Ruskin's Correspondence with Margaret Alexis Bell and the Children of Winnington Hall*, Harvard University Press, Cambridge, Mass., 1969, pp. 416-417 (letter of John Ruskin to his father, 26 August 1863). Henceforth, Burd, *The Winnington Letters*.

62. *Diaries*, II, p. 581.

63. *Diaries*, II, p. 581.

64. *Diaries*, II, p. 581.

65. CW36: 453 (letter of John Ruskin to his father, 14 September 1863).

66. CW36: 453 (letter of John Ruskin to his father, 14 September 1863).

67. CW36: 453 (letter of John Ruskin to his father, 14 September 1863).

68. CW35: 436.

69. CW35: 436.

70. CW17: lxxv (letter of John Ruskin to his father, 11 September 1863).

71. CW17: lxxv.

72. Burd, *The Winnington Letters*, p. 432.

73. Burd, *The Winnington Letters*, pp. 433-434 (letter of John Ruskin to his father, 21 September 1863).

74. Quoted in Burd, *The Winnington Letters*, p. 433, n. 3.

75. CW36: 461 (letter of John Ruskin to his father, 16 December 1863).

76. CW36: 462 (letter of John Ruskin to George Allen, 1 January 1864).

77. CW27: 281 n. 1.

Chapter 10

1. *Diaries*, II, p. 595.

2. *Diaries*, II, p. 598.

3. *Diaries*, II, p. 602.

4. *Diaries*, II, p. 609.

5. CW36: 522 (letter of John Ruskin to Charles Eliot Norton, 23 January 1867).

6. *Diaries*, II, p. 608.

7. *Diaries*, II, p. 613.

8. *Diaries*, II, p. 613.

9. *Diaries*, II, p. 614.

10. *Diaries*, II, p. 616.

11. *Diaries*, II, p. 616.

12. *Diaries*, II, p. 617.

13. *Diaries*, II, p. 619.

14. *Diaries*, II, p. 620.

15. *Diaries*, II, p. 620.

16. *Diaries*, II, p. 620.

17. *The Times*, Friday 11 October 1867, p. 9.

18. Hilton, *John Ruskin: The Later Years*, pp. 146-147.

19. *Diaries*, II, p. 644 (9 March 1868).

20. *Diaries*, II, p. 644.

21. CW35: 317-318.

22. Shapiro, *Ruskin in Italy*, p. 243 (letter of Margaret Ruskin to her son, 28 June 1845).

23. Burd, *The Winnington Letters*, p. 617 (letter of Joan Agnew to Margaret Ruskin, 9 May 1868).

24. Cynthia Gamble, "Ruskin's Northern France: 'a perpetual Paradise' Abbeville, Rouen and Amiens" in Stephen Wildman and Cynthia Gamble, *'A Perpetual Paradise': Ruskin's Northern France*, The Ruskin Library, University of Lancaster, 2002, p. 9.

25. *Diaries*, II, p. 664.

26. *Diaries*, II, p. 672.

27. John Lewis Bradley (ed.), *The Letters of John Ruskin to Lord and Lady Mount-Temple*, Ohio State University Press, 1964, pp. 225-226 (letter of John Ruskin to Mrs Cowper-Temple, 5 October 1869).

28. Hilton, *John Ruskin: The Later Years*, p. 101.

29. *Diaries* II, p. 681.

30. *Diaries*, II, p. 686.

31. *Diaries*, II, p. 686.

32. Hilton, *John Ruskin: The Later Years*, pp. 171-172.

33. *Diaries*, II, p. 693.

34. Jeffrey Richards, *Sir Henry Irving*, Hambledon & London, London, 2005, p. 92. Henceforth, Richards, *Sir Henry Irving*.

35. CW26: 328, n. 1.

36. See *Diaries*, II, p. 644.

37. CW26: 327-328.

38. See Hilton, *John Ruskin: The Later Years*, p. 180.

39. Quoted in Jeanne Clegg, *Ruskin and Venice*, Junction Books, London, 1981, p. 142. Henceforth, Clegg, *Ruskin and Venice*.

40. Clegg, *Ruskin and Venice*, p. 209 n. 24.

41. See CW20: xlix, n. 2 for tour itinerary.

42. *Diaries*, II, p. 700.

43. *Diaries*, II, p. 705.

44. *Diaries*, II, p. 705.

45. *Diaries*, II, p. 706.

46. See CW20: 185 *seq.*

47. CW27: 105.

48. CW28: 661.

49. Burd, *The Winnington Letters*, p. 670 (letter of John Ruskin to Joan Agnew, 7 December 1870).

50. Hilton, *John Ruskin: The Later Years*, pp. 130-131.

51. CW37: 35 (letter of John Ruskin to Charles Eliot Norton, 14 September 1871).

52. CW37: 35 (ibid.).

53. CW37: 35 (ibid.) The emphasis is Ruskin's.

54. CW37: 43 (letter of John Ruskin to W. H. Harrison, undated).

55. CW37: 47.

56. *Diaries*, II, p. 718.

57. *Diaries*, II, p. 732.

58. CW25: xxxvii.

59. CW19: lv.

60. See CW34: 719; CW37: 591.

61. CW30: 328.

62. Letter of Osborne Gordon to John Ruskin, 11 June 1874, Lancaster RF L7.

63. See CW34: 513-516.

64. CW34: 517 (letter of John Ruskin to Mr Chapman, 26 May 1874).

65. CW34: 517.

66. CW34: 517.

67. CW34: 517.

68. Letter of Osborne Gordon to John Ruskin, 11 June 1874, Lancaster RF L7.

69. Letter of Osborne Gordon to John Ruskin, 11 June 1874, Lancaster RF L7.

70. Letter of Osborne Gordon to John Ruskin, 11 June 1874, Lancaster RF L7.

71. Letter of Osborne Gordon to John Ruskin, 11 June 1874, Lancaster RF L7.

72. Letter of Osborne Gordon to John Ruskin, 11 June 1874, Lancaster RF L7.

73. *Diaries*, III, p. 837.

74. Van Akin Burd (ed.), *John Ruskin and Rose La Touche: Her Unpublished Diaries of 1861 and 1867*, The Clarendon Press, Oxford, 1979, p. 133.

75. CW28: 246.

76. Robert Hewison, Ian Warrell and Stephen Wildman, *Ruskin, Turner and the Pre-Raphaelites*, Tate Gallery Publishing, 2000, p. 261. See also on the same page Ruskin's pencil sketch of Rose on her deathbed.

77. See Hilton, *John Ruskin: The Later Years*, p. 325.

78. *Diaries*, III, p. 876.

79. Letter of Osborne Gordon to John Ruskin, 14 January 1876, Lancaster RF L7.

80. Letter of Osborne Gordon to John Ruskin, 14 January 1876, Lancaster RF L7.

81. Letter of Osborne Gordon to John Ruskin, 14 January 1876, Lancaster RF L7.

82. Letter of Osborne Gordon to John Ruskin, 14 January 1876, Lancaster RF L7.

83. Letter of Osborne Gordon to John Ruskin, 14 January 1876, Lancaster RF L7.

84. CW28: 637 (letter of Osborne Gordon to John Ruskin, 20 April 1876).

85. CW28: 561, 562.

86. CW28: 562.

87. CW28: 637 (letter of Osborne Gordon to John Ruskin, 20 April 1876).

88. CW28: 637.

89. CW28: 637.

90. CW28: 637.

91. CW28: 637.

92. CW28: 618.

93. He stayed in Venice from 2 November 1876 until 23 May 1877: see CW24: xxxiv for the itinerary of his continental tour.

94. CW24: 228.

95. CW24: 182.

96. CW24: 187.

97. CW24: 226.

98. Examples of their work can be found at All Souls Church, Swiss Cottage, London; Albert Memorial, London; stained-glass windows in St Stephen's Church, Rosslyn Hill, London.

99. *The Bridgnorth Journal*, Saturday 2 June 1883.

100. *The Bridgnorth Journal*, 2 June 1883.

101. CW29: 222.

102. CW29: 184.

Chapter 11

1. *The Times*, Monday 30 December 1878, p. 6.

2. Marshall, *OG*, pp. 57-58.

3. Diary of John Ruskin August 1882-January 1883, Lancaster RF Ms 23, folio 135 right hand page.

4. Published as "Mythic Schools of Painting[:] E. Burne-Jones and G. F. Watts" in CW33: 287-305.

5. Letter of John Ruskin to Joan Severn 23 May 1883, Lancaster RF L45.

6. Published as "Fairy Land [:] Mrs. Allingham and Kate Greenaway" in CW33: 327-349.

7. Letter of John Ruskin to Joan Severn 30 May 1883, Lancaster RF L45.

8. See report in *The Times*, Thursday, 31 May 1883: "The remains of the late Rev. Osborne Gordon, B.D., rector of Easthampstead, Berks, were buried yesterday afternoon at Easthampstead churchyard. Among those present were Lord Arthur Hill, Mr Walter, M.P., Sir Arthur Hayter, M.P. General Pritchard, Colonel Peel, the Dean of Christ Church, Oxford and several of the deceased's Oxford friends. The funeral service was conducted by the Dean of Christ Church."

9. Marshall, *OG*, pp. 60-61.

10. Marshall, *OG*, p. 67.

11. Marshall, *OG*, p. 67.

12. George William Kitchin, *Ruskin in Oxford and Other Studies*, London: Murray, 1904, p. 24.

13. Quoted in Marshall, *OG*, p. 9.

14. *Oxford DNB*, from Calendars of the Grants of Probate and Letters of Administration (CGPLA).

15. Probate inventory of the goods of Osborne Gordon, dated 1883, catalogue ref. D/EZ118/2, Berkshire Record Office.

16. His death was reported in *The Times* of Tuesday 3 July, 1883: "On the 28th June, Alexander John Gordon, of The Hill, near Bridgnorth".

17. Collins, *Easthampstead*, p. 92.

18. Bill and Mason, *Christ Church and Reform*, p. 131.

19. Names listed by Marshall in *OG*, introductory notice.

20. See reproduction of bust as frontispiece in Marshall, *OG*, and also the

Latin inscription.

21. M. H. Spielmann, *John Ruskin*, Cassell, London, Paris, New York & Melbourne, 1900, pp. 180-185 and p. 171 for reproduction of Dressler's bust of Ruskin.

22. Jennifer Sherwood and Nikolaus Pevsner, *Oxfordshire*, Penguin Books, Harmondsworth, 1975 [1974], p. 59.

23. CW33: 363.

24. I have transcribed the text from a photocopy of Ruskin's original draft in Collins, *Easthampstead*, p. 64.

25. CW35: 249

26. CW35: 250

27. Broseley Parish Register.

28. Newman and Pevsner, *Shropshire* (2006), p. 312.

29. John Randall, *History of Broseley* (1879), pp. 217-218.

30. Broseley Parish Register, by kind permission of the Rev. Michael Kinna.

31. John Blachford, *St Peter's Bournemouth*, Jarrold Publishing, Norwich, 2006, p. 13. This fine pulpit and also a font by Earp are in St Peter's Church, Bournemouth.

32. [Dr R. H. Moore], *The Pritchard Family and Businesses*, Pitt & Cooksey, 1190/3/1, in Shropshire Archives (S.A.), Shrewsbury.

33. S. A. 1190/3/567/1.

34. Catalogue of the sale of Stanmore Hall by Ian Haynes & Co., Halesowen.

Part Two

Chapter 12

1.   Henry James, *A Small Boy and Others*, Gibson Square Books, London, 2001, p. 144. Henceforth, *A Small Boy* (2001).

2.   Leon Edel, *Henry James. A Life*, Flamingo, London, 1996 [William Collins, London, 1985], p. 38. Henceforth, Edel, *HJ: A Life* (1996).

3.   *A Small Boy* (2001), p. 163.

4.   *A Small Boy* (2001), p. 165.

5.   *A Small Boy* (2001), p. 144.

6.   *A Small Boy* (2001), p. 182.

7.   *A Small Boy* (2001), p. 182.

8.   *A Small Boy* (2001), p. 190.

9.   *A Small Boy* (2001), pp. 190-191.

10. *A Small Boy* (2001), p. 186.

11. *A Small Boy* (2001), p. 176.

12. John Purkis, *Morris, Burne-Jones and French Gothic, being an account of a walking tour in France July to August 1855*, William Morris Society, London, 2000 [1988, 1991], p. 7.

13. Edel, *HJ: A Life* (1996), p. 226.

14. Edel, *HJ: A Life* (1996), p. 226.

15. *A Small Boy* (2001), p. 165.

16. Richards, *Sir Henry Irving*, p. 69.

17. *A Small Boy*, pp. 164-165.

18. Quoted in Cornelia Pulsifer Kelley, *The Early Development of Henry James*, University of Illinois Press, Urbana, 1965, p. 21. Henceforth, C. P. Kelley, *The Early Development of Henry James*.

19. Henry James, *The Princess Casamassima*, preface to the New York Edition of 1909, edited with an introduction by Derek Brewer, Penguin Books, 1987 [Macmillan & Co. 1886], p. 33. Henceforth, *The Princess Casamassima* (1987).

20. *The Princess Casamassima* (1987), p. 33.

21. *The Princess Casamassima* (1987), p. 33.

22. Henry James, author's preface to *The Spoils of Poynton*, Heinemann, London, 1962, pp. vii and ix.

23. CW36: xciii.

24. Stephen Wildman and John Christian; with essays by Alan Crawford and Laurence des Cars, *Edward Burne-Jones: Victorian Artist-Dreamer*, The Metropolitan Museum of Art, New York, 1998, p. 205.

25. F. W. Dupee (ed.), *Henry James Autobiography,* [*A Small Boy and Others: Notes of a Son and Brother: The Middle Years*], Princeton University Press, Princeton, New Jersey, 1983, p. 476. Henceforth, Dupee, *Henry James Autobiography* (1983). James wrote: "I had addressed in trembling hope my first fond attempt at literary criticism to Charles Eliot Norton."

26. Leon Edel (ed.), *Henry James: Selected Letters*, Cambridge, Massachusetts and Belknap, London, 1987, p. 22 (letter of Henry James to Alice James, 10 March 1869). Henceforth, Edel, *HJ SL* (1987).

27. Edel, *HJ SL* (1987), p. 22.

28. Edel, *HJ SL* (1987), p. 22.

29. Edel, *HJ SL* (1987), p. 22.

30. Edel, *HJ SL* (1987), pp. 22-23.

31. Edel, *HJ SL* (1987), p. 23.

32. Edel, *HJ SL* (1987), p. 23.

33. Edel, *HJ SL* (1987), p. 23.

34. Reproduced in Julian Treuherz, Elizabeth Prettejohn and Edwin Becker (eds), *Dante Gabriel Rossetti*, Uitgeverij Waanders b.v, Zwolle/ Van Gogh Museum, Amsterdam/National Museums Liverpool, 2003, p. 81. Henceforth, Treuherz et al., *Rossetti* exhibition catalogue. Cf. also the portrait of Swinburne by William Bell Scott, 1860, in Christine Poulson, *The Art of William Morris*, Silverdale Books, Leicester, 2004, p. 25 (at Balliol College, Oxford).

35. Edel, *HJ SL* (1987), p. 23.

36. See Treuherz et al., *Rossetti* exhibition catalogue in which the painting of Jane Morris is reproduced as fig. 63, p. 94.

37. Edel, *HJ SL* (1987), p. 23.

38. Edel, *HJ SL* (1987), p. 23.

39. Edel, *HJ SL* (1987), p. 24.

40. Edel, *HJ SL* (1987), p. 38 (letter of Henry James to John La Farge, 20 June 1869).

41. Edel, *HJ SL* (1987), p. 38.

42. Quoted by Francis O'Gorman, *Ruskin*, Sutton Publishing, Stroud, 1999, p. 14.

43. Edel, *HJ SL* (1987), p. 39.

44. Edel, *HJ: A Life* (1996), p. 95.

45. In Linda Merrill, *A Pot of Paint. Aesthetics on Trial 'Whistler v. Ruskin'*, Smithsonian Institution Press, Washington and London, 1992, p. 174.

46. Quoted in Hilton, *John Ruskin: The Later Years*, pp. 153-154.

47. Hilton, *John Ruskin: The Later Years*, p. 153.

48. C. P. Kelley, *The Early Development of Henry James*, p. 100.

49. Quoted in C. P. Kelley, *The Early Development of Henry James*, p. 103.

50. Henry James, *Transatlantic Sketches*, James R. Osgood and Company, Boston, 1875, p. 34. Henceforth, *Transatlantic Sketches*.

51. *Transatlantic Sketches*, p. 14.

52. Edel, *HJL*, II, p. 110 (letter of Henry James to Henry Adams, 5 May 1877).

53. Edel, *HJ: A Life* (1996), p. 208.

54. Edel, *HJL*, II, p. 124 (letter of Henry James to William James, 10 July 1877).

55. Edel, *HJL*, II, p. 98 (letter of Henry James to his father, 13 February 1877).

56. Quoted in C. P. Kelley, *The Early Development of Henry James*, p. 109.

57. Edel, *HJL*, II, p. 124 (letter of Henry James to William James, 10 July 1877).

58. At a dinner given by Bernard Quaritch, bookseller, to honour Burton in June 1882, Ruskin made a speech in which he acknowledged his longstanding friendship with the explorer, "whose acquaintance I have had the honour of enjoying for more years than I now care to remember" (CW37: 399).

59. Edel, *HJ: A Life* (1996), p. 209.

60. *Portraits of Places* (2001), pp. 198-207. Cf. William Powell Frith's large, crowded canvas entitled *Derby Day* of 1858 depicting a microcosm of society: pickpockets, gypsies, wealthy landowners and others.

61. *Portraits of Places* (2001), pp. 183-197.

62. Quoted in John L. Sweeney (ed.), *The Painter's Eye: Notes and Essays on the Pictorial Arts by Henry James*, University of Wisconsin Press, 1989, p. 145.

63. Edel, *HJL*, II, p. 123 (letter of Henry James to William James, 10 July 1877).

Chapter 13

1. Henry Adams, *The Education of Henry [Brooks] Adams. An Autobiography*, Constable, London, 1919, p. 204. Henceforth, *Adams Autobiography*.

2. The painting (3003mm x 4978 mm) is in the National Portrait Gallery, London.

3. *Adams Autobiography*, p. 206.

4. *VCH Shropshire*, x, p. 416.

5. *Adams Autobiography*, p. 206.

6. *Adams Autobiography*, p. 207.

7. Ernest Samuels (ed.), *Henry Adams: Selected Letters*, Cambridge, Massachusetts and Belknap Press of Harvard University Press, London, c. 1992, p. 69 (letter of Henry Adams to Charles Francis Adams, Jr., 7 October 1864). Henceforth, Samuels, *HA SL* .

8. Samuels, *HA SL*, p. 69.

9. Samuels, *HA SL*, p. 69.

10. Samuels, *HA SL*, p. 69.

11. Samuels, *HA SL*, p. 69.

12. A reference to Tennyson's poem "Aylmer's Field" (1864).

13. Samuels, *HA SL*, p. 69.

14. George Cecil Weld Forester, the second son of the first Lord Forester, was elected MP for Wenlock in 1828, a position he held for 46 years and became 'Father of the House'.

15. Samuels, *HA SL*, p. 69.

16. Samuels, *HA SL*, p. 70.

17. *Adams Autobiography*, pp. 290-291.

18. *Adams Autobiography*, p. 291.

19. Marian Adams, *The Letters of Mrs Henry Adams, 1865-1883*, Longmans & Co., London, 1937, pp. 133-134 (letter of Clover Adams to her father, 23 July 1873). Henceforth, *The Letters of Mrs Henry Adams.*

20. George Monteiro (ed.), *The Correspondence of Henry James and Henry Adams, 1877-1914*, Louisiana State University Press, Baton Rouge and London, 1992, p. 41 (letter of Henry James to Henry Adams, 15 July 1877. Henceforth, Monteiro, *Corr. HJ HA.*

21. Monteiro, *Corr. HJ HA*, p. 40 (letter of Henry James to Henry Adams, 5 June 1877).

22. Monteiro, *Corr. HJ HA*, p. 40 (letter of Henry James to Henry Adams, 5 June 1877.

23. Quoted in Monteiro, *Corr. HJ HA*, p. 40, n. 2 (from Levenson *et al.*, eds., *Letters of Henry Adams*, II, p. 307).

24. Edel, *HJL*, II, p. 123 (letter of Henry James to William James, 10 July 1877.

25. Edel, *HJL*, II, p.123 (letter of Henry James to William James, 10 July 1877.

26. For biographical details, see W. B. C. Lister, with an introduction by John R. Gretton, *A Bibliography of Murray's Handbooks for Travellers and Biographies of Authors, Editors, Revisers and Principal Contributors*, Dereham Books, Dereham, Norfolk, 1993, pp. 104, 124.

27. Monteiro, *Corr. HJ HA*, p. 41 (letter of Henry James to Henry Adams, 15 July 1877). (cf. Edel, *HJL*, II, p. 125).

Chapter 14

1. Henry James, *A Little Tour in France*, with ninety-four illustrations by Joseph Pennell, William Heinemann, London, 1900 , p. 80. Henceforth, *A Little Tour in France* (1900).

2. Henry James, *Portraits of Places*, Duckworth, London, 2001 [Macmillan, 1883] p. 239. Hereafter, *Portraits of Places* (2001).

3. Cf. *The Princess Casamassima* (1987), p. 315.

4. Rebecca West, *Henry James*, Nisbet and Co. Ltd., London, 1916, pp. 46-47.

5. Edel, *HJ: A Life* (1996), p. 215.

6. Lady Catherine Milnes Gaskell, *Spring in a Shropshire Abbey*, Smith, Elder & Co., London, 1905, p. 20. Henceforth, *Spring in a Shropshire Abbey*.

7. See Mackenzie Edward Charles Walcott, *The Four Minsters round the Wrekin: Buildwas, Haughmond, Lilleshull and Wenlock, with ground plans [and photographic views]*, Shrewsbury [printed], London, 1877 in which there is a plan showing the location of the guesthouse. See also W. F. Mumford, *Wenlock in the Middle Ages*, 1989 [1977], p. 93: henceforth, Mumford, *Wenlock in the Middle Ages*.

8. Lady Catherine Milnes Gaskell, *Friends Round the Wrekin*, Smith, Elder & Co., 1914, p. 3.

9. *The Europeans*, Penguin Classics, 1985, p. 165. Hereafter, *The Europeans* (1985).

10. Monteiro, *Corr. HJ HA*, p. 41.

11. Charles Milnes Gaskell had expressed his liking for James in a letter to Adams, who commented in his reply of 22 August 1877: "I am glad you liked Harry James, and am glad you had him to Wenlock" (quoted in Monteiro, *Corr. HJ HA*, p. 44, n. 2).

12. Monteiro, *Corr. HJ HA*, p. 41 (letter of Henry James to Henry Adams, 15 July 1877 (cf. Edel, *HJL*, II, p. 126).

13. Monteiro, *Corr. HJ HA*, p. 41 (letter of Henry James to Henry Adams, 15 July 1877 (cf. Edel, *HJL*, II, pp. 125-126).

14. See letter of Marian (Clover) Adams to her father, Dr Robert William Hooper, 8 June 1879: "Our plan was to leave London tomorrow, and put up at an inn for a few days, till we found lodgings to suit us; but Mr Gaskell and his wife, with sempiternal kindness, insist so on our going to them first that, after firmly refusing from Washington, we have had to give in. It's an outrage. Gaskell's wife has never seen us, and may find us 'quite too awfully, don't you know, odious'. But to 33 Grosvenor Street we go on Tuesday or Wednesday, they themselves not going up from Wenlock Abbey till tomorrow" (*The Letters of Mrs Henry Adams*, pp. 138-139).

15   Monteiro, *Corr. HJ HA*, pp. 41-42 (letter of Henry James to Henry Adams, 15 July 1877 (cf. Edel, *HJL*, II, p. 126).

16. *Spring in a Shropshire Abbey*, p. 176.

17. *Spring in a Shropshire Abbey*, pp. 13-14.

18. Lady Catherine's embroidery is referenced in Linda Parry (ed.), *William Morris*, Philip Wilson Publishers in association with The Victoria and Albert Museum, 1996, p. 290. I am grateful to Stephen Wildman for drawing my attention to this reference.

19. *Spring in a Shropshire Abbey*, p. 74.

20. *Portraits of Places* (2001), p. 232.

21. *Portraits of Places* (2001), p. 233.

22. Dupee, *Henry James Autobiography* (1983), p. 515.

23. Henry James, *Hawthorne*, Macmillan & Co., London, 1879, p. 42. Henceforth, *Hawthorne* (1879).

24. *Hawthorne* (1879), p. 43.

25. Waldemar Januszczak, "The rocky rehung picture show", *The Sunday Times*, 18 September 2005, p. 7 in the "Culture" supplement.

26. *Portraits of Places* (2001), pp. 238-239.

27. *Portraits of Places* (2001), p. 239.

28. See Sydney Decimus Kitson, *The Life of John Sell Cotman*, Faber and Faber, London, 1937, pp. 41-42.

29. *Spring in a Shropshire Abbey*, p. 224.

30. Murray, *A Handbook for Shropshire, Cheshire and Lancashire*, 1870, p. 41.

31. Samuels, *HA SL*, p. 171 (letter of Henry Adams to Charles Milnes Gaskell, 3 December 1882).

32. *Portraits of Places* (2001), p. 238.

33. *Portraits of Places* (2001), p. 238.

34. *Portraits of Places* (2001), p. 238.

35. *Portraits of Places* (2001), p. 238.

36. *The Princess Casamassima* (1987), p. 301.

37. *Hawthorne* (1879), p. 43.

38. *Portraits of Places* (2001), p. 240.

39. Marcel Proust, *In Search of Lost Time*, general editor Christopher Prendergast, *The Way by Swann's*, volume 1, translated and with an introduction and notes by Lydia Davis, Penguin Books, London, 2002, pp. 61-62.

40. *Portraits of Places* (2001), p. 240.

41. *Portraits of Places* (2001), p. 240.

42. *Portraits of Places* (2001), p. 240.

43. Monteiro, *Corr. HJ HA*, p. 43 (letter of Henry James to Henry Adams, 15 July 1877 (cf. Edel, *HJL*, II, p. 127).
44. *Portraits of Places* (2001), pp. 240-241.
45. *The Princess Casamassima* (1987), p. 308.
46. *The Portrait of a Lady*, Penguin Books, Harmondsworth, 1968, p. 139. Henceforth, *The Portrait of a Lady (1968)*.
47. *The Portrait of a Lady* (1968), p. 46.
48. *The Portrait of a Lady* (1968), p. 578.
49. Quoted in Mumford, *Wenlock in the Middle Ages*, p. 145.
50. *Portraits of Places* (2001), p. 239.

Chapter 15

1. Monteiro, *Corr. HJ HA*, p. 42 (letter of Henry James to Henry Adams, 15 July 1877) (cf. Edel, *HJL*, II, pp. 126-127).
2. *Portraits of Places* (2001), p. 241.
3. Monteiro, *Corr. HJ HA*, p. 42: cf. Edel, *HJL*, II, p. 127 that gives "green" instead of "*préau*". I have not been able to verify the original manuscript but the use of the French word ("*préau*" means a "courtyard") is typically Jamesian.
4. *Portraits of Places* (2001), p. 243.
5. *Portraits of Places* (2001), p. 242.
6. CW 26: 565, note 3: see also *Diaries*, III, p. 893.
7. Kelly's *Directory for Shropshire*, 1900, p. 250.
8. *A Little Tour in France* (1900), p. 263.
9. *Portraits of Places* (2001), p. 242.
10. ibid, p. 242.
11. ibid, p. 242.
12. ibid, p. 241.
13. ibid, p. 241
14. ibid, p. 241.
15. ibid, p. 241.
16. ibid, p. 241.
17. ibid, p. 242.
18. ibid, pp. 242-243.
19. ibid, p. 243.
20. ibid, p. 243.

21. ibid, p. 243.

22. ibid p. 243.

23. ibid, p. 243.

24. ibid, p. 243.

25. Quoted in Tony Tanner, *Venice Desired*, Blackwell Publishers, Oxford, 1992, pp. 158-159. Henceforth, Tanner, *Venice Desired*.

26. Edel, *HJL*, II, p. 484.

27. *A Little Tour in France* (1900), p. 187.

28. *Portraits of Places* (2001), p. 243.

29. Tony Tanner has pointed out this important theme in James's fiction: see Tanner, *Venice Desired*, p. 167.

30. Henry James, *The Aspern Papers* and *The Turn of the Screw*, edited with an introduction by Anthony Curtis, Penguin Books, Harmondsworth, 1984, p. 155. Henceforth, *The Aspern Papers* and *The Turn of the Screw* (1984).

31. *The Aspern Papers* and *The Turn of the Screw* (1984), p. 164.

32. *Portraits of Places* (2001), p. 244. Fanny Price and Emma Woodhouse are heroines of Jane Austen's *Mansfield Park* (1814) and *Emma* (1816) respectively. Evelina and Cecilia are the heroines of Fanny Burney's *Evelina* (1778) and *Cecilia* (1782) respectively.

33. *Portraits of Places* (2001), p. 245.

34. *Portraits of Places* (2001), p. 244.

35. *Portraits of Places* (2001), p. 244.

36. *A Small Boy* (2001), p. 167.

37. Edel, *HJL*, II, p. 160 (letter of Henry James to his father, 25 March 1878).

38. *The Aspern Papers* and *The Turn of the Screw* (1984), p. 47.

39. Maria Fairweather, *Madame de Staël*, Constable & Robinson, London, 2005, p. 419.

Chapter 16

1. Monteiro, *Corr. HJ HA*, p. 42 (letter of Henry James to Henry Adams, 15 July 1877 (cf. Edel, *HJL*, II, p. 127).

2. *Letters of Mrs Henry Adams*, p. 133 (letter of Marian (Clover) Adams to her father, 23 July 1873).

3. *Portraits of Places* (2001), p. 234.

4. ibid, p. 233.

5. ibid, p. 233.

6. ibid, p. 233.

7. ibid, p. 234.

8. ibid, p. 234.

9. ibid, p. 234.

10. ibid, p. 233.

11. ibid, p. 233.

12. ibid, p. 239.

13. *The Princess Casamassima* (1987), p. 338.

14. *Portraits of Places* (2001), p. 162.

15. *Portraits of Places* (2001), p. 247.

16. *Portraits of Places* (2001), p. 248.

17. Edel, *HJL*, II, p. 424 (letter of Henry James to Grace Norton, 28 July 1883).

18. Monteiro, *Corr. HJ HA*, p. 42 (Henry James to Henry Adams, 15 July 1877) (cf. Edel, *HJL*, II, p. 126).

19. Monteiro, *Corr. HJ HA*, p. 41 (letter of Henry James to Henry Adams, 15 July 1877 (cf. Edel, *HJL*, II, pp. 125-126).

20. Monteiro, *Corr. HJ HA*, p. 43 (letter of Henry James to Henry Adams, 15 July 1877) (cf. Edel, *HJL*, II, p. 128).

21. CW35: 13.

22. *The Princess Casamassima* (1987), p. 304.

23. *The Aspern Papers* and *The Turn of the Screw* (1984), p. 49.

24. *Portraits of Places* (2001), p. 167.

25. Edel, *HJ: A Life* (1996), p. 235.

26. *Portraits of Places* (2001), p. 236.

27. *Portraits of Places* (2001), p. 236.

28. *Italian Hours* (1995), p. 96.

29. *Portraits of Places* (2001), p. 239.

30. *Portraits of Places* (2001), pp. 236-237.

31. *Portraits of Places* (2001), p. 237.

32. Murray, *A Handbook for Shropshire, Cheshire and Lancashire*, 1870, p. 31.

33. *Portraits of Places* (2001), p. 237.

34. *Portraits of Places* (2001), p. 237.

35. *Portraits of Places* (2001), pp. 237-238.

36. *Portraits of Places* (2001), p. 235.

37. *Portraits of Places* (2001), p. 238.

38. *The Portrait of a Lady* (1968), p. 125.

39. *The Aspern Papers* and *The Turn of the Screw* (1984), p. 75.

40. *Portraits of Places* (2001), p. 238.

41. *The Europeans* (1985), p. 85.

42. Forrest, *The Old Houses of Wenlock*, p. 86.

43. Quoted in Tanner, *Venice Desired*, p. 158.

44. Quoted in Tanner, *Venice Desired*, p. 158.

45. Quoted in Tanner, *Venice Desired*, p. 158.

46. Henry James's preface to *The Portrait of a Lady* (1968), p. ix.

47. Edel, *HJ: A Life* (1996), p. 215.

48. Edel, *HJL*, II, p. 180. To date, I do not have information about this proposed second visit.

Chapter 17

1. *Portraits of Places* (2001), p. 268.

2. Edel, *HJL*, II, p. 198 (letter of Henry James to Alice James, written on New Year's Eve 1878 from Fryston Hall, Ferrybridge).

3. *Portraits of Places* (2001), 269.

4. *Portraits of Places* (2001), 269.

5. *Portraits of Places* (2001), 269.

6. Edel, *HJL*, II, p. 209 (letter of Henry James to Grace Norton, 4 January 1879).

7. *Portraits of Places*, p. 268.

8. Edel, *HJL*, II, p. 200 (letter of Henry James to Alice James, New Year's Eve 1878).

9. Quoted in Simon Heffer, *Moral Desperado: A Life of Thomas Carlyle*, Weidenfeld and Nicolson, London, 1995, p. 212.

10. Edel, *HJ: A Life* (1996), p. 236.

11. In *Oxford DNB*, from *Collected Letters*, 13. 80.

12. See Anne Taylor, *Laurence Oliphant 1829-1888*, Oxford University Press, Oxford, New York, Toronto and Melbourne, 1982, pp. 96-97.

13. John Batchelor, "Alfred Tennyson: Problems of Biography", *The Yearbook of English Studies*, volume 36, 2006, p. 80.

14. Edel, *HJL*, II, pp. 198-199 (letter of Henry James to Alice James, New Year's Eve 1878).

15. *Portraits of Places* (2001), p. 268.

16. Edel, *HJL*, II, p. 208 (letter of Henry James to Grace Norton, 4 January 1879).

17. Quoted in C. P. Kelley, *The Early Development of Henry James*, p. 201.

18. Edel, *HJ: A Life* (1996), p. 224.

19. Quoted in A. N. Wilson, *The Victorians*, Arrow Books, London, 2003, p. 587.

Select Bibliography

The bibliography mirrors to some extent the interdisciplinary nature of my book. I have attempted to indicate in general terms the books most relevant to each person and theme. There is inevitable overlap.

Manuscript sources

The Bodleian Library, Oxford.

The British Library, London.

The Ruskin Foundation (Ruskin Library, Lancaster University).

Shropshire Archives, Shrewsbury.

Henry Brooks Adams

Adams, Henry, *The Education of Henry [Brooks] Adams: An Autobiography,* Constable, London, 1919.

Adams, Marian, *The Letters of Mrs Henry Adams,* Longmans & Co., London, 1937.

Ford, Worthington Chauncey (ed.), *Letters of Henry Adams 1858-1891,* Constable & Co., London, 1930.

Levenson, Jacob Clavner [et al.] (eds), *The Letters of Henry Adams,* in three volumes, Belknap Press, Cambridge, Massachusetts, c. 1982.

Levenson, Jacob Clavner [et al.] (eds), *The Letters of Henry Adams,* in six volumes, Harvard University Press, Cambridge, Massachusetts, 1982-1988.

Samuels, Ernest (ed.), *Henry Adams: Selected Letters,* Belknap Press of Harvard University Press, Cambridge, Massachusetts and London, c.1992.

Edward Cheney

Cheney, Edward, *Original Documents Relating to Venetian Painters and their Pictures in the 16th Century,* c. 1873.

Cheney, Edward, *Remarks on the Illuminated Manuscripts of the Venetian Republic,* 1868.

Osborne Gordon

Bill, E. G. W. and Mason, J. F. A., *Christ Church and Reform 1850-1867,* The Clarendon Press, Oxford, 1970.

Collins, Diane, *Easthampstead, its Manor, Church and People,* Juniper Publications, Bracknell, 2000.

Gordon, Osborne, *A Sermon Preached in The Cathedral Church of Christ in Oxford on Easter Day 1861,* J. H. and Jas. Parker, Oxford & London, 1861.

Jones, Maureen (ed.), *Bridgnorth Grammar & Endowed Schools,* Five Hundred Years of Change 1503-2003, published by B.G.S. 500th Anniversary Group, 2003.

Marshall, George, Osborne Gordon. *A Memoir: with a Selection of his Writings,* Parker & Co., Oxford & London, 1885.

Simon, Oliver, *The Stained Glass in the Parish Church of St Michael and St Mary Magdalene,* Easthampstead, Berkshire, 1994.

Wakeling, Edward (ed.), *Lewis Carroll's Diaries: The Private Journals of Charles Lutwidge Dodgson,* volume 1, January to September 1855, introduction by Roger Lancelyn Green, The Lewis Carroll Society, Luton, 1993.

Henry James

Dupee, Frederick Wilcox (ed.), *Henry James: Autobiography* [*A Small Boy and Others, Notes of a Son and Brother, The Middle Years*], W. H. Allen, London, 1956.

Edel, Leon, *Henry James: A Life,* Collins, London, 1985.

Edel, Leon, *Henry James: A Life,* Flamingo, London, 1996.

Edel, Leon (ed.), *Henry James: Selected Letters,* Belknap, Cambridge, Massachusetts and London, 1987.

Edel, Leon (ed.), *Letters of Henry James,* volume 1, Harvard University Press, 1974.

Edel, Leon (ed.), *Letters of Henry James,* volume 2, Belknap Press of Harvard University Press, Cambridge, 1975.

Edel, Leon (ed.), *Letters of Henry James,* volume 3, Harvard University Press, Cambridge, 1980.

Edel, Leon (ed.), *Letters of Henry James,* volume 4, Belknap Press, Cambridge, 1984.

Horne, Philip, *Henry James: A Life in Letters,* Allen Lane, London, 1999.

James, Henry, *The Aspern Papers and The Turn of the Screw,* edited with an introduction by Anthony Curtis, Penguin Books, Harmondsworth, 1984.

James, Henry, *The Europeans,* with an introduction by Tony Tanner and notes by Patricia Crick, Penguin Books, London, 1985.

James, Henry, *Hawthorne,* Macmillan & Co., London, 1879.

James, Henry, *Italian Hours,* edited with an introduction and notes by John Auchard, Penguin Books, Harmondsworth, 1995.

James, Henry, *A Little Tour in France,* with a preface by Henry James and ninety-four illustrations by Joseph Pennell, William Heinemann, London, 1900.

James, Henry, *The Portrait of a Lady,* Penguin Books, Harmondsworth, 1968 [1963].

James, Henry, *Portraits of Places,* Duckworth, London, 2001 [Macmillan, 1883].

James, Henry, *The Princess Casamassima,* edited with an introduction by Derek Brewer, notes by Patricia Crick, Penguin Books, London 1987 [Macmillan, 1886].

James, Henry, *A Small Boy and Others,* Gibson Square Books, London, 2001.

James, Henry, *The Spoils of Poynton,* Heinemann, London, 1962.

James, Henry, *What Maisie Knew,* edited with an introduction and notes by Adrian Poole, Oxford University Press, Oxford, 1998.

Kelley, Cornelia Pulsifer, *The Early Development of Henry James,* with an introduction by Lyon N. Richardson, University of Illinois Press, Urbana, 1965.

Matthiessen, F. O. and Murdock, Kenneth B. (eds), *The Notebooks of Henry James,* Oxford University Press, New York, 1947.

Monteiro, George (ed.), *The Correspondence of Henry James and Henry Adams, 1877-1914,* Louisiana State University Press, Baton Rouge and London, 1992.

Sweeney, John L. (ed.), *The Painter's Eye: Notes and Essays on the Pictorial Arts by Henry James*, University of Wisconsin Press, 1989.

Tanner, Tony, *Venice Desired*, Blackwell Publishing, Oxford, 1992.

Treuherz, Julian, Prettejohn, Elizabeth and Becker, Edwin (eds), *Dante Gabriel Rossetti*, Uitgeverij Waanders b.v, Zwolle/Van Gogh Museum, Amsterdam/National Museums Liverpool, 2003.

West, Rebecca, *Henry James*, Nisbet and Co. Ltd., London, 1916.

John Ruskin

Batchelor, John, *John Ruskin: No Wealth But Life*, Pimlico, London, 2001 [Chatto & Windus, London, 2000].

Batchelor, John, *Lady Trevelyan and the Pre-Raphaelite Brotherhood*, Chatto & Windus, London, 2006.

Batchelor, John, "Alfred Tennyson: Problems of Biography", *The Yearbook of English Studies*, volume 36, 2006, pp. 78-95.

Bradley, John Lewis (ed.), *Ruskin's Letters from Venice 1851-1852*, Yale University Press, New Haven, 1955.

Bradley, John Lewis (ed.), *The Letters of John Ruskin to Lord and Lady Mount-Temple*, Ohio State University Press, Columbus, Ohio, 1964.

Bradley, John Lewis and Ousby, Ian (eds), *The Correspondence of John Ruskin and Charles Eliot Norton*, Cambridge University Press, Cambridge, 1987.

Burd, Van Akin (ed.), *The Ruskin Family Letters. The Correspondence of John James Ruskin, His Wife, and Their Son, John, 1801-1843*, in two volumes, Cornell University Press, Ithaca and London, 1973.

Burd, Van Akin (ed.), *The Winnington Letters. John Ruskin's Correspondence with Margaret Alexis Bell and the Children at Winnington Hall,* George Allen & Unwin, London, 1969.

Clegg, Jeanne, *Ruskin and Venice,* Junction Books, London, 1981.

Collingwood, William Gershom, *The Limestone Alps of Savoy; A Study in Physical Geology,* with an introduction by John Ruskin, George Allen, Orpington, 1884.

Collingwood, William Gershom, *The Life and Work of John Ruskin,* in two volumes, Methuen, London, 1893.

Collingwood, William Gershom, *The Life of John Ruskin,* in one volume, Methuen, London, 1905 [1900].

Collingwood, William Gershom, *Ruskin Relics,* Isbister & Co., London, 1903.

Cook, Edward Tyas, *The Life of John Ruskin,* in two volumes, George Allen, London, 1912 (second edition).

Cook, Edward Tyas and Wedderburn, Alexander (eds), *The Works of John Ruskin,* in thirty-nine volumes, George Allen, London, 1903-1912.

Dearden, James S., *John Ruskin's Camberwell,* Brentham Press, St Albans, 1990.

Dearden, James S., *Ruskin, Bembridge and Brantwood,* Keele University Press (Ryburn Publishing), Keele, 1994.

Evans, Joan and Whitehouse, John Howard (eds), *The Diaries of John Ruskin,* in three volumes, The Clarendon Press, Oxford, 1956-1959.

Feiling, Keith, *In Christ Church Hall,* Macmillan, London, 1960.

Gamble, Cynthia, "Viollet-le-Duc et Ruskin, peintres des Alpes", *La*

Revue Savoisienne, Académie Florimontane, Annecy, 1996, pp. 125-137.

Gamble, Cynthia, "John Ruskin, Eugène Viollet-le-Duc and the Alps", *The Alpine Journal,* volume 104, 1999, pp. 185-196.

Gamble, Cynthia, "Ruskin's Northern France; 'a perpetual paradise' Abbeville, Rouen and Amiens" in Wildman, Stephen and Gamble, Cynthia, *'A Perpetual Paradise': Ruskin's Northern France,* The Ruskin Library, Lancaster University, 2002.

Gamble, Cynthia, "Ruskin's Camberwell Connections and Lecture", *Camberwell Quarterly,* No. 139, October 2003, pp. 5-8.

Heffer, Simon, *Moral Desperado: A Life of Thomas Carlyle,* Weidenfeld and Nicolson, London, 1995.

Hewison, Robert, *Ruskin and Oxford: The Art of Education,* The Clarendon Press, Oxford, 1996.

Hewison, Robert, Warrell, Ian and Wildman, Stephen, *Ruskin, Turner and the Pre-Raphaelites,* Tate Gallery Publishing, London, 2000.

Hilton, Tim, *John Ruskin: The Early Years 1819-1859,* Yale University Press, New Haven and London, 2000 [1985].

Hilton, Tim, *John Ruskin: The Later Years,* Yale University Press, New Haven and London, 2000.

Hunt, John Dixon, *The Wider Sea: A Life of John Ruskin,* Dent, London, Melbourne and Toronto, 1982.

Hunt, William Holman, *Pre-Raphaelitism and the Pre-Raphaelite Brotherhood,* in two volumes, Macmillan & Co., London, 1905.

James, William (ed.), *The Order of Release: The Story of John Ruskin, Effie Gray and John Everett Millais told for the first time in their unpublished letters,* John Murray, London, 1947.

Kitchin, George William, *Ruskin in Oxford and Other Studies,* John Murray, London, 1904.

Links, J. G., *The Ruskins in Normandy. A Tour in 1848 with Murray's Handbook,* John Murray, London, 1968.

Lutyens, Mary, *Effie in Venice,* John Murray, London, 1965.

Lutyens, Mary, *Millais and the Ruskins,* John Murray, London, 1967.

Lutyens, Mary, *The Ruskins and the Grays,* John Murray, London, 1971.

Maas, Henry (ed.), *The Letters of A. E. Housman,* Rupert-Hart-Davis, London, 1971.

Merrill, Linda, *A Pot of Paint: Aesthetics on Trial 'Whistler v. Ruskin',* Smithsonian Institution Press, Washington and London, 1992.

Purkis, John, *Morris, Burne-Jones and French Gothic, being an account of a walking tour in France July to August 1855,* William Morris Society, London, 2000 [1988, 1999].

Richards, Jeffrey, *Sir Henry Irving: A Victorian Actor and his World,* Hambledon and London, London and New York, 2005.

The Ruskin Review and Bulletin, published three times a year by The Ruskin Centre, University of Lancaster.

Shapiro, Harold I. (ed.), *Ruskin in Italy. Letters to his Parents 1845,* The Clarendon Press, Oxford, 1972.

Spates, James L., "John Ruskin's Dark Star", *Bulletin of the John Rylands University Library of Manchester,* volume 82, number 1, Spring, 2000, pp. 135-191.

Spates, James L., "Ruskin in Milan, 1862", *The Journal of Pre-Raphaelite Studies,* volume 13 (New Series), Fall, 2004, pp. 17-62.

Spates, James L., foreword by Van Akin Burd, *The Imperfect Round: Helen Gill Viljoen's Life of Ruskin,* A Long View Book, 2005.

Spielmann, M. H., *John Ruskin,* Cassell, London, Paris, New York & Melbourne, 1900.

Taylor, Anne, *Laurence Oliphant 1829-1888,* Oxford University Press, Oxford, New York, Toronto and Melbourne, 1982.

West, Algernon, *Recollections 1832 to 1886,* in two volumes, Smith, Elder & Co., London, 1899.

Wildman, Stephen and Christian, John; with essays by Alan Crawford and Laurence des Cars, *Edward Burne-Jones: Victorian Artist-Dreamer,* The Metropolitan Museum of Art, New York, 1998

Wildman, Stephen and Gamble, Cynthia, *"A Perpetual Paradise": Ruskin's Northern France,* The Ruskin Library, Lancaster University, 2002.

Wilson, A. N., *The Victorians,* Arrow Books, London, 2003.

Topography

Ballu, Yves, *À la conquête du Mont-Blanc,* Gallimard, Paris, 1993.

Bellamy, Vivien, *A History of Much Wenlock,* Shropshire Books, Shrewsbury, 2001.

Bellamy, Vivien, *The Making of Shrewsbury: The History of a Border Town,* Pen & Sword Books, Barnsley, 2004.

Borrow, George, *Wild Wales: Its People, Language and Scenery,* with an introduction by Cecil Price, Fontana [London], 1977 [Collins, 1862].

Creighton, Mandell, *The Story of Some English Shires,* The Religious

Tract Society, London, 1897.

Emery, Anthony, *Great Medieval Houses of England and Wales,* volume II, Cambridge University Press, 2000.

Fitzsimons, Raymund, *The Baron of Piccadilly: The Travels and Entertainments of Albert Smith 1816-1860,* Geoffrey Bles, London, 1967.

Forbes, James D., *Travels through the Alps,* revised and annotated by W. A. B. Coolidge, Adam and Charles Black, London, 1900.

Forrest, H. E., *The Old Houses of Wenlock and Wenlock Edge,* Wilding & Son, Shrewsbury, 1922 (third edition) [1914, 1915].

Gaskell, Lady Catherine Milnes, *Spring in a Shropshire Abbey,* Smith, Elder & Co., London, 1905.

Gaskell, Lady Catherine Milnes, *Friends Round the Wrekin,* Smith, Elder & Co., London, 1914.

A Handbook for Shropshire, Cheshire, and Lancashire, with map, John Murray, London, 1870.

A Handbook for Shropshire and Cheshire, with map, new (second) edition, John Murray, London, 1879.

A Handbook for Residents and Travellers in Shropshire and Cheshire, third edition, revised, with maps and plans, John Murray, London, 1897.

A Handbook for Travellers in Berks, Bucks, and Oxfordshire, including a particular description of the University and City of Oxford, and the descent of the Thames to Maidenhead and Windsor; with a travelling map and plans, John Murray, London, 1860.

A Handbook for Travellers in Berks, Bucks and Oxfordshire, [as above], second edition, revised, John Murray, London, 1872.

A Handbook for Travellers in Berks, Bucks and Oxfordshire, [as above], third edition, revised, John Murray, London, 1882.

Ionides, Julia L. and Howell, Peter G., *The Old Houses of Shropshire in the 19th Century: The Watercolour Albums of Frances Stackhouse Acton,* The Dog Rose Press, Ludlow, 2006.

Jones, Ken, *The Wenlock Branch: Wellington to Craven Arms,* The Oakwood Press, Usk, 1998.

Kitson, Sydney Decimus, *The Life of John Sell Cotman,* Faber and Faber, London, 1937.

Lister, W. Brian Collins, *A Bibliography of Murray's Handbooks for Travellers,* Dereham Books, Dereham, Norfolk, 1993.

Lloyd, David, *The Concise History of Ludlow,* Merlin Unwin Books, Ludlow, 2005.

Lloyd, David, foreword by The Earl of Powis, *Ludlow Castle: A History and a Guide,* no date, no publisher.

Mercer, Eric, *English Architecture to 1900: The Shropshire Experience,* Logaston Press, Little Logaston, Herefordshire, 2003.

Mumford, William F., *Wenlock in the Middle Ages,* published by Mrs E. Mumford, 1989 [1977].

Parker, John Henry, *Some Account of Domestic Architecture in England: from Richard II to Henry VIII,* Parker, Oxford, 1859.

Pevsner, Nikolaus, *Berkshire,* Penguin Books, 1998 [1966].

Pevsner, Nikolaus and Sherwood, Jennifer, *Oxfordshire,* Penguin Books, Harmondsworth, 1974.

Pevsner, Nikolaus, *Shropshire,* Yale University Press, New Haven and

London, 2002 [Penguin Books, 1958].

Pevsner, Nikolaus and Newman, John, *Shropshire*, Yale University Press, New Haven and London, 2006.

Pinnell, Julie, *Wenlock Priory*, English Heritage, London, 2001 [1999].

Randall, John, *History of Broseley*, 1879.

Randall, John, *Old Sports and Sportsmen: or, the Willey Country*, London, 1873.

Randall's Tourist's Guide to Wenlock, with photographic & wood illustrations, being a Complete Handbook to Places of Interest in the Town, and Containing a Full Description and History of the Priory; printed and published by John Randall, Madeley, Lawley and Wenlock, 1875.

The Victoria History of the Counties of England: A History of Shropshire, vol. II, 1973 (ed. A. T. Gaydon); vol. III, 1979 (ed. G. C. Baugh); vol. IV, 1989 (ed. G. C. Baugh); vol. VIII, 1968 (ed. A. T. Gaydon); vol. X, 1998 (ed. G. C. Baugh); vol. XI, 1985 (ed. G. C. Baugh).

Walcott, Mackenzie Edward Charles, *The Four Minsters round the Wrekin: Buildwas, Haughmond, Lilleshull and Wenlock, with ground plans [and photographic views]*, Shrewsbury [printed], London, 1877.

Sale catalogues

Catalogue of the sale of Pictures belonging to Capel Cure, at Christie's on 29 April 1885.

Catalogue of the sale of Prints and Drawings belonging to Capel Cure, at Sotheby's on 29 April 1885.

Catalogue of the sale of the Collection formed by Edward Cheney of Objects of Antiquity of the Renaissance and of Later Times, at Christie's, Thursday 4 May and Friday 5 May 1905.

Catalogue of the sale of the Collection of Important Pictures by Old Masters formed by Edward Cheney of Badger Hall (the property of Francis Capel-Cure), at Christie's, 8 King Street, London, Saturday 6 May 1905 at one o'clock.

Catalogue of the sale of items belonging to Francis Capel-Cure at Sotheby's, 11-13 May 1905.

Catalogue of the sale of items belonging to H.[erbert] Pritchard Gordon at Sotheby's on 10 May 1933.

Catalogue of the Christie's sale of items in the collection of Lewis Motley, held at Wenlock Abbey on 25 October 1982.

Directories and dictionaries

Bénézit, Emmanuel (1854-1920), *Dictionnaire critique et documentaire des peintres, sculpteurs, dessinateurs et graveurs de tous les temps et de tous les pays,* par un groupe d'écrivains spécialistes français et étrangers sous la direction de E. Bénézit, avec nombreuses reproductions hors texte d'après les maîtres, Roger et Chernoviz, Paris, 1911-1923.

Burke, Bernard, *A Genealogical and Heraldic History of the Landed Gentry of Great Britain and Ireland,* fifth edition, Harrison, London, 1871.

Crockford's Clerical Directory, Church House Publishing, London, annual publication.

Dictionary of National Biography, edited by Leslie Stephen and Sidney Lee, Smith, Elder & Co., London, 1890.

Oxford Dictionary of National Biography, in association with the British Academy: from the earliest times to the year 2000, edited by H.

C. G. Matthew and Brian Harrison, in 61 volumes, Oxford University Press, Oxford, 2004.

The Dictionary of Welsh Biography down to 1940, under the auspices of the Honourable Society of Cymmrodorion (Editors, Sir John Edward Lloyd and R.T.Jenkins), London, 1959.

Joll, Evelyn, Butlin, Martin and Herrmann, Luke (eds), *The Oxford Companion to J. M. W. Turner,* Oxford University Press, Oxford, New York and other places, 2001.

Kelly's Directory of Shropshire, 1900.

Mallalieu, Huon Lancelot, *The Dictionary of British Watercolour Artists up to 1920,* third edition, in two volumes, Antique Collectors' Club, Woodbridge, 2002.

Pigot's Directory of Shrewsbury, 1839.

Who's Who of British Members of Parliament 1832-1885, volume 1, compiled by Michael Stenton, Harvester Press, Hassocks, Sussex, 1976.

Who's Who of British Members of Parliament 1886-1918, volume 2, compiled by Michael Stenton, Harvester Press, Sussex, 1978.

Index